Noam Chomsky
AT WAR WITH ASIA

AK
PRESS
EDINBURGH · LONDON · OAKLAND

At War With Asia
by Noam Chomsky
ISBN 1-902593-89-8

Copyright 1969, 1970, and 2005 by Noam Chomsky
www.chomsky.info
For rights, contact: arnove@chomsky.net

AK Press
674-A 23rd Street
Oakland, CA 94612-1163
USA
(510) 208-1700
www.akpress.org
akpress@akpress.org

AK Press U.K.
PO Box 12766
Edinburgh, EH8 9YE
Scotland
(0131) 555-5165
www.akuk.com
ak@akedin.demon.co.uk

The addresses above would be delighted to provide you with the latest complete AK catalog, featuring several thousand books, pamphlets, zines, audio products, video products and stylish apparel published and distributed by AK Press. Alternatively, visit our websites for the complete catalog, latest news and updates, events and secure ordering.

Library of Congress Control Number: 2003113038

Printed in Canada on recycled paper at a union plant.

Acknowledgement
"After Pinkville," "Cambodia," "Laos," and "North Vietnam" appeared originally in a slightly different form, in *The New York Review of Books*. *At War With Asia* was originally published in 1970 by Pantheon Books/Random House.

Cover design by John Yates

Table of Contents

1. Indochina and the American Crisis   1

2. After Pinkville   61

3. Cambodia   89

4. Laos   145

5. North Vietnam   201

6. On War Crimes   223

AT WAR WITH ASIA

Chapter 1
Indochina and the American Crisis

I

IN 1947, COMMENTING on the rising tide of "anti-Communist" hysteria in the United States, John K. Fairbank made the following perceptive observations:

> Our fear of Communism, partly as an expression of our general fear of the future, will continue to inspire us to aggressive anti-Communist policies in Asia and elsewhere, [and] the American people will be led to think and may honestly believe that the support of anti-Communist governments in Asia will somehow defend the American way of life. This line of American policy will lead to American aid to establish regimes which attempt to suppress the popular movements in Indonesia, Indochina, the Philippines, and China.... Thus, after setting out to fight Communism in Asia, the American people will be obliged in the end to fight the peoples of Asia.
>
> This American aggression abroad will be associated with an increasing trend toward anti-Communist authoritarianism within the United States, which its victims will call fascism and which may eventually make it impossible to have discussions like this one today. This American fascism will come, if it comes, because American liberals have joined the American public in a fear of Communism from abroad rather than fascism at home as the chief totalitarian menace.[1]

These remarks have proved to be accurate. The events of April 1970 reveal, once again, how the policy of "anti-Communism" draws the American government, step by fateful step, into an endless war against the peoples of Asia, and, as a natural concomitant, toward harsh repression and defiance of law at home.

What is the nature and source of these "aggressive anti-Communist policies"? The British economist Joan Robinson has described the American crusade against Communism in the following terms:

It is obvious enough that the United States crusade against Communism is a campaign against development. By means of it the American people have been led to acquiesce in the maintenance of a huge war machine and its use by threat or actual force to try to suppress every popular movement that aims to overthrow ancient or modern tyranny and begin to find a way to overcome poverty and establish national self-respect. In those countries whose governments have been prepared to accept American support, "aid" is given in a form which may do more to inhibit development than to promote it.[2]

Rhetoric aside, the underlying assumption is formulated not very differently by the makers of American policy. Consider, for example, how the threat of Communism to the American system is defined in an extensive study sponsored by the Woodrow Wilson Foundation and the National Planning Association,[3] a study that involved a representative segment of the tiny elite that largely determines foreign policy, whoever is technically in office. The primary threat of Communism, as they see it, is the economic transformation of the Communist powers "in ways which reduce their willingness and ability to complement the industrial economies of the West." Correspondingly, the American crusade against Communism is not a campaign against all forms of development, but only against the effort of indigenous movements to extricate their societies from the integrated world system dominated largely by American capital, and to use their resources for their own social and economic development. A Korean journalist writing in Japan put the matter precisely in discussing his own country: "The economic policy of the Park Administration seemingly draws admiration not because its economic construction is being carried out in a firm and reasonable manner, but because South Korea is pursuing an 'open door' economic policy and offers abundant low-cost labor."[4]

What results from the continued "willingness" (spurred by occasional intervention and subversion) to complement the great industrial economies is seen most clearly in the case of Latin America, traditionally a preserve of the United States. The 1960s, one recalls, were to be a "decade of development" under the Alliance for Progress. It might be argued that the second half of the decade provides an unfair test, given the exigencies of the Vietnam War. Consider then the first five years. The record was summarized by the editor of *Inter-American Economic Affairs*:

During that period [1960–1965] the rate of economic growth dropped sharply from the average for 1950–55 and 1955–60 and the change in the growth rate per capita was even more adverse. During that period the distribution of income became even more unsatisfactory as the gap between the rich and poor widened appreciably. During most of the period a very heavy proportion of the disbursements went to military regimes which had overthrown constitutional governments, and at the end of the period, with almost half of the population under military rule, a significant portion of the aid was going *not* to assist "free men and free governments" [in Alliance rhetoric] but rather to hold in power regimes to which the people had lost their freedom.[5]

Surveying the situation today, Frederick Clairmonte reports that:

United States corporations and their multinational subsidiaries currently control between 70–90% of the raw material resources of Latin America, and more than 60% of its industrial plant. Its public utilities, its banking, commerce and foreign trade relationships are in the hands of U.S. corporations or their subsidiaries.[6]

He cites the report of a Brazilian industrial commission, sponsored by the government but never published in Brazil:

…in 1968 foreign capital controlled 40% of the nation's capital market, 62% of its foreign trade, 82% of its maritime transport, 100% of motor vehicle output, 100% of tire production, more than 80% of the pharmaceutical industry, nearly 50% of the chemical industry, 59% of machine production, 62% of auto parts factories, 48% of aluminum, 90% of cement and 77% of the overseas airlines … half the foreign capital comes from the United States [followed by German, English, French, and Swiss capital].

One recalls the statement of the Chairman of the House Foreign Affairs Committee in 1965, celebrating the overthrow of the Goulart government:

Every critic of foreign aid is confronted with the fact that the Armed Forces of Brazil threw out the Goulart government and that U.S. military aid was a major factor in giving these forces an indoctrination in the principles of democracy and a pro-U.S. orientation. Many of these officers were trained in the United States under the AID program. They knew that democracy was better than communism.[7]

The outstanding Latin American correspondent of *Le Monde* explains in more detail how the Brazilian military elite conceives the principles of democracy and a pro-United States orientation:

> Accepting the principle of "total war against subversion," the doctrine of national security considers that the "underdeveloped countries must aid the leading State of the Christian world to defend civilization by furnishing it with primary materials."[8]

Other effects of the love for democracy might be cited, for example, the benefits to the American steel industry of a protected Latin American market (guaranteed by tied loans), or simply the profitability of investment: profit remittances and other returns on investment were three times the average annual inflow of direct investment (including reinvestment of profits) from 1960 to 1966.[9]

The ideology of anti-Communism has served as a highly effective technique of popular mobilization in support of American policies of intervention and subversion in the postwar period—an average of one such episode every eighteen months, as one author notes.[10] It is an ideology adapted to an era when the civilizing mission of the white race can no longer be invoked. Thus when the United States conquered the Philippines from its own population at the turn of the century, it was stoutly bearing the White Man's Burden, whereas today in Indochina it is defending the Free World against the savage Communists. In fact, in both cases, it is merely fulfilling the prophecy of Brooks Adams who proclaimed, three-quarters of a century ago, that "Our geographical position, our wealth, and our energy pre-eminently fit us to enter upon the development of Eastern Asia and to reduce it to part of our own economic system."[11] Although many American scholars and ideologists refuse to admit it, the Vietnam war is simply a catastrophic episode, a grim and costly failure in this long-term effort to reduce Eastern Asia and much of the rest of the world to part of the American-dominated economic system. The foreign editor of *Look* magazine put the matter quite accurately when he wrote that in Vietnam "we have overreached ourselves. America's historic westward-driving wave has crested"[12]—temporarily, at least.

A generation ago, few Americans failed to perceive the hypocrisy and self-delusion of Japanese leaders such as Tojo and Matsuoka when they explained their invasion of China as an altruistic gesture by Japan, which was "paying the price that leadership of Asia demands" and attempting to save Asia from the twin evils of Communism and dismemberment by the imperial powers of the West. Japan, they insisted, sought only to create a "co-prosperity sphere" in which its capital and technological resources would contribute to the development of the entire region, to the creation of an "earthly paradise." Surely no one could accuse the Japanese of crass economic motives. Was it not obvious that Japan was spending more on the war in China than it could possibly gain in return, protecting the true nationalists of China from Communist bandits and imperialist agents?[13] Similarly, today American critics of the war carefully explain the absurdity of the assumption that material interests led to the "tragic error" of Vietnam—surely the United States is spending more on the war in Indochina than it can possibly hope to gain in return. And today, Japanese observers can perceive clearly that the American government is engaged "in continuing French suppression of the Vietnamese people's struggle for independence"; they understand that "behind this concept of shielding Asia from domination by any single power, whether prewar Japan or present-day China, there appears to be a hidden American desire itself to play the role of top dog in Asia."[14] The Japanese correspondent of the *Far Eastern Economic Review*, Koji Nakamura, puts the matter plainly and simply (May 28, 1970):

> In Japanese eyes the American behavior and action in Indochina is a "xeroxed copy" of the Japanese behavior and action in China not many years ago which eventually led to the rise and fall of an Imperial Japan.

What he fails to add, however, is that Imperial Japan was not the world's mightiest military and industrial power.

Quite generally, the leaders of imperialist powers and their spokesmen have been able to persuade themselves—and the domestic population, so long as the costs are not too high—of the benevolence and rationality of the measures they undertake to extend their power. As John Adams once said, "Power always thinks it has a great soul and vast views beyond the comprehension of the weak; and that it is doing God's service when it is violating all his laws."[15] There is no reason to expect Americans to be immune to this historical process of self-delusion, and in fact, discussions of American policy are replete with references to its deeply moral character—misplaced moralism, in the eyes of many critics.

The American self-image is expressed with great clarity by former Ambassador Charles Bohlen in a recent essay on postwar American policy. Commenting on the postwar years, he writes:

> … one of the difficulties of explaining this policy even in the early days, and even more now, is that our policy is not rooted in any national material interest of the United States, as most foreign policies of other countries in the past have been.[16]

The political commentator TRB of *The New Republic*, strongly opposed to the war, writes that "we are a deeply moral nation (don't let anybody tell you the contrary)."[17] Referring to "Johnson trying to carry the Great Society everywhere, Kennedy seeking to eliminate revolutionary wars," he comments, "Do not ridicule such idealism." The rhetoric may be inflated, but the idealism, he insists, is beyond question:

> The moral pull for the U.S. to go on rescue missions will always be enormous. There are a dozen such spots today. Our conscience aches for them. But our capacity? It is probably limited….

The lesson he draws from Vietnam is that our capacity is limited. This is a rescue mission that we should not have undertaken. We should have resisted the moral pull. And he surely represents a fair segment of enlightened American opinion in this interpretation of what he regards, of course, as the tragedy of our intervention in Vietnam.

TRB also expresses widely held feelings when he writes of the "agonizing moral dilemma" we now face. The problem is: What is our primary duty? Is it to "South Vietnamese who might be massacred if we quit? or to the 150–200 American boys who lose their lives weekly if we stay? I don't think the U.S. has ever before faced such a question."

What of the South Vietnamese who might be massacred if our collaborators were to win, or those who are now being massacred by our military actions? It is remarkable that they do not appear to figure in our moral dilemma and are not so much as mentioned by TRB (though he admits that the North Vietnamese victims of American bombing might have "thought they were atrocities too").

TRB is right not to ridicule the feelings of those who would support virtually any act committed by their government out of a sense of idealism. He is right, as well, to point to the agonizing moral dilemma. It is not without historical precedent. It is, for example, a dilemma that might have been posed by German moralists in 1944, had they been faced with the demand that they withdraw from France. What of the collaborators who might be massacred if we quit—who were, in fact, massacred in the thousands when France was abandoned by the Wehrmacht? TRB is also right in saying, as he does, that "people can vote in other ways than at the polling booth—by defending themselves, say, or by dying for their country: that [he writes] would be evidence that South Vietnam really is a country." And he testifies to the amazing blindness of this deeply moral nation in that he simply cannot perceive that there are those in South Vietnam who have been dying for their country and defending it, with indescribable heroism, against the blows of the idealists who seek to eliminate revolutionary wars everywhere, to carry the Great Society everywhere.

Returning to an earlier day, during the period of its industrial dominance Britain advocated economic liberalism, not merely on grounds of the material advantages that such policies afford to the dominant power, but on universal grounds, protectionism being conceived, in Palmerston's phrase, as "a principle of fatal injury to the country and inimical to the prosperity of every country to whose affairs it may be applied."[18] Similarly, in the period following World War II the United States has tended to adhere to this doctrine (highly selectively, to be sure) insofar as it guarantees American ascendancy, and to urge others to accept free and unconstrained economic relations.[19] This was natural enough. The United States emerged from the second World War with overwhelming power relative to other industrial societies. Its industrial production had quadrupled, while every other major industrial society had been devastated or severely crippled. Gabriel Kolko, in an extremely important study, has shown in detail how the United States proceeded, during the war, to lay the groundwork for a postwar economic empire, particularly at the expense of our ally

Great Britain.[20] Similarly, postwar loans were used to compel the British to dismantle the imperial preference system and restrict nationalization.[21] As William Clayton, then Under-Secretary of State for Economic Affairs, put it: "We loaded the British loan negotiations with all the conditions that the traffic would bear." LaFeber formulates the general outlines of America's European policy, as advocated by the American executive branch:

> ... a rejuvenated Europe could offer many advantages to the United States: eradicate the threat of continuing nationalization and spreading socialism by releasing and stimulating the investment of private capital, maintain demand for American exports, encourage Europeans to produce strategic goods which the United States could buy and stockpile, preserve European and American control over Middle Eastern oil supplies from militant nationalism which might endanger the weakened European holdings, and free Europeans from economic problems so they could help the United States militarily. [P. 51.]

Meanwhile, "The economic relationship with Latin America and Canada could be assumed; none had to be developed" (p. 10). As Henry Stimson put it rather nicely, in trying to work out a strategy for breaking down European regional systems while preserving our own: "I think that it's not asking too much to have our little region over here [i.e., South America] which never has bothered anybody."[22] Where it was possible, unequal treaties were imposed, as in the Philippines.

As for Western and Southern Europe, the popular forces of the Resistance were broken, in part by force,[23] and the Marshall Plan successfully reconstructed European capitalism. A highly sympathetic commentator describes the goals of this program as follows:

> While there were humanitarian and economic justifications for the Marshall Plan, the strategic importance of keeping Western Europe out of the Soviet orbit was its ultimate if not its sole justification. In strategic terms, the Marshall Plan represented a commitment of American resources to the protection of Western Europe against the expansion of Soviet influence and control.[24]

The Marshall Plan also laid the basis for the integration of much of the world economy, largely, though not wholly, on American terms. Japan was reconstructed as an industrial power with an essentially colonial hinterland. A good argument can be given in support of the analysis of "critical Japanese commentators" that "Japan was to be developed not only as a military base against China and the Soviet Union, but also as an industrial base supporting the counterrevolutionary cause in Southeast Asia," a policy that was opposed not only by Russia but also by virtually all the members of the Far Eastern Commission.[25] The American hopes of dominating this system have received a setback because of the unexpected costs and failures of the Vietnam war. How significant this will be in the long run remains to be seen.

The overriding goal of American policy has been to construct a system of societies that are open to free economic intervention by private enterprise (which in many ways is publicly subsidized). The goal was formulated clearly by George Ball, who "urged a greater unification of the world economy to give full play to the benefits of multinational corporations," which are "a distinctly American development." "Through such corporations," he observed, "it has become possible for the first time to use the world's resources with maximum efficiency"—for the benefit of whom, he does not reveal.[26] It is hardly surprising that the world-dominant power should oppose the resort to state controls by its weaker neighbors or that it should speak of "economic liberalism" and the benefits of unifying the world economy. Nor is it surprising that others see the matter rather differently. Thus a Tanzanian planner comments:

> A country whose industrial development depends on foreign investments cannot adequately control its own destiny. It might succeed in attaining a successful take-off, but its economy might be likened to an unmanned aircraft whose course and safety are maintained by remote controls. It is a flying economy with no pilot aboard. The foreign investors who control it from a distance might decide to do anything with it.[27]

Words that might be spoken as well in South Korea, Canada, even England, and many other countries today.

That such subservience creates and perpetuates unbalanced development and severe underdevelopment has been demonstrated in many studies.[28] Such effects do not pass unnoticed within the imperialist powers themselves. The study *The Political Economy of American Foreign Policy* (see note 3) refers to some of the effects of economic liberalism on the under-developed countries with this comment:

> However, as the example of the United States suggests, this is proba-bly not the way their resources would have been used had these coun-tries been fully independent and had local enterprise existed capable of managing its own development. [P. 29.]

And Alfred Marshall, for one, observes: "The brilliant genius and national enthusiasm of List stand in contrast to the insular narrowness and self-confidence of the Ricardian school ... [for] ... he showed that in Germany and still more in America, many of its indirect effects [free trade, in the early nineteenth century] were evils...."[29] But by and large, the dominant world powers easily manage to construct a self-image of benevolence and rationality, the United States not excepted.

The unification of the world economy by American-based multina-tional corporations poses a threat to national sovereignty, but more signif-icantly, to the possibility for social progress within even the more powerful societies. The problem is, quite naturally, of deep concern to organized labor. The head of one of Great Britain's largest unions, Hugh Scanlon, has recently discussed "the power of international corporations to hamstring and browbeat the interests of organized labour." He cites *Fortune* magazine on the scale of these institutions:

> The hard financial core of capitalism is composed of not more than 60 firms, partnerships or corporations, owned or controlled by 1000 men.... In fact recent forecasts claim that in 25 years 200 multina-tional firms will completely dominate production and trade and account for over 75 per cent of the total corporate assets of the capi-talist world.[30]

The scale of these institutions is such, he writes, that they can "obtain an overwhelming bargaining power with any government." Furthermore, their power and ability to transfer operations from one country to another can be used as a weapon against labor—as an example he cites the recent Ford strike, when the threat to transfer operations from England to Belgium was used in exactly this way. Evidently, only an international labor organization (with, as Scanlon emphasizes, "real grass roots on the shop floor") could begin to deal with this threat, which surely is severe.

In the less developed societies other means are employed to prevent balanced independent development. The imperial powers have consistently exploited and exacerbated ethnic rivalries and hostilities, and have tried to develop native elites that would control the local population while enriching themselves through their relations with the imperial power. Josue de Castro observes that "productive forces [are] strangled by the domination of alienated [i.e., Western-educated] elites, whose interests do not coincide with those of the disinherited masses."[31] The goal of the imperial power is to create a class of bureaucrats and a colonial bourgeoisie that will collaborate in the administration and exploitation of the country. As Keith Buchanan points out, citing de Castro's remark, "Such elite groups today constitute one of the heaviest millstones around the necks of some of the emerging Southeast Asian peoples." Nominal political independence may have little or no effect on the underdevelopment caused by colonial dependence. Buchanan observes:

> In this prolongation of dependent and "underdeveloped" status the new elites, the colonial bourgeoisie created by the European restructuring of colonial societies, play an essential role; this, as we have seen, is a group which profited by, still profits by, the exploitation of the colonial peoples—their fellow-countrymen. This group, which now controls effective political power in Southeast Asia, has neither the vision nor, for obvious reasons, the desire to strike out and create, through the medium of planned societies based on a humanistic socialism, a fuller and more autonomous life for their people; only in Cambodia is there a dedicated attempt to follow this path. [No more—N.C.] And since these countries are now an area on which the conflict between the West and the Soviet Bloc is projected, the whole military establishment of the West, and its associated economic, cultural and political mechanisms, is used to buttress the elite groups who rule them. These groups are kept in power as a barrier against the changes the creation of a decent society would involve, against the changes we for some reason fear, and the aid we give is used too often to create a Potemkin-façade of prestige development (Bangkok or Kuala Lumpur offer classic examples of this) behind which the stagnation of whole areas continues.[32]

The social and economic effects of such tendencies in Southeast Asia are reviewed in a recent paper by two Yale University economists.[33]

Surveying the situation in the Philippines, Thailand, Malaya, and Singapore, they note

> the persistence of virtual stagnation in the hinterland, in which the majority of the people live, in contrast to the rapid growth of the metropoli; Bangkok, Manila, and Kuala Lumpur. Widening inequality is also visible within the metropoli in the form of industrial dualism: an organized and heavily protected manufacturing sector coexists with a large crafts sector where most of the urban people are employed or where there exists disguised unemployment.

Despite political independence, there is "increased dependency on the goods and the technology of the West." Many of the recently developed consumer-goods industries are, furthermore, subsidiaries of multinational corporations. Economic policies favor consumer goods for the privileged, while a pool of cheap labor provides services for the middle and upper classes. While the countryside stagnates, the overcrowded cities decay behind the façade of wealth. A recent United Nations report notes that "the conjunction of rapid population growth ... with widespread unemployment and family poverty has led to a further precipitous decline in urban living conditions, which in many large Asian cities have reached a stage of depression and disorder that practically defies description."[34] To cite one illustrative example, in Bangkok, a superficially affluent metropolis of three million, most people have no sanitation facilities, while color television is now available throughout the country. Bangkok, Bell and Resnick comment, "has become less and less a part of Thailand and more a part of the West." Of course the process has been accelerated by the American use of Bangkok as a rest-and-recreation center for the Vietnam war, and Thailand in general as a sanctuary for the attack on the countries of Indochina. The corruption of Bangkok is, in fact, immediately evident even to the casual visitor. Furthermore, "about half of the increase of the gross domestic product from 1965 to 1967 was attributable to military spending by the U.S. within Thailand, which has only further lopsided the pattern of development," and, incidentally, led to considerable fears among the Thai elite concerning the future, in the event of an American de-escalation of the war.[35]

Needless to say, this subservience to foreign interests breeds corruption on a vast scale. To cite just one example, the previously cited review of "The Korean Question" by an anti-Communist Korean journalist living in Japan[36] maintains that the present Park administration had earned the worst reputation of any Korean government with regard to political corruption and injustice. Kim claims that "a foreign credit of $10 million shrinks to $6 million before it becomes available for its intended purpose: 20 per cent of the original amount goes to political funds and another 20 per cent disappears in bribes for government officials from low-echelon clerks up to ministers." The same observations hold for other less developed Asian countries that remain within the "integrated world system" of modern capitalism.

The vested interest in American imperialism that is developing in such countries as Japan, South Korea, Thailand, and Singapore is also a potentially dangerous feature of modern American imperialism in Southeast Asia. American power modifies the social and economic structure of countries that become partners in its Asian wars, and consequently threatens true independence in complex ways. Even the aid program has this effect. In 1967, Michael Leifer wrote: "The urban elite [of Cambodia]—accustomed to a high standard of living sustained by American aid—is now finding it difficult to adjust to economic austerity" caused by the termination of this program in 1963 on Sihanouk's initiative.[37] Similarly, the termination of American military assistance led to disaffection among the military. This disaffection of the military and the urban elite was a contributing factor to the coup of March 18, 1970, which toppled Sihanouk and plunged Cambodia into a civil war, and the Indochina war. (See the comments by Keith Buchanan cited previously, page 11, and Chapter 3.)

The American crusade against Communism is in part an effort to prevent independent economic development, but, as Joan Robinson also noted, it functions in other ways as well. It provides the psychological climate in which a continuing public subsidy can be provided to technologically advanced sectors of American industry for "maintenance of a huge war machine." Only a population that fears for its survival can be induced to consent to this subsidy, which has become a central factor in the

American postwar economy. This, indeed, was the primary economic lesson of World War II. New Deal measures had smoothed many of the rough edges of the great depression, but had not succeeded in bringing it to an end. The depression was overcome by wartime government spending, and this lesson was not lost on those who own and manage the economy. Business historian Alfred Chandler describes the economic lessons of World War II as follows:

> The government spent far more than the most enthusiastic New Dealer had ever proposed. Most of the output of the expenditures was destroyed or left on the battlefields of Europe and Asia. But the resulting increased demand sent the nation into a period of prosperity the like of which had never before been seen. Moreover, the supplying of huge armies and navies fighting the most massive war of all time required a tight, centralized control of the national economy. This effort brought corporate managers to Washington to carry out one of the most complex pieces of economic planning in history. That experience lessened the ideological fears over the government's role in stabilizing the economy.

The ensuing Cold War, the crusade against Communism, carried further the depoliticization of American society and created the psychological climate in which the government is able to intervene, in part through fiscal policies, public works, and public services, but very largely through war spending, to preserve "economic health." The government acts as "a coordinator of last resort" when "managers are unable to maintain a high level of aggregate demand."[38] Charles E. Wilson, president of General Electric, was undoubtedly motivated in part by a sense of economic realism when he proposed a "permanent war economy" in 1944.[39] As another business historian writes, enlightened corporate managers, far from fearing government intervention in the economy, view "the New Economics as a technique for increasing corporate viability."[40] And the primary technique of intervention is, quite naturally, war spending. Indeed, it is not easy, with the best of will, to imagine other forms of government-induced production that will not harm but will rather enhance the interests and power of the private empires that control the economy, that are endlessly expandable, and that will, at the same time, be tolerated by the mass of the population, which has to foot the bill.

The managers of the publicly subsidized war industries are pleasingly frank about the matter. Bernard Nossiter has published a remarkable series of articles in which he reports a number of interviews with representatives of this system of militarized state capitalism. Samuel F. Downer, financial vice-president of the LTV Aerospace Corporation, explained in the following words why "the post-war [i.e., post-Vietnam war] world must be bolstered with military orders":

> It's basic. Its selling appeal is defense of the home. This is one of the greatest appeals the politicians have to adjusting the system. If you're the President and you need a control factor in the economy, and you need to sell this factor, you can't sell Harlem and Watts but you can sell self-preservation, a new environment. We're going to increase defense budgets as long as those bastards in Russia are ahead of us. The American people understand this.[41]

Of course, those bastards aren't exactly ahead of us in this deadly and cynical game, but that is only a minor embarrassment to the thesis. In times of need, it is always possible to call upon Dean Rusk, Hubert Humphrey, and other luminaries to warn of the billion Chinese, armed to the teeth and setting out on world conquest.

Many commentators have noted the dependence of the American economy on Third World resources, particularly nonferrous metals, as one factor in explaining the American crusade against independent national development.[42] These resources are required, to a large extent, for war production. Harry Magdoff notes that "three quarters of the imported materials included in the stockpile program come from the underdeveloped areas." He illustrates this dependence by an analysis of critical materials needed for jet engines. The strategic character of the materials is a factor, along with general considerations of profitability and control, in making the American government wary of trusting to trade relations with independent nations to acquire its needed raw materials.

Military power is needed to control the empire. The empire is seen as a necessity to guarantee military power. Militarization of the economy is a primary factor in maintaining "economic health." The threat of war, the constant "danger" of domestic insurgency in many parts of the world, helps maintain the appropriate psychological climate of psychosis and conformism. Such mutually supporting factors create a system that is highly resistant to change, despite its irrationality and the costs it imposes on the citizenry (almost 70 per cent of taxes now are used to pay for past, present, and future wars), not to speak of the threat to continued survival.

The role of the Cold War in this system as a technique of domestic control should not be overlooked. Of course, Russian imperialism is not an invention of American ideologists. It is real enough, as the Hungarians and Czechs can testify. What is an invention is the uses to which it was put, for example, by Dean Acheson in 1950[43] or Walt Rostow a decade later, when they pretended that the Vietnam war was an example of Russian imperialism; or by the Johnson administration in 1965 when it justified the Dominican intervention with reference to the "Sino-Soviet military bloc"; or by "an entire generation of leaders" who, as Townsend Hoopes puts it, were "conditioned by the tensions of the Cold War years" and thus could not perceive that the triumph of the national revolution in Vietnam would not be "a triumph for Moscow and Peking"[44]—a most remarkable blindness on the part of literate men; or by Eugene Rostow, who, in a recent book that was widely praised by American liberals,[45] outlined the series of challenges to world order in the modern era: Napoleon, Kaiser Wilhelm, Hitler—and continuing in the postwar world (among others), general strikes in France and Italy, the civil war in Greece,[46] and the attack on South Vietnam where, he writes, *Russia* "has put us to severe tests" in its efforts to spread Communism by the sword.

One can continue indefinitely. I mean to suggest that the Cold War is highly functional for the American elite as well as for its Soviet counterpart, who, in a similar way, sends its armies into Czechoslovakia to ward off Western imperialism. It serves to provide an ideology for empire, and to mobilize support for the government-subsidized system of military state capitalism. It is predictable, then, that opportunities to end the Cold War will be side-stepped, and that challenges to Cold War ideology will be bitterly resisted.

In many ways, American society is indeed open and liberal values are preserved. However, as the poor and the black know well, the liberal veneer can be thin. Mark Twain once wrote: "It is by the goodness of God that in our country we have those three unspeakably precious things: freedom of speech, freedom of conscience, and the prudence never to practice either of them."[47] Those who lack the prudence may well pay the cost.

A crucial element of the evolving postwar system is the increasing centralization of control in the economy and political life of the postwar world. A recent report by the staff of the Federal Trade Commission notes: "By the end of 1968, the 200 largest industrial corporations controlled over 60 per cent of the total assets held by all manufacturing corporations." In 1941, the same amount of power was spread over a thousand corporations. The report notes further that the top two hundred corporations are partially linked with one another and with other corporations in ways that may prevent or discourage independent behavior in market decisions.[48] These corporations are, furthermore, increasingly becoming international in the scope of their operations.

At the same time, in every parliamentary democracy, the role of parliament in policy formation is diminishing. The House Armed Services Committee described the role of Congress as "that of a sometimes querulous but essentially kindly uncle who complains while furiously puffing on his pipe but who finally, as everyone expects, gives in and hands over the allowance."[49] Careful studies of civil-military decisions show that this is an accurate perception. Harold Stein, Professor at the Woodrow Wilson School of Princeton University, writes that since World War II

> The basic determination of foreign-military policy, of military expenditures and organization, and of weapons has been made by civilians in the Executive Branch, usually with the President in active control. Congress has exercised an occasionally restraining but never a guiding hand.[50]

Senator Arthur Vandenberg, twenty years ago, expressed his fear that the American Chief Executive would become "the number one war lord of the earth."[51] That has since occurred. The clearest example, perhaps, was President Johnson's decision to escalate the war in Vietnam in February 1965, in cynical disregard of the expressed will of the electorate.[52] The recent invasion of Cambodia is a further step in this erosion of parliamentary power, so blatant that it has finally called forth significant gestures of senatorial opposition. These incidents reveal with perfect clarity the role of the public, acting through the parliamentary system, in decisions about peace and war.

Furthermore, these processes of centralization of control in economic and political life are closely related, by virtue of the interpenetration of the executive branch of the government and the corporate elite. Richard Barnet cites his study of the men "who have set the framework of America's national-security policy." Most of the top four hundred decision makers, he writes, "have come from executive suites and law offices within shouting distance of one another in fifteen city blocks in New York, Washington, Detroit, Chicago, and Boston."[53]

In general, democratic decision-making in a capitalist democracy is severely limited by the very fact that the commercial, financial, and industrial systems—the central institutions of the society—are in law and in principle excluded from public control or participation, except in the indirect ways in which any system of authority, no matter how autocratic, must be responsive to the public will. The tendencies toward concentration of power just noted, and now commonly discussed, further underscore the fundamental incompatibility of democracy and capitalism, particularly in its modern centralized form. The reliance of this system on production for war with the ideological mobilization of the population that is required, the paranoid fears that must be induced if the system is to be viable, simply indicates the severity of the current American crisis—a world crisis, given American power.

II

THE PEOPLE OF INDOCHINA have, for twenty years, been the victims of the American crisis. For twenty years, the United States has been attempting to maintain Western control over Indochina, first by support of the French, and then, when they proved inadequate to the task, through its own efforts. During this period there have been many modifications of tactics, and even occasional revision of goals as earlier hopes proved unrealizable. At first, there were recognizable and clearly presented material interests that motivated the American intervention in Indochina. I shall return to some of these later on. As time progressed and American involvement deepened, ideological factors became increasingly dominant. By now, a rational calculation of material interest would presumably dictate that the United States abandon Indochina to its own people, and influential segments of the American corporate elite itself are urging that this venture be "liquidated," as bad business, if for no other reason. Unfortunately, the anti-Communist crusade, so deeply rooted in the American system of postwar imperial state capitalism, cannot be turned on and off at will. Only a political leader of great courage and skill could extricate the United States from Indochina, even if the will were there. Hence even if the dominant segments of American society decide that the war is no longer a paying proposition, there is no guarantee that they will be able to bring this particular case of "anti-Communist" aggression to an end—and they are far from having reached this decision, it appears. Even today the hope remains that a military victory can be achieved, if only domestic protest can be stilled. There is little indication of any change of strategy, though new tactics are being proposed to achieve the long-range goal of dominating Indochina.

The original support for French imperialism was justified by the general ideology of anti-Communism. Dean Acheson's State Department decided that Ho Chi Minh was acting as an agent of Soviet imperialism in 1950, thus showing a remarkable grasp of the realities of international affairs (a degree of insight demonstrated also by then Assistant Secretary of State Dean Rusk in his famous and often-quoted remark that China, in 1951, was "a colonial Russian government—a Slavic Manchukuo on a large scale—it is not the government of China. It does not pass the first test. It is not Chinese."). An official State Department document explained:

> The United States government, convinced that neither national independence nor democratic evolution can exist in any area dominated by Soviet imperialism, considers the situation to be such as to warrant its according economic aid and military equipment to the Associated States of Indochina [i.e., the French colonial governments] and to France in order to assist them in restoring stability and permitting these states to pursue their peaceful and democratic development.[54]

After Dien Bien Phu the French were no longer able to maintain their effort. The Geneva Conference of 1954, so it appeared, established a sound and reasonable structure for the settlement of the affairs of

Indochina on the basis of peace, independence, and neutrality. The United States, however, had other ideas.

On May 3, 1954, as he departed from the international conference in Geneva, Secretary of State Dulles told the head of the French delegation, Jean Chauvel, that "above all, the Red River and Mekong deltas must be held, in order to prepare for the coming counterattack in two years' time."[55] Throughout, Dulles' attitude was quite negative. He strongly opposed the proposed neutralization of Laos and Cambodia, and appears to have tried to sabotage the negotiations. Anthony Eden understood his attitude as follows:

> As I reported to London at the time, the Americans seemed clearly apprehensive of reaching any agreement, however innocuous, with the Communists.[56]

Chauvel gave the following description of American intentions:

> The Americans can only accept the Geneva agreements provisionally. They have reconciled themselves to "respecting" them during the stated two-year period until the elections are held. That is, during these two years they will react to any Communist venture directed against the state of affairs defined in the agreements. But they are in no way prepared to let things take their course when the time comes. As far as they are concerned, the general elections must be prevented by means of any excuse whatsoever. The only purpose of the Geneva agreements, as they see them, is to provide a cover for the political, economic, and military preparations for the conquest. In May, Dulles thought the preparations would take two years. This re-conquest must be achieved, if not through war, then at least by the threat of war; therefore, the pact must create an international force designed either to wage war well or to make the threat of war effective.[57]

Dulles' motivations are outlined by Walter LaFeber in a recent summary of the development of American policy in Indochina:

> We became involved in Indochina twenty long years ago not because we were primarily concerned about that area, but because we were concerned about two other problems. These two problems were Japan and Western Europe. We were concerned about Japan because we wanted the Japanese to become, over a period of time, the bulwark against revolutions and Communist China. In 1950 we negotiated a

security pact with Japan. Between 1950 and 1954 a series of intelligent, persuasive statements by president Eisenhower and John Foster Dulles emphasized that Southeast Asia was important to the United States because Southeast Asian markets were important to Japanese industrial growth. Without a viable, pro-West Japan, there could be no effective containment of Asian Communism. In a private meeting of the Council of Foreign Relations in October, 1950, Dulles, then a key State Department policy-maker, argued that Japan must either exploit an open Southeast Asia or else she would turn towards her traditional markets of China. Because of the American determination to isolate China, such Sino-Japanese relations could not be tolerated. Southeast Asia would have to remain open…. [In 1954] Indochina continued to be regarded by Dulles, now Secretary of State, as of importance in the overall Asiatic picture whose focus was Japan. The European policy was changed slightly: Indochina became important because the manner in which we maintained anti-Communist forces there would demonstrate our commitment to the containment policy in Europe.[58]

Thus the American policy in Indochina was seen as a central component in American global strategy. A few years ago, LaFeber observed that when Eisenhower announced his "falling dominoes" theory on April 7, 1954, he referred specifically to Japan:

[Communist success in Indochina] takes away, in its economic aspects, that region that Japan must have as a trading area or Japan, in turn, will have only one place in the world to go—that is, toward the Communist areas in order to live. So, the possible consequences of the loss are just incalculable to the free world.

LaFeber added: "This thesis became a controlling assumption: the loss of Vietnam would mean the economic undermining and probable loss of Japan to Communist markets and ultimately to Communist influence if not control."[59]

Similar concerns were voiced, in 1955, by the prestigious Study Group cited earlier. Their report observes:

Japanese industry has long since outgrown its meager domestic resource-base and must find expanding overseas sources of food, fuel and industrial materials which can be purchased with expanding exports of manufactures. In the interwar period, the Japanese industrialists threw in their lot with the militarists in an effort to solve this problem though imperialism. Today the same problem faces them again in much aggravated form. The Japanese economy has now been shorn of its protected colonial markets, investment outlets and food and raw materials sources, and its trade with the Chinese mainland has been reduced to a trickle.[60]

The last reference is perhaps a bit disingenuous. There is reason to believe that American pressure was a factor in the reduction of the China trade. A recent study by Chitoshi Yanaga observes:

> At a closed regional meeting of American ambassadors in Asia in early March [1955], Secretary of State Dulles outlined American diplomatic strategy, a major goal of which was to develop markets for Japan in Southeast Asia *in order to counteract Communist trade efforts and to promote trade between Japan and Southeast Asian countries.*[61]

This was the culmination of a series of discussions over the preceding year which, in Yanaga's words, endorsed the view "that in the execution of Japan's plan of economic cooperation, the United States and the countries of Southeast Asia were inseparably tied to Japan."

The Study Group continues as follows:

> The history of the 1930's should be a warning to the West, and especially to the United States, that failure to make sufficient economic opportunity for the expansion of Japan's exports and for Japanese economic growth can be disastrous for the security of the West and the peace of the world. The logical way to open this opportunity would be to make possible greater Japanese participation in the development of Southern Asia. [P. 135.]

Elsewhere, the report notes that the concern of the United States "for expanding the sources of primary products and increasing the markets for industrial exports" in the underdeveloped countries "is primarily a function of our political and military concern for the economic health and military strength of Western Europe and Japan" (pp. 226–27); "these industrial economies can enjoy adequate rates of growth only if they can achieve a rapid and sustained increase of industrial exports and primary imports at satisfactory terms of trade" (p. 236); correspondingly, spokesmen for the less developed countries continually point out that the deterioration of the terms of trade, from their point of view, is a major factor in perpetuating their underdevelopment.

Of course, these discussions of political and economic advantages for the industrial societies, and how to guarantee them, are also spiced liberally with references to the humane and civilized goals of the West, whose "institutions express—however imperfectly—those universal ideals of human freedom, individual worth, and economic and social justice which the middle classes of the underdeveloped countries may yet come to value as much as, if not more than, material progress" (p. 161; meanwhile, "The aim of economic activity in the West is the maximization of money income—in one or another of its forms—by individuals through the investment of capital or of labor on one's own account or for, and under the direction of, others"—p. 143). The realization of these ideals is threatened in many ways: by collectivist totalitarianism, by the British "excessively egalitarian pattern of income distribution—excessive, that is, from the standpoint of savings, labor incentives and labor mobility,"[62] by irrational, Communist-inspired land redistribution as in Guatemala under Arbenz (p. 165), by the "nationalistic totalitarian or crypto-communist regimes" which "nearly succeeded in consolidating their rule" in such countries as Iran and Guatemala in the early 1950s (p. 180), and so on. Still, there is every possibility that "the millhands of Calcutta, the peasants of Egypt and the Indians of Guatemala" can "become politically more reliable and economically more cooperative members of the free world community," exercising the "capacity for self-control, for rational and morally valid choices, and for responsible actions" (pp. 154–57), under the guidance of native elites which the United States will establish and support and under the active leadership of the United States, which can no longer merely play the role of an infrequent and impartial arbiter in international affairs.[63]

Although the Indochina war in part develops through its own dynamics—the President, as noted earlier, is hardly likely to be willing to face the domestic political consequences of an American defeat, even if the alternative is a possible global war—it may be that the "controlling assumption" that LaFeber persuasively identified remains an important factor in accounting for the persistence of the American effort to control Southeast Asia.

Returning to 1954, after the Geneva Conference the United States quickly seized control of South Vietnam, eliminating British and French influence and establishing the Diem dictatorship, which, in a sense, still persists.[64] As the Indian diplomat B. S. N. Murti of the International Control Commission put it, "in September, 1954, it was the United States, not the Vietnamese people, who decided that Ngo Dinh Diem would continue to be the President of South Vietnam."[65] With substantial American assistance and liberal use of force and terror, Diem succeeded in imposing his rule and subverting the Geneva agreements, while rejecting all diplomatic efforts and blocking even minimal contacts with North Vietnam.[66] By 1959, the situation was such that a high American official in Saigon could report: "The Viet-Minh ... can make a strong case that the United States is effectively replacing France as the new master of Free Vietnam."[67]

Meanwhile, the United States created the Southeast Asia Treaty Organization (SEATO); its "principal purpose," according to Dulles, "was to provide our President legal authority to intervene in Indochina."[68]

Efforts to bring Cambodia into the American anti-Communist alliance were unavailing. Cambodia's American-supported neighbors, South Vietnam and Thailand, blockaded the Cambodian coast and carried out border incursions in the late 1950s, and attempted, probably with American aid, to overthrow Sihanouk in 1959, but without success.

In Laos, however, American subversion succeeded in toppling the coalition government and finally imposing the regime of the military dictator Phoumi Nosavan in 1959, recapitulating what the United States had achieved in Thailand a decade earlier.[69] However, the consequences in Laos were so appalling, from the point of view of the American government, that it undertook a new approach in 1961 and joined in the second Geneva conference which, in 1962, established the basis for neutralization of Laos and the formation of a new Government of National Union. This coalition once again collapsed. The Royal Lao Government and the Pathet Lao have traded accusations as to the cause, and there is much that remains unclear. By 1964 a new civil war was underway, with the United States supporting the Royal Lao Government and the Democratic Republic of Vietnam (North Vietnam) supporting the Pathet Lao.

In Vietnam, the succession of American-supported regimes had, by 1965, lost the war in province after province to local South Vietnamese resistance forces (which the Americans call "Viet Cong"), including South Vietnamese who returned from North Vietnam after the final breakdown of the Geneva agreements (from 1959, according to American government sources). Since even the vast American support efforts of the early 1960s were unavailing, the United States sent what amounted to an occupying army in 1965 and subsequent years, and began the intensive and regular bombardment of North and South Vietnam in early February 1965. The first North Vietnamese units were detected in South Vietnam in April 1965, according to the Pentagon.[70]

George Kahin summarizes the events of this period as follows:

> Any dispassionate examination of the relevant data makes clear that insurrectionary activity against the Saigon government is southern-rooted, began in the south at southern initiative in response to southern demands. It commenced not as a consequence of any dictate from Hanoi, but in fact was initially contrary to Hanoi's injunctions. The NLF finally gave political articulation and leadership to an already advanced and well-developed, widespread reaction in the south against the harshness and heavy-handedness of Diem's Saigon government. It represented an assertion of leadership by southern Vietminh veterans no longer willing to accept the restraint so long urged by Hanoi.[71]

It is useful to note that although American government propaganda invariably speaks of "aggression from the North," the documentary evidence presented by American officials and academic advisers is entirely in support of Kahin's summary, and in fact these same individuals generally concede as much in more technical discussions.[72]

The Tet offensive of January 1968 led to a reassessment of American strategy. To some influential policy makers, it indicated that the strategy of military victory was not feasible. Under-Secretary of the Air Force Townsend Hoopes drafted a memorandum in March 1968, in which he concluded:

Anything resembling a clear-cut military victory in Vietnam appears possible only at the price of literally destroying SVN, tearing apart the social and political fabric of our own country, alienating our European friends, and gravely weakening the whole free world structure of relations of alliances.[73]

This point of view had a certain influence, but was not adopted. Hoopes puts it as follows:

Military victory had been foreclosed both by events and the decisions of March 31, yet half the government, tacitly encouraged by the President, continued its ardent pursuit. And because military victory was not firmly put aside as an unreality, the idea of an "independent South Vietnam free of communist influence" continued to circulate in influential places as a valid, viable objective of US policy. Until October, when Clifford, Harriman, and Vance succeeded in bringing off a total bombing halt, the bombing effort was not really curtailed, but only geographically rearranged; statistically, there was an intensification.[74]

It would have been more accurate to say that in October the bombing effort was also geographically rearranged, and was, again, intensified. The planes released from the bombardment of North Vietnam were shifted to Laotian targets and the bombing—including heavy bombardment of civilian targets in northern Laos—reached its highest peak of the war in early 1969.

It is useful to recall, as well, the American reaction in South Vietnam to the termination of the regular bombing of the North and the opening of negotiations in Paris in November 1968. Douglas Robinson quoted military sources that outlined plans to use the warplanes freed from daily missions over North Vietnam "for increased air strikes to support ground actions in the South."[75] Moreover:

In the Gulf of Tonkin, American warships began to steam toward positions off the coast of South Vietnam. Military leaders said that the battleship New Jersey and the other cruisers and destroyers that had been used to bombard the North Vietnamese coast would now be used for the military operation in the South.

—as was reported shortly after. But the most cynical aspect of American military planning was indicated in the "extremely important gain" anticipated by the Allied military command:

> If the North Vietnamese do not try to build up their forces as a result of the bombing halt … at least a division of American troops would be freed to carry out an operation long thought necessary by the military—the ferreting out of Vietcong leaders and cadres in Communist-dominated villages and hamlets around South Vietnam.

Thus if the "Communists" show their sincerity by restricting their military activities in the South, we reciprocate by using our military forces to eradicate the political and administrative structure of the National Liberation Front, to deprive it of what South Vietnamese Prime Minister Tran Van Do had earlier described as "a political way to take over South Vietnam," namely, "the integration of the Front," its acceptance as a political party—sure disaster for the Saigon regime, which professed itself, then as now, to be unable to organize South Vietnam politically.

General Abrams explained the matter clearly to his senior commanders: "The North Vietnamese personnel and units are totally dependent … for their existence as well as their military operations … [on] the political, administrative and paramilitary structure…." It is this indigenous South Vietnamese structure "on which his whole movement depends." "So, you should go out and work against them and find them"—a proper goal for the American army of occupation.[76] The United States military command quickly reported some measure of success, an improvement in the kill-ratio, attributed to "the pressure being maintained by allied forces" which were seeking "to attack the entire North Vietnamese-Vietcong system in South Vietnam."[77]

The New York Times on November 23, 1968, cites Allied officials as pointing out "that a decrease in the activity of regular enemy forces logically leads to an increase in allied activity against guerrillas," and particularly against "the Vietcong infrastructure, which is where so much of it really starts." The report describes an operation in which 3,000 civilians were evacuated and "painstakingly screened" by intelligence officers (100 "enemy forces" dead, about a dozen suspected Viet Cong identified). On a facing page, the *Times* quotes President Johnson: "We cannot have productive talks in an atmosphere where the cities are being shelled and where the DMZ is being abused."

On December 14, 1968, *The New York Times* commented editorially on the fact that "Since the bombing halt, the enemy has initiated only one battalion-sized assault [while] by comparison last month American troops mounted 63 battalion operations and South Vietnam staged 664 such campaigns" in an effort "to extend South Vietnamese Government control over disputed areas and territory long controlled by the Vietcong." I. F. Stone checked these figures with the Pentagon (they were not challenged) and discovered further that "the tempo of offensive operations from our side had gone up about 25% in December over November." The number of actions initiated by the "enemy" was classified, for reasons unexplained, though hardly obscure.[78] With the advent of the Nixon administration, "accelerated pacification" has been continued in this manner. Surely the Vietnamese or the American people would have to be naive to the point of near imbecility to put any faith in the good intentions of the American government.

In fact, the cynicism of the American response to the opportunities for peace in 1968 merely recapitulates, in another form, the reaction to Geneva in 1954. The record is quite clear that the Viet Minh, the forces that had fought and defeated the French, accepted the Geneva Accords in good faith and made a serious effort to initiate discussions that would lead to the elections promised in 1956. The American-instituted regime in the South took advantage of this naiveté to institute an extensive repression in which thousands were killed and tens of thousands imprisoned. By 1959 a good part of the former Viet Minh political structure had been wiped out. In contrast, there were apparently very few cases of political reprisal in the North, nor has the American government or its Saigon subsidiary made any specific claim to the contrary. For details, see the references cited above, and many other sources. In the elections of 1967 neither Communists nor neutralists whose activities might be interpreted (by the government) as sympathetic to the Communists were permitted to participate. Since then repression has proceeded unabated. Under the circumstances, the National Liberation Front (now the Provisional Revolutionary Government of South Vietnam) can certainly not accept any solution (cease-fire, or some election formula) that leaves control of the South in the hands of the Saigon authorities. This would amount to suicide—literally. Thus all of the formulas that have been proposed, however vaguely, by the United States in the Paris negotiations are totally unacceptable, since all, in one form or another, require that the Viet Cong lay down their arms, trusting to the good intentions of the Saigon government and the United States, an obvious absurdity.

Since the curtailment of regular bombing of North Vietnam in November 1968, the United States has further escalated the war in Laos, both on the ground and in the air, and has recently invaded Cambodia. At the time of the Nixon inaugural, the *U.S. News & World Report* (January 27, 1969) reported that "those most deeply involved in overall strategy" foresee a slow reduction of United States forces in Vietnam to 200,000 men by the end of 1971, as "the basis for a long-haul, low-cost effort in Vietnam that could continue indefinitely."[79] Since that time, the American Expeditionary Force in South Vietnam has been reduced to below half a million men and there is talk of further withdrawals. From the rather vague reports from Washington, it appears that the present intention is to leave a force of perhaps a quarter of a million American soldiers along with the approximately 70,000 troops that the United States has brought in from South Korea, Thailand, Australia, and New Zealand, operating from the huge American bases in South Vietnam and supported by the Pacific Naval and Air Command with its sanctuaries scattered from Thailand to Okinawa. There is no indication that the intensive bombardment of Indochina will be in any way reduced or that any efforts will be made to reach a political settlement. On the contrary, it is likely that the "technological war" will intensify, since it involves few American casualties and is therefore felt to be tolerable at home. A fair estimate is that military and subsequent political victory, in the sense described by Hoopes (see note 73), continue to be the aim of American policy.

However, the United States, despite its formidable military resources, does not dominate the situation. The war has now expanded over all of Indochina. The United States finds itself sustaining regimes in South Vietnam, Laos, and Cambodia that can command little domestic support. A Viet-Lao-Khmer alliance of popular liberation forces is in formation, backed strongly by China. The war may spread to other areas of Southeast Asia—in particular, the United States can hardly hope to continue to use Thailand as a privileged sanctuary for its Indochina war, as it has been doing since early 1964, without a response from those peoples whom it is attacking. Thailand now has troops engaged in South Vietnam, Laos, and Cambodia, in part for counterinsurgency training under American guidance, but in part, no doubt, because of the guerrilla threat that results from its use as an American sanctuary, and that intensifies as it sends troops to help combat insurgency in the countries of Indochina. The current situation is outlined in a recent report from Bangkok, as the Thai see it:

> *Eastern frontiers in danger:* on the maps all the frontiers situated to the east of the country today are bordered with red, the red of the guerrilla. All along the Mekong which, for almost 700 kilometers, borders the country, the army faces incursions from guerrillas coming from Laos. In the north operations continue against guerrilla forces that maintain at present a close cooperation with the Lao fighters of the red Prince Souphanouvong. Bangkok has replied by sending its own advisers to aid the Royal Lao Army.
>
> To the south pro-Chinese guerrillas operate on both sides of the Malaysian frontier. The Thai and Malaysian armies carry out coordinated operations against them. But it is the frontier of Cambodia which may pose the greatest dangers. Bangkok is only 200 kilometers from Cambodia; and the fall of Prince Sihanouk, in precipitating pro-Communist troops of several origins (Vietnamese, Cambodian) into the interior of Cambodia, has opened to "subversion" the vast plains drained by the Menam and the tributaries of the Mekong.[80]

The American bases are also menaced, the report continues, not only the air bases at Udorn and Ubon, not far from the Laotian border, but also the great aeronaval base at Sattahip, which is only about 100 miles from Cambodia. UPI reports that Thailand has put its forces on "full alert" along the Cambodian border, where General Prapas Charusathien, commander of the Thai army, describes the situation as "serious." The presence of Communist troops in Cambodia, he says, represents the biggest threat to Thailand's security (i.e., the security of the Thai elite) in the past fifty years. Moreover, a Chinese-built all-weather highway under construction in northern Laos, said to be protected by Chinese troops and anti-aircraft, may also someday be used for support of Thai guerrillas or even direct invasion if the United States should escalate again elsewhere. In the far north of Thailand near the border of Laos and Burma and not far from China an American battalion, recently arrived from Vietnam, is reported to be constructing a jungle road to the border post of Hin Teak, in an area where three to four thousand Nationalist Chinese are said to be operating: fighting Communists, guarding the frontier, protecting the opium cara-vans, and sending spies and commandos into southern China.[81] From the far north to the Gulf of Siam, the Thai border is likely to be increasingly troubled and the Thai elite threatened in its rule of the country that has been, for many years, America's major base for its Southeast Asian wars.

Furthermore, American provocation of China has been serious. To cite just the most dramatic case, from 1965 to 1968 the air war against North Vietnam was in part directed against internal Chinese communica-tion lines, namely, the rail and road connections that were the sole con-nection between southwestern China and the rest of China, and that hap-pen to pass through North Vietnam near Hanoi. If the United States were to escalate to the point where the destruction of the Pathet Lao, the National Liberation Front, the Sihanouk government and its emerging local army, or the Democratic Republic of Vietnam appeared likely, direct Chinese intervention might follow. The Soviet Union, though unlikely to intervene in force in Indochina, might well react elsewhere in an effort to maintain its prestige and authority—perhaps in the Middle East, where a highly inflammatory situation persists.

It is quite possible that at the present and projected level of American involvement in the Indochina war, the American position may suddenly collapse or slowly erode. In the past, perceived threats have led to highly erratic behavior on the part of the American government, Franz Schurmann has recently commented on this recurrent pattern:

> The air war over Laos began on May 17, 1964, after a crisis of little more than a day caused by the fall of a minuscule Laotian town called Tha Thom, apparently but not really to the Pathet Lao. The most notoriously sudden decision of all was Tonkin Gulf. Hardly had the conflicting reports on the second clash with North Vietnamese PT boats come into Washington than the word went out to launch mas-

sive air strikes against North Vietnam. The most critical escalation of
all, the February 7 air attack on North Vietnam which launched the
bombing war, was decided on within twelve hours of the Vietcong
attack on Pleiku.[82]

Other examples might be cited. Jonathan Mirsky and Stephen
Stonefield give a detailed discussion of one incident, which they summa-
rize as follows:

> After a CIA-sponsored Lao leader provoked a clash during the 1962
> Geneva "cease-fire," the Kennedy Administration seriously consid-
> ered a nuclear attack on the Chinese Mainland, although its own mil-
> itary observer on the scene reported no foreign troops engaged other
> than American Special Forces.[83]

One recalls, of course, the Cuban missile crisis of the same year, when the
Kennedy administration was willing to face what it considered an
extremely high risk of nuclear war in order to establish the principle that
we have the right to maintain missiles on the Russian border (obsolescent
missiles, which had already been ordered withdrawn, unknown to the
Russians), but that they do not have the equivalent right. Thus
Khrushchev's offer that all these missiles should be withdrawn provoked
highly irrational reactions, and was rejected.

It is not unlikely that the Nixon administration might be led to desperate measures, particularly if domestic turmoil and loss of confidence
continue, along with the internal economic crisis that is closely related to
the Indochina war. Speculating about this possibility, Richard Barnet
warns—quite plausibly—of the danger that the United States government
might resort to the use of nuclear weapons. He points out that as of 1968,
there were 5,500 nuclear weapons in the Southeast Asia area and recalls
some of President Nixon's earlier pronouncements, for example, the following:

> The weapons which were used during the Korean war and World War
> II are obsolete. Our artillery and our tactical Air Force in the Pacific
> are now equipped with atomic explosives which can and will be used
> on military targets with precision and effectiveness.
>
> It is foolish to talk about the possibility that the weapons which
> might be used in the event war breaks out in the Pacific would be lim-
> ited to the conventional Korean and World War II types of explosives.

Our forces could not fight an effective war in the Pacific with those types of explosives if they wanted to. Tactical atomic explosives are now conventional and will be used against the military targets of any aggressive force.[84]

The President is not alone in such recommendations. To cite a further example, Hanson Baldwin, military commentator for *The New York Times*, has urged that in the post-Vietnam era we be prepared to "escalate technologically rather than with manpower" as we "bolster movements under attack and secure them against creeping Communism." Such escalation, he suggests, might involve the use "of small nuclear devices for *defensive* purposes."[85] Particularly interesting is the concept of "defensive purposes"—as we bolster a weak government against creeping Communism. Surety no rational or realistic person will discount the possibility that the United States might suddenly resort to nuclear weapons. Those who retain the instinct for survival, not to speak of minimal concern for their fellow man, will seek ways to act before rather than after the event.

III

THE AMERICAN WAR IN Indochina has been based on two principles: physical destruction in areas that are beyond the reach of American troops, and the use of what are euphemistically called "population control measures" in areas that can be occupied by American forces or the forces that they train, supply, advise, and provide with air and artillery support. Since 1959 forced relocation has been undertaken to concentrate the population. Population removal through defoliation began in 1961, according to one Vietnamese eyewitness.[86] Long reports that "It proved easier to order fliers to spray crops from the air than to send in ground troops to force the people out by setting fire to their fields and houses." Later, population removal was carried out largely by air and artillery bombardment, particularly after the establishment of vast free-fire zones. To put the matter in the simplest and most dispassionate terms, massacre and forced evacuation of the peasantry, combined with rigorous control over those forced under American rule, is the essence of American strategy in Vietnam.[87]

The facts are easily established, and the reasons are also fairly clear: there is no other technique that can be effective against a "people's war." The reasons for the success of the "people's war" are also not obscure. Years

ago the strongly anti-Communist Australian reporter Denis Warner, who
knows Southeast Asia well, observed that "in hundreds of villages all over
South-East Asia the only people working at the grass roots for an uplift in
people's living standards are the Communists."[88] In his judgment, this is a
"monstrous trick," but his judgment does not seem to be shared by the
peasants of Vietnam. United States government documents suffice to show
the effects of this grass-roots work, which forced the United States to resort
to violence and terror.[89]

Observing the American response to the "people's war," one recalls
once again the Philippine campaign at the turn of the century. For example, when President Theodore Roosevelt gave orders to pacify Samar,
General "Jake" Smith ordered that Samar be transformed into "a howling
wilderness." "I want no prisoners," he ordered.[90] "I wish you to kill and
burn; the more you burn and kill the better it will please me."[91]

For a clear explanation of the theory behind the American strategy in
Vietnam, one can turn to an important essay by Professor Samuel
Huntington, Chairman of the Department of Government of Harvard
University and Chairman of the Council on Vietnamese Studies of the
Southeast Asia Development Advisory Group (SEADAG).[92] He writes:
"In an absent-minded way the United States in Vietnam may well have
stumbled upon the answer to 'wars of national liberation.'" The answer to
such wars is "forced-draft urbanization and modernization which rapidly
brings the country in question out of the phase in which a rural revolutionary movement can hope to generate sufficient strength to come to
power." He presents a more detailed description of "the answer" we have
stumbled upon in a comment on Sir Robert Thompson's contention that
People's Revolutionary War is immune to "the direct application of
mechanical and conventional power." This Professor Huntington denies:

> In the light of recent events, this statement needs to be seriously qual-
> ified. For if the "direct application of mechanical and conventional
> power" takes place on such a massive scale as to produce a massive
> migration from countryside to city, the basic assumptions underlying
> the Maoist doctrine of revolutionary war no longer operate. The
> Maoist-inspired rural revolution is undercut by the American-spon-
> sored urban revolution.

He also notes that the Viet Cong remains "a powerful force which cannot be dislodged from its constituency so long as the constituency continues to exist."

These comments, no doubt accurate, provide a succinct explanation for American strategy. Since the Viet Cong is a powerful force which cannot be dislodged from its constituency so long as the constituency continues to exist, the United States command has resorted to military force, causing the migration of rural population to refugee camps[93] and urban slums where, it is hoped, the Viet Cong constituency can be properly controlled.

No sentimentalist, Huntington expresses no qualms, no judgment at all about such methods (which clearly involve war crimes as defined by Nuremberg Principle VI, for example). His approach follows the principle enunciated by two counterinsurgency theorists recently: "All the dilemmas [of counterinsurgency] are practical and as neutral in an ethical sense as the laws of physics."[94] Thus Huntington uses such terms as "urbanization" to refer to the process by which we drive the Viet Cong "constituency" into refugee camps and cities, and he speaks of the "American-sponsored urban revolution," the "*social* revolution," that we have brought about in this way. So successful is "urbanization," he might have added, that the population density of Saigon is now estimated at more than twice that of Tokyo. Lucky Vietnamese.

After describing how we may have stumbled upon the answer to peasant revolutions, Huntington adds this paragraph:

> Time in South Viet Nam is increasingly on the side of the Government. But in the short run, with half the population still in the countryside, the Viet Cong will remain a powerful force which cannot be dislodged from its constituency so long as the constituency continues to exist. Peace in the immediate future must hence be based on accommodation.

Obviously, if the Viet Cong constituency will continue to exist *in the short run*, it follows that *in the immediate future*, if there is to be peace, it must be based on accommodation (or American withdrawal, which is rejected as "misplaced moralism"). This is not a policy proposal, but rather, indubitably, an immediate consequence of the assumption that the Viet Cong will remain a powerful force. Why this assumption? Huntington explains:

> To eliminate Viet Cong control in these areas would be an expensive, time-consuming and frustrating task. It would require a much larger and more intense military and pacification effort than is currently contemplated by Saigon and Washington.

Since "the answer to 'wars of national liberation'" will, in this instance, require an effort that is "expensive, time-consuming and frustrating," and since Saigon and Washington cannot or will not take the necessary steps, evidently another approach must be sought. Therefore Huntington proposes that the Viet Cong accept an arrangement rather like that of the Hoa Hao (who, he asserts, went through the typical evolution: development of social and political consciousness, confrontation with the central government, defeat by the central government, withdrawal from the national political scene, accommodation). Given the present "rates of urbanization and of modernization," his prognosis is that the Viet Cong "could now degenerate into the protest of a declining rural minority increasingly dependent upon outside support" (though at one time, prior to "urbanization and modernization," the Viet Cong "had the potential for developing into a truly comprehensive revolutionary force with an appeal to both rural and urban groups").

Suppose, however, that the NLF refuses to be satisfied with the generous offer of some degree of local control within the framework of national power set by the United States military and the Saigon authorities it has installed. Suppose that the NLF is unwilling to accept an "accommodation" under which it is likely to degenerate into a declining rural minority. Then, Mr. Huntington explains, we can make it clear that "this confrontation cannot succeed." He does not list the methods, but they can easily be imagined.

Thus, although the general answer to peasant revolution may be beyond our grasp in the short run, given present political realities, we may still be able to impose (by force) an "accommodation" that is likely to lead to the political solution that we have determined to be appropriate. Nothing could indicate more clearly the persistence of what can only be described as colonialist assumptions, pragmatically attuned to the political and economic constraints within which policy makers are forced to operate.

Huntington illustrates his premises further in some remarks about the Dominican intervention of 1965.[95] In evaluating an intervention, he explains, "results are all that count." Thus the Dominican intervention appears to have been a success, even in the eyes of those who felt in 1965 that there were no "good political and moral grounds ... whatsoever for intervening in the Dominican Republic." Why? Because "whether or not there was a threat of communist takeover on the island, we were able to go in, restore order, negotiate a truce among conflicting parties, hold reasonably honest elections which the right man won,[96] withdraw our troops, and promote a very considerable amount of social and economic reform." Thus the intervention was consistent with the general purposes and methods of intervention, namely, the attempt "to minimize violence and instability in foreign countries" (though not, of course, to minimize the kind of violence carried out by our friends in Indonesia, where hundreds of thousands were massacred,[97] or the kind we and our allies perpetrate in Vietnam; nor to support the kind of stability we find in North Vietnam, which has "probably the most stable government in Southeast Asia"—a "bitter truth but a real one," according to Professor Huntington).

Similarly in Vietnam, if all goes well, we may ultimately be able to cope with the problems of "urbanization" or to reverse the process: "After the war, massive government programs will be required either to resettle migrants in rural areas or to rebuild the cities and promote peacetime urban employment."[98] And with luck, we may be able to arrange matters so that the "right man" wins in a "reasonably honest election."[99] Meanwhile we continue, absent-mindedly, to contribute to the theory and practice of political development by artillery and aerial bombardment in the rural areas. As Huntington explains it, we thereby help the GVN to bridge the gap to the countryside, from which it is "divorced," by "inducing substantial migration of people from the countryside to the cities" and by promoting economic development.[100]

The problem of lack of resolve on the home front touched upon by Professor Huntington in the comments quoted above has concerned other government advisers as well. Thus Huntington's colleague Professor Ithiel

Pool, then Chairman of the Department of Political Science at MIT and a Defense Department consultant who also directs research on pacification and urban insurgency, discussed the interrelation of Vietnam policy and domestic attitudes at the Stevenson Institute Conference to which I have already referred.[101] Pool observes that "our worst mistake in Vietnam clearly was to initiate the bombing of the north." The explanation is interesting:

> Before that started, it was my view that the United States as a democracy could not stand the moral protest that would arise if we rained death from the skies upon an area where there was no war. After the bombing started, I decided I had been in error. For a while there seemed to be no outcry of protest, but time brought it on. Now I would return to my original view with an important modification, namely, time. Public reactions do not come immediately. Many actions that public opinion would otherwise make impossible are possible if they are short-term. I believe we can fairly say that unless it is severely provoked or unless the war succeeds fast, a democracy cannot choose war as an instrument of policy.

This is spoken in the tone of a true scientist correcting a few of the variables that entered into his computations—and to be sure, Professor Pool is scornful of those "anti-intellectuals" such as Senator Fulbright, who do not comprehend "the vital importance of applied social science for making the actions of our government in foreign areas more rational and humane than they have been." In contrast to the anti-intellectuals, the applied social scientist understands that it is perfectly proper to "rain death from the skies upon an area where there was no war," so long as we "succeed fast." If victory is delayed, "the cohesion of the democratic community" will be destroyed by the choice of war as an instrument of policy. Furthermore, we cannot abandon this instrument of policy, for we must "come to realize that we can live in safety only in a world in which the political systems of all states are democratic and pacifically oriented"—like ours. Though it would be preferable "to influence political outcomes" without the use of force, we must continue to be ready "to cope with dangerous armed ideologies" as in Vietnam, at least until the various "aspects of our value system"—in particular, its "pacific orientation"—spread more widely throughout the world.

It would seem to follow, then, that our failure in Vietnam is traceable to a serious inadequacy in our own political system: its inability to contain the moral outrage that resulted when we began to rain death on a country where there was no war. This is precisely the conclusion reached by Professor Pool, who is not short on logic: "… we are paying an inordinate price for our goals" and "in that sense we certainly have failed—but more in the United States than in Vietnam. The agonizing political lesson that racks this country is that there has been a failure of our own political system." The performance of our political system has been "disappointing" and "gloomy" (but not too gloomy, since "there is no evidence that either the government or the majority of the public are ready to withdraw abruptly in disarray from Vietnam"). Our system has proved incapable of dealing with the "intensity of dissent" which, along with other factors, threatens domestic stability. "These are failings of which we usually accuse the Vietnamese, but the criticism is more fairly addressed against ourselves."

In short, a democratic community is incapable of waging aggressive war in a brutal manner, and this is a *failure of democracy*. What is wrong is not the policy of raining death on an area where there is no war, still less the far more intensive bombardment of South Vietnam, which goes unmentioned. What is wrong is the inability of a democratic system to contain the inevitable dissent and moral outrage. The conclusion appears obvious, and we may ask how long it will be before at least some influential voices in liberal America will explain the necessity for removing the major impediment to the achievement of what Professor Pool refers to as "our national goals."

Huntington, incidentally, appears to share the qualms of his colleague regarding the inadequacies of democracy as a political system in a period when, as Pool puts it, we feel "massively threatened." Thus he recommends that our "involvements" be kept "reasonably limited, discreet, and *covert*" (my italics) and he feels that even the "shift toward introversion in our society" may have "side benefits," in that the "more limited forms of foreign involvement" to which we will be restricted will be facilitated "in the sense that there will be less public attention and concern directed to these issues."[102]

The plain fact is that a democracy cannot fight a brutal, drawn-out war of aggression. Most people are not gangsters. Unless public concern can be deflected, unless intervention is discreet and covert, there will be protest, disaffection, and resistance. Either the war will have to go, or the democracy.

IV

IN SEPTEMBER 1967, THE Inter-University Council of the Student Unions of Can Tho University, Van Hanh University, Saigon University, and Dalat University directed an open letter to President Johnson in which they wrote:

> The American intervention in the Vietnamese internal situation since after the Geneva Accord in 1954 has made the Vietnamese people regard the United States as replacing the French colonizers. The American policy, instead of helping the Vietnamese people, only pushes them into a destructive and bloody war. The Vietnamese people, principally in the countryside, have been living in misery, and because of the American intervention the country has been split and its struggling force reduced…. If Mr. President and your government continue their policy of supporting the individuals without consideration of the Vietnamese people's aspirations, we will consider the United States of America as an aggressor instead of an ally fighting for Independence, Peace and Unification of our country.[103]

In June 1968, the Students' Association of Saigon submitted the following manifesto:

> After the Tet offensive, the majority of South Vietnamese people saw that the country was about to undergo a historic change. After years of incessant fighting, the conflict cannot be solved by a military victory. On the contrary, the bombardments have caused more and more damage, exhausted the energy of the people and the national potentials. Up till now this destruction continues due to foreign imperialism. The national civilization has become therefore desperate. Aware of the danger of total extermination and seen for themselves how the bombardments have murdered the people, destroyed painstakingly erected constructions, the Representative Council of Saigon Students, before history, before the people, before the whole student community whose only aim is to serve the people, solemnly declares: It is now the

moment to solve the Vietnamese conflict, to avoid the total extermination of the Vietnamese people....[104]

Within a few weeks, the official newspaper of the Students' Association was closed and its editor sentenced by a military tribunal to five years at hard labor, where he joined the President of the General Association of Saigon Students and many of the other officers of the Association, as well as Truong Dinh Dzu and innumerable others. According to the Saigon Daily News, there are 100,000 persons in South Vietnamese jails, suffering such conditions as these:

> The Can Tho provincial jail [which] was built by the French for 500 prisoners is now used to keep over 2,000. Other prisons through the country are in a similar situation. Detainees have no room to sit. Legs of most prisoners have been swollen for having to stand on their feet to sleep....[105]

The *Saigon Daily News* was suspended by the government on November 14, the tenth newspaper closed in twenty days.

In September 1968, Professor Ly Chanh Trung delivered a speech at the Saigon Student Union Center explaining why he wanted peace. I quote the initial paragraphs:

> I want peace, first of all, because I am a Vietnamese. Being a Vietnamese, I cannot stand anymore the sight of Vietnamese blood continuing to be spilled more and more each day—not only the blood of the soldiers on both sides, but also the blood of hundreds of thousands of innocent civilians, of old men and old women, of women and children—while a number of other Vietnamese unconcernedly seek after money and eat and make merry in a dissolute manner, as if they were living in Paris or New York, or, to be more exact, on another planet, since the inhabitants of Paris and New York may well concern themselves with the present war in Viet Nam more than they do.
>
> Being a Vietnamese, I can no longer put up with the sight of foreigners who presume to have the right to destroy my country, with the most modern and terrible means, and all in the name of "protecting the freedom" of the people of southern Viet Nam—that is to say, a kind of "freedom" which the inhabitants of the southern part of Viet Nam have been throwing up and vomiting out for the last ten years already, without yet being able to swallow.

Surely, there are many Americans who honestly believe that they have come here to "protect freedom," and I sincerely thank them [for their good intentions]. But they are mistaken, or have been cheated, because if the inhabitants of the southern part of Viet Nam had truly experienced freedom as an automatic result of independence, then they would have had more than enough strength to protect their own freedom without having to inconvenience anybody at all! But, unfortunately, the inhabitants of the southern part of Viet Nam have not been able to enjoy freedom, and have not had the chance to be the masters of their own destiny, precisely because the Americans, in the name of the protectors of freedom, have, in fact, been protecting regimes which stamp out that freedom.

And when these regimes crumbled or failed, not because of "Communist terrorism" but because of their own decomposure, powerlessness, and lack of justice, the only way Americans then knew to "protect freedom" was by the several millions of tons of bombs used to crush to pieces the very land of Viet Nam, and by the gigantic streams of dollars which deluge Vietnamese society in the south—that is to say, by destroying the very roots of the material and spiritual foundations of this country.[106]

On October 15, 1969, ninety-three Catholic priests and intellectuals now residing in France together with "a great number of Catholics in Vietnam" (whose names were not published for fear of retaliation by the Saigon government) published an open letter on the occasion of the Moratorium, in which they wrote:

How can the U.S.A. be wicked enough to wish to exterminate all of our people to defend an idea, a theory, which time has adequately demonstrated to have only been a myth and never a reality? ... Those whom the U.S.A. accuses in its ignorance as Communists, are in reality our relatives, our brothers, our sisters, our friends dispersed in villages and hamlets. They are only peasants, workers, peddlers, hairdressers, and herdsmen. They ask only one thing: to be masters of their own home and to gain a livelihood by the sweat of their brow.[107]

I can obviously not presume to judge how widespread such sentiments may be among the people of South Vietnam. I doubt that any Westerners have the slightest idea what is happening in the teeming slums of Saigon, or among the millions of refugees, or in the villages of Vietnam.

In Vientiane a few weeks ago I met two Americans who had lived for several years in Vietnam, not in American compounds, but in intimate involvement with the Vietnamese. One, a former IVS volunteer, had worked closely with Vietnamese youth in Saigon. They impressed me greatly with their understanding and intelligence, and even more by the sympathetic concern that they felt for the character and unique quality of Vietnamese life and culture. Both had left Saigon, with deep regrets, because of the hostility toward Americans which, they report, only the most insensitive observer can now fail to perceive, sentiments so widespread and deeply felt that life is intolerable for any American who hopes for more than superficial contact with Vietnamese society. I heard many similar comments from reporters who had worked in South Vietnam. One would surely conclude, from such observations, that the information reaching Americans is of highly dubious quality.

Other sources support this conclusion. Consider a recent study by Harvey Meyerson on the Delta province of Vinh Long where he spent much of 1967 and early 1968. He returned in December 1968 to investigate the reports of great American success in the "accelerated pacification" program. A primary indicator of success, he notes, is the number of Viet Cong defectors, which rose sharply beginning in August 1968. The sharp rise coincided with a remarkable innovation, the "third party inducement program," whereby "cash rewards were offered to persons who induced Viet Cong to defect." Studying the defectors, Meyerson made some curious discoveries. For one thing, almost all were quite recent recruits to the Viet Cong. In fact, many appeared to be peasants whose identity cards had been taken by the Viet Cong after the Tet offensive, and who were faced with the option of either imprisonment by the government, or "defection," with its various material rewards. Third, it appeared that the "third party inducement program" was serving as an excellent device to funnel funds to "inducers" (hence, no doubt, ultimately to the Viet Cong in many cases) after the inevitable siphoning off by government officials down the line. But most interesting was the discovery that of 145 "defectors" analyzed in one group, no less than 142 elected to return to their home hamlets. As Meyerson notes, a true defector who returned to his home hamlet "would live in constant fear of Viet Cong reprisal."

Presumably, then, the "defection" was carried out with the connivance or at the initiative of the Viet Cong. The Americans in charge of the programs were aware of none of this. Meyerson concludes:

> The Viet Cong in Vinh Long may have been collapsing. But if this was the case, the Americans in Vinh Long did not know about it. They could not know about it. They were living in a dream world.[108]

Quite apart from the specific study of Vietnam, one can draw on the general colonialist experience. Gandhi, at his trial in 1922, explained how "a subtle but effective system of terrorism and an organized display of force on the one hand, and the deprivation of all powers of retaliation and self-defense on the other, had emasculated the people and induced in them the habit of simulation."[109] Hence the exasperation so commonly expressed by the colonial administrator, unable to secure the active cooperation of the natives whom he wishes only to help, though they always endeavor, as Lord Cromer of India noticed, "to say what is pleasant to the interrogator, especially if he occupies some post of authority."[110] The Americans in Vietnam are not the first invaders to have to learn this lesson.

A Vietnamese scholar living near Saigon observes that what the Vietnamese hold most against the Americans is the social demoralization that they have caused:

> Whether they mean to or not, they destroy what we hold most dear: family, friendships, our way of expression. Consciously or not, the Vietnamese see their intervention that way…. Even the girl in the bar who has money now, who lives in town and never wants to return to the country, feels a sense of guilt…. Even after five or ten years of work she still feels ill at ease, alienated. Something is missing, and she knows it. She would give up all the advantages and her independence if she could rediscover that something.

The Viet Cong, he observes, represent "a desire to return to normal," so "the Vietnamese feel in a confused way. But for the NLF there is obviously no question of restoring the thieves' honour or the rules of piracy of the past."[111]

The aimless, hopeless character of Saigon, the decay and demoralization, are the constant themes of those who try to describe the life of the city, as it can be seen by an outsider:

Saigon today stands as an example of what Indochina has become with American occupation. To a visitor it is a hellhole of noise, filth and misery which no one should become accustomed to. Every street is jammed with Hondas. And on the dirty, broken pavements they stand in gleaming ranks for sale. The bargirls on the streets with American soldiers are defiant, passing a battery of abuse from their own people....[112] The Vietnamese families squatting in shacks along the railway line smell as though they are rotting. In the orphanages the children displaced and lost by the movement of the war are lifeless, stinking lumps of humanity. In one sweltering room crammed with 30 cots last week I saw a baby with a ping-pong ball swelling under its arm: "bubonic plague," the fat slattern minding the children said laconically. Officially there is no plague in Saigon.[113] ... In Saigon the legacy of American occupation is an emasculated, Westernised city devoid of character. A people without nationhood.[114]

Saigon, as noted earlier, is now estimated to have more than twice the population density of Tokyo. According to recent reports, the trees that lined the boulevards have been destroyed by pollution and perhaps also defoliants, by fumes from containers that are used for fires. Gangs of homeless youth roam the city. The IVS worker I mentioned earlier reports that the situation is reminiscent of the turmoil that preceded the fall of Diem. Demonstrations by students and wounded war veterans have been reported regularly in the press. The schools and universities have been closed.

The ever-present corruption continues unabated. What is described as "the most colossal case of currency smuggling and corruption in the country's modern history" was discovered a few weeks ago by customs officers at Tan Son Nhut Airbase. According to two Vietnamese senators, the ring of smugglers involves top officials and three of the four most powerful generals in the Thieu regime: General Dang van Quang, Thieu's assistant in charge of national security and pacification; General Do Cao Tri, whose troops are now destroying Cambodian villages in the "Parrot's Beak"; and Cao Van Vien, Chief of Staff of the armed forces. General Tri, who is currently one of the American heroes[115] (and, like most of the others, a former officer under the French in the First Indochina War), is further alleged to be deeply involved in graft in the provinces within his "zone of influence."[116]

But the real corruption is deeper and more subtle. A useful indication of the true nature of the "American-sponsored urban revolution," as it affects the more privileged, is given by Don Luce and John Sommer:

> When students at Saigon's teacher training college were asked to list 15 occupations in an English examination, almost every student included launderer, car washer, bargirl, shoeshine boy, soldier, interpreter, and journalist. Almost none of the students thought to write down doctor, engineer, industrial administrator, farm manager, or even their own chosen profession, teacher. The economy has become oriented towards services catering to the foreign soldiers.[117]

Such is the social revolution that we have brought to the elite of South Vietnam, those who have been selected as our partners. One recalls again other episodes in the history of colonialism. When the United States conquered the Philippines, domestic upper-class collaborators expressed their enthusiasm for American rule in such terms as these:

> After peace is established, all our efforts will be directed to Americanizing ourselves; to cause a knowledge of the English language to be extended and generalized in the Philippines, in order that through its agency the American spirit may take possession of us, and that we may so adopt its principles, its political customs, and its peculiar civilization that our redemption may be complete and radical.[118]

This "loss of identity," as is commonly noted, remains one of the most profound problems of the Philippines. Commenting on Latin America, Claude Julien detects a related phenomenon:

> The revolt of Latin American students is not directed only against dictatorial regimes that are corrupt and inefficient—nor only against the exploitation by the foreigner of the economic and human resources of their country—but also against the cultural colonization that touches them at the deepest level of their being. And this is perhaps why their revolt is more virulent than that of the worker or peasant organizations that experience primarily economic colonization.[119]

For the same reason, cultural colonization, if it succeeds, is the most deplorable in its long-term effects.

The Vietnamese scholar whose remarks were quoted earlier (see page 44) concluded his discussion by saying:

> Mine is a country you either respect or destroy, there is no half measure. Up until now, no one has managed to destroy it.

Vietnam has endured many wars, many conquests. Its resistance to American aggression can be described, with no exaggeration, as a colossal triumph of the human spirit. But there is a limit to human endurance, and it may some day be reached even in Vietnam if the world, and the American people, permit this monstrous war to continue.

V

TWO OF THE ESSAYS that follow were written in late 1969 and early 1970. Three were written upon my return from a brief trip to Indochina in April 1970, as was most of this introductory chapter.

At the Bangkok airport I picked up several books to help pass the hours of the flight home across the Pacific. Among them was a novel by Kurt Vonnegut in which one of the characters, a psychiatrist, discusses a disease that he calls "samaritrophia," defined as "hysterical indifference to the troubles of those less fortunate than oneself." A person afflicted by samaritrophia follows the path of enlightened self-interest. His flag is "the black and white Jolly Roger, with these words written beneath the skull and crossbones: 'The hell with you, Jack, I've got mine.'"

Vonnegut apologizes to the reader for bothering to give a name to this disease, which is "virtually as common among healthy Americans as noses." But, he points out, the disease is particularly evil in its consequences when the person afflicted formerly thought of himself as benevolent and concerned for his fellows. Then, when his conscience is subdued, he can become a mad dog, savage and vicious.

As I have already observed, like most of their predecessors in imperialist ventures, Americans have tended to regard their involvements in other countries—Southeast Asia in particular—as an exercise in benevolence. Now there is too much information available for a literate person, for a person with access to a television set, to retain any such belief. Surely everyone now realizes that Song My was merely the tip of an iceberg. One awaits, daily, the revelation of new atrocities, sure to come. One day we read the account by a former helicopter pilot, David Bressem, of the massacre of thirty-three peasants thirty miles from Song My.[120] The next, we may come across the news that the American First Infantry Division has branded its insignia in the Vietnamese landscape, bulldozing a mile and a half of jungle—an act that is low on the atrocity scale, no doubt, but that is nevertheless revealing in the contempt it shows for the land and the people that the United States government treats as playthings.[121] We may read a letter from an AFSC field worker who watches American soldiers firing aimlessly into the rice paddies where peasants are visibly working—"practicing," she and her companion are informed by an American sergeant.[122] Or we may see the NLF report of a recent sweep in Quang Nam Province in which, it is claimed, in two days (November 11, 12, 1969) 700 civilians were massacred in five villages, with 1,000 houses burned down and thousands of hectares of crops devastated[123]—such reports have proved accurate in the past. Or we may merely look at Pentagon statistics on bombardment: from 1965 through 1969, 4.5 million tons of bombs, nine times the total tonnage expended in the Pacific theater in World War II, and this only half the tonnage of ordnance expended in Indochina; in Laos alone, today, the equivalent of several Hiroshima explosions a month, much of it on civilian targets.[124]

What will be the effect of these disclosures? Perhaps, one still hopes, they may bring the American people to force their government to desist. Or perhaps they will simply lead to habituation, to deepening our hysterical indifference to the troubles of those who defend themselves with valor but who cannot, of course, strike back at the aggressor.

I need hardly emphasize that there is a domestic analogue. The war has contributed to a serious economic crisis.[125] According to a recent calculation, it costs half a million dollars to kill one Viet Cong soldier, an amount equal to the federal funds which could support 3,400 people in school or college or build at least 50 housing units; and about $40 million for a heavy B-52 raid, a sum that could purchase 3 four-hundred-bed hospitals or 27 elementary schools or about 4,050 housing units.[126] The cost of ordnance expended currently in the bombardment of Laos alone apparently averages several million dollars a day.[127] While traveling in North Vietnam I was shown a bridge, still standing uneasily, that was attacked daily from

1965 until the termination of the regular bombing, with 99 American jets lost—the cost in planes lost alone must be on the order of half a billion dollars, to destroy one bridge.[128] Even America's productive system cannot sustain these vast, lunatic expenditures without domestic consequences. As unemployment and inflation grow, as our resources are wasted in destruction and preparation for new wars, American blacks, Mexicans, Puerto Ricans, and others are increasingly locked into the hopeless conditions of urban misery and stagnation, and, as we now know, there is large-scale malnutrition, even starvation, in rural America. The words "The hell with you, Jack, I've got mine" become assimilated into the patterns of racism of the relatively affluent white society, and they become the last line of defense of those who feel themselves immediately threatened, in their own tenuous economic situation, by the reserve army of unemployed and dispossessed, pressing on them from the deeper poverty and misery of the ghettos.

To anyone with eyes to see, it is clear that the present prospects are for a long, endless war, perhaps a general war with the peoples of Asia, if the American people are willing to settle into passivity and tolerate it.

There is some acute commentary on the matter in a recent *New Yorker* editorial.[129] The editors point out that opponents of the war have won all the arguments, but they have also "found that it is inadequate to repeat these arguments." Why?

> Perhaps one reason is that the gap between the official explanations and the realities we are faced with daily on television and in the newspapers has become so staggeringly huge and so obvious that when one persists in making these points one feels almost ludicrously simple-minded.... It is as though the public had shrugged its shoulders and decided to accept the war as something that cannot be affected by human effort. The war has outlived the *issue* of the war ... the actual conduct of the war is developing according to a completely separate set of rules, determined by the conditions of unspeakable brutality and confusion in Vietnam itself.

There is surely some truth to this. It is hardly necessary, at this point, to win the debate over whether the war is brutal, monstrous, a war of destruction against the peasants of Indochina. Nevertheless, the real debate over Vietnam, is, in my opinion, yet to come. Within the main-stream of American opinion, hawks and doves divide over the question whether the American people can stay the course until victory, or whether polarization and discord in American society make this effort inadvisable, not in our national interest. This question is real enough, but it is not the one that we should be discussing. In this debate the hawks may, in fact, be right. The all-too-human samaritrophia may, in fact, ultimately vindicate them in their cause. That America has the power to obliterate Indochina is not, after all, in doubt, and who can predict what might happen if those generals of whom James Gavin recently warned succeed in embroiling us in a war against China—the ultimate enemy, in their paranoid fantasies.[130]

For those concerned with peace, there are several tasks. The first is to shift the terms of the debate to an entirely different issue. The proper question is not whether the United States can win at an acceptable cost, but whether it should be involved at all in the internal affairs of Indochina. Until this becomes the unique and overriding issue, the debate over Vietnam will scarcely have begun.

The second task is to understand clearly, and explain clearly, what is really happening in Indochina.

And the third, and most important, is to work incessantly to bring home to hawks and doves alike that the American people will not stay the course, that the society will become ungovernable if the American war in Indochina continues or expands. For those who wish to work within the narrow margins of the political system, there is now a very real and quite rare opportunity, given the willingness of some members of Congress to cut off appropriations for the war. But surely these are not the limits of legitimate protest. A person who takes seriously the responsibilities of citizenship will refuse to be a passive accomplice in crimes against peace and against humanity, and will undertake and support direct resistance to the lawless violence of the state.

A few weeks in Southeast Asia merely confirm, with vivid and unforgettable impressions, what anyone can discover for himself by careful reading and attention to contemporary events. The American involvement in Indochina is tragic for all concerned. It is deeply rooted in global American policies that have persisted, without serious change, since World War II and that are still operative today. Given the anti-Communist obsessions that have so distorted and narrowed American life, the easiest course for any political leader will be to adjust tactics and try once again, quite apart from the underlying material interests that once clearly motivated the American intervention and still are not without force, quite apart from the pressure of the military and others with a vested interest in policies that, once undertaken, are difficult to abandon. This being so, public apathy and limited, intermittent concern may be all that are required to guarantee that we shall find ourselves at war with Asia.

The people of Asia are, of course, the pitiful victims of these policies. But the United States will not escape. It is unlikely that we can continue indefinitely on this mad course without severe domestic depression and regimentation. For those who hope to rule the world, to win what some scholars like to call "the game of world domination,"[131] American policies in Southeast Asia may appear rational. To the citizens of the empire, at home and abroad, they bring only pain and sorrow. In this respect we are reliving the history of earlier imperial systems. We have had many opportunities to escape this trap and still do today. Failure to take advantage of these opportunities, continued submission to indoctrination and indifference to the fate of others, will surely spell disaster for much of the human race.

Notes

1 Cited by Jim Peck in an excellent discussion of Asian scholarship in postwar America, in *Bulletin of Concerned Asian Scholars*, Vol. 2, No. 3 (April–July 1970). Address: 1737 Cambridge Street, Cambridge, Mass. 02138.

2 "Contrasts in Economic Development," in Neal D. Houghton, ed., *Struggle Against History: U.S. Foreign Policy in an Age of Revolution* (New York, Washington Square Press, 1968).

3 William Y. Elliott, ed., *The Political Economy of American Foreign Policy* (New York, Henry Holt & Co., 1955), p. 42.

4 Kim Sam-kyu, "The Korean Question," *Japan Quarterly*, January 1970. For a discussion of the takeover of the South Korean economy by great international corporations, largely Japanese, see *AMPO*, Nos. 3–4 (March 1970), a publication of Beheiren (The Japan "Peace for Vietnam" Committee), Ishii Building, 6-44 Kagurazaka, Shinjuku, Tokyo, Japan. The report shows in detail how South Korea is being converted into a "subcontractor to Japan manufacturing those goods which can not be produced at a profit inside Japan, with its higher wage scale and its labor shortage." Japan, the report continues, is "returning to the path it traveled once before, 60 years ago."

5 Simon Hanson, *Five Years of the Alliance for Progress* (Washington, D.C., Inter-American Affairs Press, 1967), p. 1. For a detailed corroborative case study of the "showcase of the Alliance," see *Colombia—A Case History of US Aid*, Staff of the Committee on Foreign Relations, United States Senate (Washington, D.C., Government Printing Office, 1969).

6 *Latin America: Meditations from Afar*, Stockholm University Institute for National Economic Studies, 1970.

7 *Congressional Record*, May 24, 1965, p. 10840. Cited in Harry Magdoff, *The Age of Imperialism: The Economics of U.S. Foreign Policy* (New York, Monthly Review Press, 1969), p. 121.

8 Marcel Niedergang, *Le Monde Weekly Selection*, December 12–18, 1968. Quotes are from the professors of the military college who, he writes, have constructed "a manichean vision of the world: the Communist East against the Christian West."

9 United Nations Commission for Latin America, cited by Clairmonte, *op. cit.*

10 Richard Barnet, *Intervention and Revolution: The U.S. in the Third World* (New York, Meridian Books, 1969), p. 10.

11 Quoted in Akira Iriye, *Across the Pacific: An Inner History of American-East Asian Relations* (New York, Harcourt, Brace & World, 1967), p. 77. Adams' ideas greatly intrigued Oliver Wendell Holmes, who wrote admiringly: "He thinks this war [the Philippine War] is the first gun in the battle for the ownership of the world." Cited by Frank Freidel, in *Dissent in Three American Wars* (Cambridge, Harvard University Press, 1970), p. 77.

12 Robert Moskin, *Look*, November 18, 1968.

13 For discussion, see my essay "The Revolutionary Pacifism of A. J. Muste," in *American Power and the New Mandarins* (New York, Pantheon Books, 1969), pp. 159–220.

14 Kyozo Mori and Shizuo Maruyama, respectively, in *Japan Quarterly*, April–June, 1970. The former is the editorial adviser, the latter an editorial writer, for Japan's leading newspaper, the conservative *Asahi Shimbun*.

15 Quoted by Walter LaFeber, *American, Russia, and the Cold War, 1945–1966* (New York, John Wiley & Sons, 1967), p. 133.

16 *The Transformation of American Foreign Policy* (New York, W. W. Norton & Company, 1969), pp. 95–96.

17 September 27, 1969.

18 Quoted by Frederick Clairmonte, *Economic Liberalism and Underdevelopment* (Bombay, Asia Publishing House, 1960), p. 54, in an illuminating discussion of the contrast between the views of spokesmen for more and less developed nations with regard to proper economic policies.

19 An exception, of course, is the American-led economic warfare against the societies that had extricated themselves from the world capitalist economy. For a review, see Gunnar Adler-Karlsson, *Western Economic Warfare: 1947–1967* (Stockholm, Almqvist & Wiksell, 1968).

20 *The Politics of War: The World and U.S. Foreign Policy* (New York, Random House, 1968).

21 See LaFeber, *op. cit.*

22 Kolko, *op. cit.*, p. 471.

23 See *ibid.* On the important role of American organized labor, see Ronald Radosh, *The American Labor Movement and Foreign Policy* (New York, Random House, 1969).

24 Paul Hammond, in Harold Stein, ed., *American Civil-Military Decisions* (A Twentieth Century Fund Study; University, Ala., University of Alabama Press, 1963), p. 472.

25 John W. Dower, "Occupied Japan and the American Lake, 1945–1950," in Edward Friedman and Mark Selden, eds., *America's Asia*, (New York, Pantheon, 1971). See also his essay on the United States-Japan military relationship in the *Bulletin of Concerned Asian Scholars*, Vol. 2, No. I (October 1969). For still earlier background, see Kolko, *op. cit.* On the role of the Korean and Vietnam wars as a spur to industrial development in Japan and other Asian countries allied to the United States, see Tadashi Kawata, "Post-Vietnam Economic Development in Southeast Asia," in *Peace Research in Japan*, a publication of the Japan Peace Research Group, 1969.

26 *New York Times*, May 6, 1967. Cited in a perceptive article by Paul Mattick, "The American Economy," *International Socialist Journal*, February 1968.

27 Cited by Clairmonte, *Latin America*.

28 See, for example, Clairmonte, *Economic Liberalism and Underdevelopment*. Also, André Gunder Frank, *Capitalism and Underdevelopment in Latin America* (New York, Monthly Review Press, 1967); *Latin America: Underdevelopment or Revolution* (New York, Monthly Review Press, 1970).

29 Cited in Clairmonte, *Economic Liberalism and Underdevelopment*, p. 66. Marshall is speaking of Friedrich List, who, inspired by the protectionist policies of Alexander Hamilton and others, urged that industrializing Germany reject the economic liberalism advocated by industrially dominant Great Britain. The obvious example of the advantages of extrication from the imperial economic system is Japan, which alone of the Asian nations prior to World War II succeeded in maintaining its independence and developing a self-sustaining industrial economy.

30 "International Combines Versus the Unions," *Bulletin* of the Institute for Workers' Control, Vol. 1, No. 4, 1969. Address: 45 Gamble Street, Forest Road West, Nottingham.

31 "La formation humaine—clé du développement," *Le Monde diplomatique*, March 1968.

32 "Southeast Asia-Predeveloped or Underdeveloped?" in *Looking North: Readings in Asian Geography*, published by the Manawatu Branch, New Zealand Geographical Society, undated.

33 Peter F. Bell and Stephen A. Resnick, "The Contradictions of Post-war Development in Southeast Asia," *The Journal of Contemporary Asia* (London), Vol. 1, No. 1 (June 1970). I quote from a preprint of this forthcoming essay.

34 *UN Review of the Social Situation in the ECAFE Region* (Bangkok, 1970), cited by Bell and Resnick.

35 See the "Economic Survey of Asia and the Pacific," *New York Times*, January 17, 1969, the article headed *Thais see peace as a mixed blessing*. The survey notes that "an end to the fighting [in Vietnam] would pose a grave threat to Thailand's economy." And if the Americans decide to maintain their military presence in Thailand, "the Thais will be faced with the even more difficult choice between a continued boom and further deterioration of their traditional society."

36 Kim Sam-kyu, *op. cit.*

37 *Cambodia: The Search for Security* (New York, Frederick A. Praeger, 1967), p. 8. See also Daniel Roy, "Le coup de Phnom-Penh," *Le Monde diplomatique*, April 1970, for further discussion.

38 Alfred D. Chandler, Jr., "The Role of Business in the United States: A Historical Survey," *Daedalus*, Winter, 1969.

39 Cited by Richard Barnet, *The Economy of Death* (New York, Atheneum Publishers, 1969), p. 116, an excellent and concise study of the evolution of this system.

40 Joseph Monsen, "The American Business View," *Daedalus*, Winter, 1969.

41 Bernard Nossiter, *Washington Post*, December 8, 1968.

42 See, for example, Claude Julien, *L'Empire américain* (Paris, Bernard Grasset, 1968); Harry Magdoff, *op. cit.*; Gabriel Kolko, *The Roots of American Foreign Policy* (Boston, Beacon Press, 1969).

43 On Acheson's role, see the excellent review article by Ronald Steel, *New York Review*, February 12, 1970.

44 "The Nuremberg Suggestion," *Washington Monthly*, January 1970. For similar statements, see Hoopes', *The Limits of Intervention* (New York, David McKay Co., 1969).

45 *Law, Power, and the Pursuit of Peace* (Lincoln, University of Nebraska Press, 1968).

46 It will be recalled that the British conquered Greece from its own population and that the United States took over when the British could no longer afford to sustain domestic repression in the country, while Stalin refused to support the guerrillas and, in fact, repeatedly urged them to desist. For discussion, see Gabriel Kolko, *Politics of War*; Richard Barnet, *Intervention and Revolution*.

47 Quoted by Howard Zinn, *Disobedience and Democracy: Nine Fallacies on Law and Order* (New York, Vintage Books, 1969), p. 75.

48 *Economic Concentration*, Hearings before the Subcommittee on Antitrust and Monopoly of the Committee on the Judiciary, United States Senate, 91st Congress, 1st Session (1969), Part 8A. See also pages 17f. above.

49 Quoted by Arthur S. Miller, "Toward the 'Techno-corporate' State?—An Essay in American Constitutionalism," *Villanova Law Review*, Vol. 14, No. 1 (Fall, 1968), p. 43, from H. R. Rep. No. 1406, 87th Congress, 2d Session (1962), p. 7.

50 Introduction to Stein, ed., *American Civil-Military Decisions*. For further discussion of this process and its roots in the planning role of the executive under state capitalism, see Michael Kidron, *Western Capitalism Since the War* (London, Weidenfeld & Nicolson, 1968).

51 Quoted by LaFeber, *op. cit.*, p. 79.

52 A decision that was apparently advocated by unanimous decision of the President's advisers even prior to the election. See James Thomson's remarks in Richard M. Pfeffer, ed., *No More Vietnams? The War and the Future of American Foreign Policy* (New York, Harper & Row, 1969), published for the Adlai Stevenson Institute of International Affairs; and in "How Could Vietnam Happen?" *Atlantic Monthly*, April 1968, reprinted in Robert Manning and Michael Janeway, eds., *Who We Are: An Atlantic Chronicle of the United States and Vietnam 1966–1969* (Boston, Little, Brown and Co., 1969).

53 *The Economy of Death*, p. 97. The role of the law firms that cater to corporate interests as representatives of the general interest of the corporate elite, rather than of some specific segment of it, has been widely discussed in recent years. For more discussion of these matters see Gabriel Kolko, *The Roots of American Foreign Policy*; Ralph Miliband, *The State in Capitalist Society* (London, Weidenfeld & Nicolson, 1969); David Horowitz, ed., *Corporations and the Cold War* (New York, Monthly Review Press, 1969).

54 Quoted by Ronald Steel, *op. cit.*, who also cites Rusk's brilliant observation. It conceivably might be argued—to compound the irony—that Russia *was* in fact attempting to create a "Slavic Manchukuo" in Manchuria, at the expense of China. There has, in fact, been some speculation that this may have been one factor in the Kao Kang purge of 1954. See Klaus Mehnert, *Peking and Moscow* (New York, Mentor Books, 1964), pp. 275–76; and also Franz Schurmann and Orville Schell, eds., *The China Reader*, Vol. 3, *Communist China* (New York, Vintage Books, 1967), p. 87.

55 Philippe Devillers and Jean Lacouture, *End of a War: Indochina, 1954* (New York, Frederick A. Praeger, 1969), p. 142.

56 *Full Circle* (London, Cassell & Company, 1960), pp. 142–43.

57 Cited in Devillers and Lacouture, *op. cit.*, pp. 322–23. See also pp. 289, 389.

58 "The Indochina War," speech at Cornell University, in *Indochina War Information Packet*, distributed by the Committee of Concerned Asian Scholars, Cornell University, Glad Day Press, Ithaca, N.Y., 1970.

59 "Our Illusory Affair with Japan," *The Nation*, March 11, 1968. As indicated by the title, LaFeber regards this as now wholly irrational, for reasons that he develops further in the speech just cited. A similar analysis has been developed by others since. See the references of note 25. Also, Harry Magdoff, *op. cit.*; Peter Wiley, "Vietnam and the Pacific Rim Strategy," *Leviathan*, June 1969; and Mike Klare, "The Great South Asian War," *The Nation*, March 9, 1970, and "The Sun Never Sets on America's Empire," *Commonweal*, May 22, 1970, both reprinted by the North American Congress on Latin America, P.O. Box 57, Cathedral Station, New York, N.Y. 10025.

60 *The Political Economy of American Foreign Policy*, p. 134.

61 *Big Business in Japanese Politics* (New Haven, Conn., Yale University Press, 1968), pp. 265–66. My italics.

62 P. 107. To counter these tendencies, the United States must find ways to "mitigate the obstacles to British economic growth," in particular, "the damaging effect on labor mobility and labor incentives of the too-great equalization of wage rates on a national basis. This practice—which persists today—reflects the power of the British trade unions and the preoccupation of their leadership with a static, egalitarian conception of economic equity and with an 'architectural' conception of the right to work, virtually to the exclusion of any concern for the growth of the national product." Presumably, the international corporations may find ways to overcome these obstacles to rationality, in the ways noted earlier; see page 10. Still, "constructive wage and social welfare policies are obviously needed to *mitigate industrial unrest*" (p. 167). My italics.

63 Pp. 211–12. Further, the United States has the right of intervention, even in ways that are "reminiscent of colonialism" (see P. 225). "Considerable American freedom of action is now essential to the security and progress of the West and of the whole free world." Any diminution of this freedom (say by international federal institutions) might "run the risk of paralyzing the political will of the West during a period in which such paralysis could mean the end of Western civilization" (p. 322). This may require us to support "older ruling groups" who "have seen clearly that their future independence lies in alliance with the West" (p. 171). And so on.

64   See Chapter 2, page 79. The social base and character of the Thieu government are remark-ably similar to that of the Diemist regime.

65   *Vietnam Divided: The Unfinished Struggle* (New York, Asia Publishing House, 1964), p. 145. Cited by Devillers and Lacouture, *op. cit.*, p. 397.

66   In retrospect, it is interesting to recall that the American representative Walter Bedell Smith in his declaration at Geneva stated that the United States "takes note" of paragraphs 1 to 12 of the Final Declaration of the Geneva Conference and "will refrain from the threat or the use of force to disturb them," pointedly omitting paragraph 13, which provides for diplomatic measures to ensure that the agreements are respected.

67   Lawrence Morrison, Chief of Industry Division and Mining, U.S.O.M., Saigon, 1955–1957, in Richard W. Lindholm, ed., *Vietnam: The First Five Years* (East Lansing, Michigan State University Press, 1959), p. 215. For a succinct review of this period, with excellent analytical commentary, see Gabriel Kolko, *The Roots of American Foreign Policy.*

68   Quoted by C. L. Sulzberger, *New York Times*, June 3, 1964; cited by Victor Bator, *Vietnam: A Diplomatic Tragedy* (Dobbs Ferry, N.Y., Oceana Publications, 1965), p. 220.

69   On Laos, see Arthur Dommen, *Conflict in Laos: The Politics of Neutralization* (New York, Frederick A. Praeger, 1964), and Hugh Toye, *Laos: Buffer State or Battleground* (New York, Oxford University Press, 1968). On Thailand, see Frank Darling, *Thailand and the United States* (Washington, D.C., Public Affairs Press, 1965). See my *American Power and the New Mandarins*, pp. 61ff., for summary and discussion.

70   On the North Vietnamese involvement in the war in the South, as represented by American government sources, see Theodore Draper, *Abuse of Power* (New York, The Viking Press, 1967). See also chapter 4, pp.163–167.

71   "The American Involvement in Vietnam" (May 1970), in *Indochina War Information Packet.* For extensive evidence, see George M. Kahin and John W. Lewis, *The United States in Vietnam* (New York, The Dial Press, 1967).

72   Much evidence on this score is presented in my *American Power and the New Mandarins*. To cite just one more recent example, consider the casual observation by Ithiel Pool that in 1964, "the only capable political structure in Vietnam [was] the Viet Cong," and that it was then "obvious that except for American forces the Viet Cong would take over Vietnam." He is impressed, however, by the fact that after the American invasion this is no longer so obvi-ous, and this in his view justifies the intervention. In Pfeffer, ed., *No More Vietnams?*, pp. 146–47. See also N. Leites and C. Wolf, *Rebellion and Authority* (RAND Corporation Research Study; Chicago, Markham Publishing Company, 1970), p. 17: "… the Viet Cong would presumably have won in 1965 had it not been for massive American intervention." The point is generally conceded.

73   Cited in his *Limits of Intervention*, p. 195. He describes military victory as having been the implicit goal of American policy at least since 1965. It "appears to be a necessary precondi-tion for the realization of a U.S. political objective which defines 'free choice' for the people of SVN as a process necessarily excluding the NLF/VC from participation in either elections or government" (p. 187). This is a perfectly accurate characterization of American political and military goals.

74   *Ibid.*, p. 228.

75   *New York Times*, November 2, 1968.

76   *Christian Science Monitor*, October 23, 1968.

77   *New York Times*, November 22, 1968.

78   *I. F. Stone's Weekly*, February 10, 1969.

79   Quoted in *I. F. Stone's Weekly*, February 10, 1969. Both the phraseology and the tactics, it appears, derive from Sir Robert Thompson, who seems to be President Nixon's favorite strategist. See Thompson's *No Exit from Vietnam* (New York, David McKay Co., 1969).

80   Gérard Le Quang, *France-Soir*, May 29, 1970. The realism of these fears of the Thai elite is another question.

81   *New York Times*, June 6, 1970; *Far Eastern Economic Review*, May 28, 1970; Jacques Doyon, *Figaro*, June 10, 1970.

82   *The Nation*, June 1, 1970. He speculates that the sudden decision to invade the "Fishhook" area of Cambodia may have been an administration effort to head off a Pentagon plan to attack Sihanoukville, an act that might have had severe international consequences. It might be questioned whether such incidents as those cited illustrate the erratic and irrational behavior of the American government, or whether in fact the incidents were simply chosen as the occasion for implementing plans motivated by the persistent goal of achieving control of the region.

83   "The United States in Laos, 1945–1962," in Friedman and Selden, eds., *America's Asia*.

84   *Hard Times*, May 25, 1970. This comment was made in a speech before the Executive Club of Chicago, March 17, 1955, when Nixon was Vice-President. It appears in James Keogh, *This Is Nixon* (New York, G. P. Putnam's Sons, 1956), p. 137.

85   *New York Times Magazine*, June 9, 1968. If we cannot do this, he says, we had better "call it quits."

86   Ngo Vinh Long, "The Vietnam War and its Implications for Southeast Asia," speech given on March 27, 1970, at the Conference of Southeast Asian Students at Indiana University, reprinted in *Thời-Báo Gà*, No. 9 (April 1970), a journal of Vietnamese students in the United States, 76a Pleasant Street, Cambridge, Mass. Mr. Long was part of a land-survey expedition in 1959–1963 which, he reports, took him to virtually every part of the country.

87   For many references and citations, see my *American Power and the New Mandarins*; Edward S. Herman, *"Atrocities" in Vietnam: Myths and Realities* (Boston, Pilgrim Press, 1970); *In the Name of America* (Annandale, Va., Turnpike Press, 1968), published by Clergy and Laymen Concerned About Vietnam; the material presented; and other sources too numerous to mention.

88   *The Lost Confucian: Vietnam, South-East Asia and the West* (A Penguin Special; London, Angus & Robertson, 1964), p. 312.

89   For many references, see my *American Power and the New Mandarins*. For a serious and, in my opinion, persuasive analysis see Mark Selden, "The National Liberation Front and the Transformation of Vietnamese Society," *Bulletin of Concerned Asian Scholars*, Vol. 2, No. 1 (October 1969), and a more extended version: "People's War and the Transformation of Peasant Society: China and Vietnam," in Friedman and Selden, eds., *America's Asia*; and also Gérard Chaliand, *The Peasants of North Vietnam*, (Harmondsworth, Eng., Penguin Books, 1969).

90   Compare the report in the *New York Times*, March 28, 1970: "Four young infantry officers said under oath today that United States Army policy, as they understand it, is not to take prisoners in combat operations in Vietnam."

91   Cited in Teodoro A. Agoacillo and Oscar M. Alfonso, *History of the Filipino People* (Quezon City, Malaya Books, 1961), p. 272. General Smith was later court-martialed and retired from the service. No action was taken against those who ordered the pacification of Samar. The parallel between the Philippine and Vietnam campaigns is, incidentally, frequently noted by Philippine nationalists. See, for example, Renato Constantino's introduction to James H. Blount, *The American Occupation of the Philippines* (Quezon City, Malaya Books, 1968); Hernando J. Abaya, *The Untold Philippine Story* (Quezon City, Malaya Books, 1968).

92   "The Bases of Accommodation," *Foreign Affairs*, Vol. 46, No. 4 (July 1968).

93   Some of which caused Senator Young, after a visit, "to think about what we denounced in World War II when we talked about Dachau and other concentration camps in Germany." *Congressional Record*, February 1, 1968, p. S1791.

94   George K. Tanham and Dennis J. Duncanson, "Some Dilemmas of Counterinsurgency," *Foreign Affairs*, Vol. 48, No. 1 (October 1969).

95   In Pfeffer, ed., *No More Vietnams?*, pp. 1f., 219, 227.

96   The wrong man having been confined to his home by threat of terror. The "social and economic reform" since are described by G. A. Geyer in *The New Republic*, May 30, 1970: "The US poured in aid and investments after the 1965 invasion. But development didn't keep track with the 3.8 per thousand population growth rate. By this year the $280 per capita income was still lower than it was in 1964, and unemployment has jumped to between 30 and 50 percent. During this four-year period, about 500 persons died mysteriously and not so mysteriously (one of Balaguer's top military officers recently machine-gunned a Boschist taxi-driver at noon on a busy street) in this country of about 4.5 million persons. All but about 30 of the dead come from the PRD [Boschist] and the farther Left."

97   On the contrary, a distinguished group of American scholars cite the "dramatic changes" in Indonesia as a great triumph for American policy. See my *American Power and the New Mandarins*, pp. 33ff., for discussion.

98   Huntington, *op. cit.*

99   Huntington explains how it might be done in a paper given at the May 1969 meeting of the Council on Vietnamese Studies, "Getting Ready for Political Competition in South Vietnam." The idea is to convince the NLF to accept some degree of local control while leaving national power in the hands of the United States and the South Vietnamese government. The United States, he urges, must be directly involved, more so than in the post-Geneva period or after the fall of Diem. As a prerequisite for "political competition," the NLF must accept "the formal authority of the GVN as the national government." He then suggests various techniques that the United States might use to counter the unfortunate fact that "The NLF is, after all, the most powerful purely political national organization"—e.g., covert means, economic assistance, subsidies to media, pork-barrel projects, manipulation of the electoral system, etc.

100 Huntington, "Getting Ready for Political Competition in South Vietnam."

101 Pfeffer, ed., *No More Vietnams?*, pp. 205f., 214, 142.

102 *Ibid.*, p. 255. Pool and Huntington take exception to this discussion of their views. See their letters in the *New York Review*, February 13, 1969, and February 26, 1970, and my responses, the latter largely reproduced here.

103 The letter is quoted, with slightly different (but materially the same) wording, in Don Luce and John Sommer, *Viet Nam: The Unheard Voices* (Ithaca, N.Y., Cornell University Press, 1969), pp. 258–59. For the initial passage I use the wording given by Ngo Vinh Long in the speech cited (see note 86). According to Mr. Long, the student unions of these universities represent most of the 30,000 university students in South Vietnam.

104 Published in *tintuong*, journal of the Overseas Vietnamese Buddhist Association, Paris, August 1968. The text is unedited.

105 *News, Views*, Vol., 1, No. 5 (September 1968), a publication of former members of the International Voluntary Services. For more recent information on these matters see Alfred Hassler, *Saigon, USA* (New York, Baron, 1970).

106 In the *CCAS Newsletter*, now the *Bulletin of Concerned Asian Scholars*, Vol. 2, No. 3 (March 1969). Professor Trung is described as one of the foremost Catholic intellectuals and most famous professors in South Vietnam. The introductory comment notes that the speech was

a courageous act, many having been imprisoned before and since for voicing such sentiments.

107 Long, *op. cit.* Long also cites an article by a Vietnamese officer in the Political Warfare Section appearing in a Saigon magazine, September 1969, in which "he says that the only reason why the Saigon government drafts so many people into the army is to keep a check on them."

108 Harvey Meyerson, *Vinh Long* (Boston, Houghton Mifflin Company, 1970), pp. 193–200.

109 Archibald P. Thornton, *Doctrines of Imperialism* (New York, John Wiley & Sons, 1965), p. 180.

110 *Political and Literary Essays* (London, 1913), p. 83, cited in Thornton.

111 Jean-Claude Pomonti, "The Sweet Smell of Decay," *Le Monde Weekly Selection*, May 20, 1970. Note that this too is a non-Communist Vietnamese voice.

112 According to a report published in the Austrian journal *Volksstimme* (November 22, 1969), in early 1969 there were 34,000 prostitutes registered with the police in this population of 3.5 million, from age twelve up. Thousands of police agents and government officials are said to be enriching themselves from the traffic in licenses. Reprinted in *Vietnam Courier* (Hanoi), March 23, 1970.

113 Dr. Alje Vennema, Director of the Canadian Government's Medical Mission to Vietnam, reports that plague was detected in 1964, followed by an epidemic in early 1965 and a "terrific epidemic" in the summer and again in 1966. It continues to be "a very big problem," as is cholera. By 1968 the World Health Organization announced that bubonic plague had reached epidemic proportions in South Vietnam. See Malvern Lumsden, *The Vietnamese People and the Impact of War*, Report No. 3 (December, 1969), published by the Institute for Peace and Conflict Research, Onsgaardsvey 13, DK-2900 Hellerup, Denmark.

114 Victoria Brittain, *New Statesman*, May 1, 1970. For a description of conditions in a South Vietnamese hospital, see Patricia Penn, *New Statesman*, May 29, 1970.

115 See the personal portrait by James Sterba, "A Fighting General," *New York Times*, June 4, 1970.

116 Phi-Bang, "Corruption-elite?" *Far Eastern Economic Review*, May 7, 1970.

117 *Op. cit.,* p. 286. Even Samuel Huntington, who takes such pride in the "social revolution," speaks of the "often heart-rending" social costs of "urbanization."

118 T. H. Pardo de Tavera, one of the first Filipino members of the American Government Philippine Commission, quoted by Constantino, in Blount, *op. cit.*, p. 22.

119 *Op. cit.,* p. 299.

120 *New York Times*, April 7, 1970; *Washington Star*, April 8, 1970.

121 I heard this story in Vientiane, with a group of war correspondents who were trading such incidents from personal experience. The incident is mentioned in the *New Yorker*, April 18, 1970, p. 34.

122 *Quaker Service*, National Edition (Spring, 1970), published by the American Friends Service Committee, 160 North 15th Street, Philadelphia, Pa.

123 *South Viet Nam in Struggle*, No. 53 (February 1, 1970).

124 For a recent effort at an estimate, difficult in this secret war, see Peter Dale Scott, "Cambodia—Why We Can't Stop," *New York Review*, June 18, 1970.

125 See, for example, the comments by Paul Samuelson, reported in the *Boston Globe*, June 1, 1970.

126 "The 'Short' War in Cambodia, Week 4, May 18–24," *Bay Area Institute Newsletter*, 9 Sutter Street, Suite 300, San Francisco. The analysis is based on cited government reports.

127 According to government figures, 300 strike sorties in northern Laos use about $1 million worth of ordnance (Hearings before the Subcommittee on United States Security Agreements and Commitments Abroad of the Committee on Foreign Relations, United States Senate, 91st Congress, 1st Session, October 20–28, 1969, released April 1970, p. 556). The number of sorties is classified. The Pathet Lao information office in Hanoi reports 630 sorties a day, at present, and other sources indicate that this is a fair, possibly a conservative estimate. See the reference of note 124 for a higher estimate. Also Chapter 4, note 37, for a high government source. Much of this is over northern Laos, far removed from the Ho Chi Minh Trail. *Newsweek* estimated the cost of American bombing in Laos at $1 billion a year, on March 31, 1969. Beginning in April or May 1969, there was a "heavy increase" in the bombardment (Senate Hearings, pp. 501–2), approximately doubling the number of strikes. There was another sharp increase in August (*ibid.*, p. 504). According to Senator Symington, in northern Laos "in some months in 1969 the strikes doubled, in others, tripled" (*ibid.*, p. 464). The reason appears to have been a decline in infiltration on the Ho Chi Minh Trail. The military claims that another reason was increased North Vietnamese offensive operations, but it is difficult to find support for this allegation.

128 One with a sense of the macabre might try to estimate how much the United States government actually spent in the attempt to destroy this one bridge. I do not even mention the loss to the Vietnamese, or the death of the pilots, most of whom were killed in action.

129 April 18, 1970.

130 Part of his recent congressional testimony on this matter, unfortunately not presented in the *New York Times* or *Washington Post*, is cited by Scott, *op. cit.*, along with comments of others who have called for the use of nuclear weapons in the past. Bernard Fall also warned of those who hope that "the Viet-Nam affair could be transformed into a 'golden opportunity' to 'solve' the Red Chinese problem as well." *Viet-Nam Witness: 1953-66* (New York, Frederick A. Praeger, 1966), p. 203.

131 Walter Isard, in Isard, ed., *Vietnam: Some Basic Issues and Alternatives* (Cambridge, Mass., Schenkman Publishing Company, 1969), a publication of the Peace Research Society (International) in which various scholars try to develop policies that will assist American leaders in more effective use of American power, this being a legitimate objective for value-free scientists because of the underlying axiom that the foreign policy of the United States has been "characterized" by "good-intentioned leaders and policy makers."

Chapter 2
After Pinkville

ON OCTOBER 15, 1965, an estimated 70,000 people took part in large-scale antiwar demonstrations. The demonstrators heard pleas for an end to the bombing of North Vietnam and for a serious commitment to negotiations, in response to the negotiation offers from North Vietnam and United Nations efforts to settle the war. To be more precise, this is what they heard if they heard anything at all. On the Boston Common, for example, they heard not a word from the speakers, who were drowned out by hecklers and counter-demonstrators.

On the Senate floor, Senator Mansfield denounced the "sense of utter irresponsibility" shown by the demonstrators, while Everett Dirksen said the demonstrations were "enough to make any person loyal to his country weep." Richard Nixon wrote, in a letter to *The New York Times*, October 29, that "victory for the Viet Cong ... would mean ultimately the destruction of freedom of speech for all men for all time not only in Asia but in the United States as well"—nothing less.

In a sense, Senator Mansfield was right in speaking of the sense of utter irresponsibility shown by demonstrators. They should have been demanding, not an end to the bombing of North Vietnam and negotiations, but a complete and immediate withdrawal of all American troops and matériel—an end to any forceful interference in the internal affairs of Vietnam or any other nation. They should not merely have been demanding that the United States adhere to international law and its own treaty obligations—thus removing itself forthwith from Vietnam; but they should also have exercised their right and duty to resist the violence of the state, which was as vicious in practice as it was illegal in principle.

In October 1967, there were, once again, mass demonstrations against the war, this time in Washington and at the Pentagon. A few months earlier, still larger, though less militant, demonstrations had taken place in New York. The Tet offensive, shortly after, revealed that American military strategy was "foolish to the point of insanity."[1] It also revealed to the public that government propaganda was either an illusion or a fraud, Moreover, an international monetary crisis threatened, attributable in part to Vietnam.

In retrospect, it seems possible that the war could have been ended if popular pressure had been maintained. But many radicals felt that the war was over, that it had become, in any case, a "liberal issue," and they turned to other concerns. Those who had demanded no more than an end to the bombing of North Vietnam and a commitment to negotiations saw their demands being realized, and lapsed into silence.

These demands, however, had always been beside the point. As to negotiations, there is, in fact, very little to negotiate. As long as an American army of occupation remains in Vietnam, the war will continue. Withdrawal of American troops must be a unilateral act, as the invasion of Vietnam by the American government was a unilateral act in the first place. Those who had been calling for "negotiations now" were deluding themselves and others, just as those who now call for a cease-fire that will leave an American expeditionary force in Vietnam are not facing reality.

As to the bombing of North Vietnam, this had always been a side show, in large measure a propaganda cover for the American invasion of the South. The United States government could not admit that it was invading South Vietnam to protect from its own population a government that we had installed. Therefore it was rescuing the South Vietnamese from "aggression." But then surely it must strike at the "source of aggression." Hence the bombing of North Vietnam. This, at least, seems the most rational explanation for the bombing of North Vietnam in February 1965, at a time when no North Vietnamese troops were in the South, so far as was known, and there was a bare trickle of supplies.

To be sure, those who are "in the know" have different explanations for the bombing of North Vietnam. Consider, for example, the explanation offered by Sir Robert Thompson, the British counterinsurgency expert who has been for many years a close adviser of the American army in South Vietnam—a man who is, incidentally, much admired by American social scientists who like to consider themselves "tough-minded, hard-nosed realists," no doubt because of his utter contempt for democracy and his relatively pure colonialist attitudes. In the British newspaper the *Guardian,* May 19, 1969, his views are explained as follows:

> He also condemns the bombing of the North. The United States Air Force in 1965 was having great budgetary problems, because the army was the only one that had a war on its hands and was thus getting all the money. "So the Air Force had to get in, and you had the bombing of North Vietnam … the budgetary problems of the Air Force were then solved."

In his *No Exit from Vietnam* (1969), he explains more graphically the attractiveness of air power:

> One can so easily imagine the Commander of the Strategic Air Command striding up and down his operations room wondering how he could get in on the act. With all that power available and an enormous investment doing nothing, it is not surprising that reasons and means had to be found for their engagement. The war was therefore waged in a manner which enabled this massive air armada to be used round the clock…. In this way the war could be fought as an American war without the previous frustrations of cooperating with the Vietnamese. [P. 135.]

Or consider the explanation for the bombing of the North offered by Adam Yarmolinsky, Principal Deputy Assistant Secretary of Defense for International Security Affairs, 1965–66, previous Special Assistant to the Secretary of Defense. According to his analysis, the strategic bombing of North Vietnam "produced no military advantages except for its putative favorable impact on morale in the south. But [this step] was taken, at least in part, because it was one of the things that the United States military forces were best prepared to do."[2]

So North Vietnam was flattened and impelled to send troops to the South, as it did a few months after the bombing began, if the Department of Defense can be believed.

Since the bombing of North Vietnam "produced no military advantages" and was extremely costly, it could be stopped with little difficulty and little effect on the American war in South Vietnam. And so it was, in two steps: on April 1, 1969, when the regular bombing was restricted to the southern part of North Vietnam, and on November 1, when it was halted. At the same time, the total American bombing, now restricted to Laos and South Vietnam, was increased in April and increased again in November. By March 1969 the total level of bombardment had reached 130,000 tons a month—nearly two Hiroshimas a week in South Vietnam and Laos, defenseless countries. And Melvin Laird's projection for the next twelve to eighteen months was the same.[3] The redistribution (and intensification) of bombing and the largely empty negotiations stilled domestic protest for a time and permitted the war to go on as before.

We can now look back over the failure of the "peace movement" to sustain and intensify its protest over the past four years. By now, defoliation has been carried out over an area the size of Massachusetts, with what effect no one has any real idea. The bombardment of Vietnam far exceeds the bombardment of Korea or anything in World War II. The number of Vietnamese killed or driven from their homes cannot be seriously estimated.

It is important to understand that the massacre of the rural population of Vietnam and their forced evacuation is not an accidental by-product of the war. Rather it is of the very essence of American strategy. The theory behind it has been explained with great clarity and explicitness, for example by Professor Samuel Huntington, Chairman of the Government Department at Harvard and at the time (1968) Chairman of the Council on Vietnamese Studies of the Southeast Asia Development Advisory Group. Writing in *Foreign Affairs*, he explains that the Viet Cong is "a powerful force which cannot be dislodged from its constituency so long as the constituency continues to exist." The conclusion is obvious, and he does not shrink from it. We can ensure that the constituency ceases to exist by "'direct application of mechanical and conventional power'… on such a massive scale as to produce a massive migration from countryside to city," where the Viet Cong constituency—the rural population—can, it is hoped, be controlled in refugee camps and suburban slums around Saigon.

Technically, the process is known as "urbanization" or "modernization." It is described, with the proper contempt, by Daniel Ellsberg, a Department of Defense consultant on pacification in South Vietnam, who concludes, from his extensive on-the-spot observations, that "we have, of course, demolished the society of Vietnam," that "the bombing of the South has gone on long enough to disrupt the society of South Vietnam enormously and probably permanently"; he speaks of the "people who have been driven to Saigon by what Huntington regards as our 'modernizing instruments' in Vietnam, bombs and artillery."[4] Reporters have long been aware of the nature of these tactics, aware that "by now the sheer weight of years of firepower, massive sweeps, and grand forced population shifts have reduced the population base of the NLF,"[5] so that conceivably, by brute force, we may still hope to "win."

One thing is clear: so long as an organized social life can be maintained in South Vietnam, the NLF will be a powerful, probably dominant force. This is the dilemma which has always plagued American policy, and which has made it impossible for us to permit even the most rudimentary democratic institutions in South Vietnam. For these reasons we have been forced to the solution outlined by Professor Huntington: to crush the people's war, we must eliminate the people.

A second thing is tolerably clear: there has been no modification in this policy. Once again, as two years ago, there is mounting popular protest against the war. Once again, a tactical adjustment is being devised that will permit Washington to pursue its dual goal, to pacify the people of South Vietnam while pacifying the American people also. The first of these tasks has not been accomplished too well. The second, to our shame, has been managed quite successfully, for the most part. Now we hear that the burden of fighting the war is to be shifted away from the American infantry to the B-52s and fighter-bombers and a mercenary force of Vietnamese. Only a token force of between 200,000 and 300,000 men, backed by the Pacific Naval and Air Command, will be retained, indefinitely, to ensure that the Vietnamese have the right of self-determination.

At a recent press conference, Averell Harriman explained that the North Vietnamese cannot believe that we really intend to abandon the huge military bases we have constructed in Vietnam, such as the one at Cam Ranh Bay (*Village Voice*, November 27, 1969). Knowledgeable American observers have found it equally difficult to believe this. For example, as long ago as August 27, 1965, James Reston wrote in *The New York Times*:

The United States bases and supply areas are being constructed on a scale far larger than is necessary to care for the present level of American forces ... In fact, the United States base at Cam Ranh ... is being developed into another Okinawa, not merely for the purposes of this war, but as a major power complex from which American officials hope a wider alliance of Asian nations, with the help of the United States, will eventually be able to contain the expansion of China.

The phrase "contain the expansion of China" must be understood as code for the unpronounceable expression, "repress movements for national independence and social reconstruction in Southeast Asia."

Premier Eisaku Sato, in a speech described by American officials as part of a joint Japanese-American policy statement, announced that we are entering a "new Pacific age" in which "a new order will be created by Japan and the United States" (*New York Times*, November 22, 1969). His words, one must assume, were chosen advisedly. To perpetuate this new order we will need military bases such as that at Cam Ranh Bay, which can play the role of the Canal Zone in the Western Hemisphere. There we can base our own forces and train those of our loyal dependencies.

We will no doubt soon proceed to construct an "Inter-Asian" army that can protect helpless governments from their own populations, much as the Brazilians were called in to legitimize our Dominican intervention. Where popular rebellion is in progress, these forces can gain valuable experience. Thus a senior American officer at Camp Bearcat in South Vietnam, where Thai units are based, explains that "they are infusing their army with experience they could never get in their own homeland.... They are coordinating their own piece of real estate." And a Thai colonel adds: "If my country ever has the same subversion, I'll have to fight there. I want to practice here" (*New York Times*, December 3, 1969). Surely Reston was right in 1965 in speculating about our long-range plans for the South Vietnamese bases, from which our "token force" of a quarter of a million men will operate in the seventies.[6]

Who can complain about a quarter of a million men, a force that can be compared, let us say, with the Japanese army of 160,000 which invaded north China in 1937, in an act of aggression that scandalized the civilized world and set the stage for the Pacific phase of World War II? In fact, counterinsurgency experts like Sir Robert Thompson have long argued that the American forces were far too large to be effective, and have advocated a "low-cost, long-haul strategy" of a sort which will now very likely be adopted by the Nixon administration, if, once again, the American people will trust their leaders and settle into passivity.

As American combat troops are withdrawn, their place, it is hoped, will be taken by a more effective force of Vietnamese—just as Czechoslovakia is controlled, it is reported, by fewer than 100,000 Russian troops. Meanwhile, the war will no doubt be escalated technologically. It will become more "capital intensive."[7] Some of the prospects were revealed in a speech by Chief of Staff William Westmoreland, reported in the *Christian Science Monitor* (October 27, 1969) under the heading: "Technologically the Vietnam war has been a great success." General Westmoreland "sees machines carrying more and more of the burden." He says:

> I see an army built into and around an integrated area control system that exploits the advanced technology of communications, sensors, fire direction, and the required automatic data processing—a system that is sensitive to the dynamics of the ever-changing battlefield—a system that materially assists the tactical commander in making sound and timely decisions.

Further details are presented by Leonard Sullivan, Deputy Director of Research and Development for Southeast Asian Matters:[8]

> These developments open up some very exciting horizons as to what we can do five or ten years from now: When one realizes that we can detect anything that perspires, moves, carries metal, makes a noise, or is hotter or colder than its surroundings, one begins to see the potential. This is the beginning of instrumentation of the entire battlefield. Eventually, we will be able to tell when anybody shoots, what he is shooting at, and where he was shooting from. You begin to get a "Year 2000" vision of an electronic map with little lights that flash for different kinds of activity. This is what we require for this "porous" war, where the friendly and the enemy are all mixed together.

Note the time scale that is projected for Vietnam. News reports reveal some of the early stages of these exciting developments. The *Times*,

November 22, 1969 (city edition), reports a plan to use remote-controlled unmanned aircraft as supply transports for combat areas. On October 1, the *Times* explains that:

> The landscape of Vietnam and the border regions are studded with electronic sensors that beep information into the banks of computers. Radar, cameras, infrared detectors and a growing array of more exotic devices contribute to the mass of information. Not long ago reconnaissance planes began carrying television cameras.

The data goes into the Combined Intelligence Center near Tan Son Nhut Air Base: "Day and night in its antiseptic interior a family of blinking, whirring computers devours, digests and spews out a Gargantuan diet of information about the enemy," the better to serve the "conglomerate of allied civil and military organizations that work together to destroy the Vietcong's underground government"—freely admitted to have been the most authentic popular social structure in South Vietnam prior to the American effort to demolish the society of Vietnam. One can understand the gloating of Douglas Pike: "The tactics that delivered victory in the Viet Minh war, however impressive once, had been relegated by science to the military history textbook."[9]

What this means is, to put it simply, that we intend to turn the land of Vietnam into an automated murder machine. The techniques of which Westmoreland, Sullivan, and Pike are so proud are, of course, designed for use against a special kind of enemy: one who is too weak to retaliate, whose land can be occupied. These "Year 2000" devices, which Westmoreland describes as a quantum jump in warfare are fit only for colonial wars. There is surely an element of lunacy in this technocratic nightmare. And if we are still at all capable of honesty, we will, with little difficulty, identify its antecedents.

Our science may yet succeed in bringing to reality the fears of Bernard Fall—no alarmist, and fundamentally in favor of the war during its early years—who wrote in one of his last essays that "Vietnam as a cultural and historic entity ... is threatened with extinction ... the countryside literally dies under the blows of the largest military machine ever unleashed on an area of this size." The South Vietnamese minister of information wrote in 1968 that ordinary Vietnamese would continue "to be horrified and embittered at the way the Americans fight their war.... Our peasants will remember their cratered rice fields and defoliated forests, devastated by an alien air force that seems at war with the very land of Vietnam."[10]

American reporters have told us the same thing so often that it is almost superfluous to quote. Tom Buckley—to mention only the most recent—describes the delta and the central lowlands:

> ... bomb craters beyond counting, the dead gray and black fields, forests that have been defoliated and scorched by napalm, land that has been plowed flat to destroy Vietcong hiding places. And everywhere can be seen the piles of ashes forming the outlines of huts and houses, to show where hamlets once stood.[11]

The truth about defoliants is only beginning to emerge, with the discovery that one of the two primary agents used is "potentially dangerous, but needing further study" while the other causes cancer and birth defects, and probably mental retardation. Both will continue to be used in Vietnam against enemy "training and regroupment centers"—i.e., anywhere we please, throughout the countryside.[12]

Of course it may be argued that the American government did not know, in 1961, that these agents were so dangerous. That is true. It was merely an experiment. Virtually nothing was known about what the effects might be. Perhaps there would be no ill effects, or perhaps—at the other extreme—Vietnam would become unfit for human life, or a race of mutants and mental retardates would be created. How could we know, without trying? In such ways "the tactics that delivered victory in the Viet Minh war, however impressive once, had been relegated by science to the military history textbook."

To see what may lie ahead, I'd like to turn away from Vietnam to a less familiar case. It has been claimed that Vietnam is the second most heavily bombarded country in history. The most intensively bombarded, so it seems, is Laos. According to *Le Monde*, "North Vietnam was more heavily bombed than Korea; Laos is now being bombed even more than North Vietnam. And this battering has been going on for over five years.... The United States Air Force carries out more than 12,500 raids a month."[13] On the same day, October 1, 1969, *The New York Times* announced its discovery that in Laos, "the rebel economy and social fabric" are now the main target of the American bombardment, which is claimed to be a success:

> Refugees from the Plaine des Jarres area say that during recent months most open spaces have been evacuated. Both civilians and soldiers have retreated into the forests or hills and frequently spend most of the daylight hours in caves or tunnels. Refugees said they could only plow their fields at night because they were unsafe during the day. "So long as the United States bombing continues at its new level," a European diplomat said here this week, "so-called Communist territory is little but a shooting range." The bombing, by creating refugees, deprives the Communists of their chief source of food and transport. The population of the Pathet Lao zone has been declining for several years and the Pathet Lao find it increasingly difficult to fight a "people's war" with fewer and fewer people.

The world's most advanced society has found the answer to people's war: eliminate the people.

It is, incidentally, remarkable that the *Times* can so blandly announce that the rebel economy and social fabric are the main target of the American bombardment. It is remarkable that this claim, which, if correct, sets American policy at the moral level of Nazi Germany, can be merely noted in a casual comment, with—so far as I know—no public reaction of horror and indignation.

Still, it is good that the American press has discovered that the rebel economy and social fabric are the target of the American bombardment of Laos. Perhaps we will be spared the pretense that our targets are steel and concrete, or that the bombing is "the most restrained in modern warfare" (as McGeorge Bundy so elegantly put it at the time when virtually every structure in North Vietnam, outside of the centers of Hanoi and Haiphong, was being demolished).

The discovery has been mysteriously delayed. For example, in July 1968 the Southeast Asia expert of *Le Monde*, Jacques Decornoy, published detailed reports of his visits to the liberated areas of Laos: "… a world without noise, for the surrounding villages have disappeared, the inhabitants themselves living hidden in the mountains … it is dangerous to lean out at any time of the night or day" because of the ceaseless bombardment which leads to "the scientific destruction of the areas held by the enemy." "The Americans are trying to 'break' the Laotian Left, both psychologically and, if possible, physically." The nature of their relentless attack "can only be explained if the target is the central administration of the Neo Lao Hak Sat"—the political organization that won handily in 1958 in the only unrigged election in Laos. This electoral victory inspired the American effort at subversion that led to the Laotian crisis of the early sixties, which still persists.

Decornoy describes "the motionless ruins and deserted houses" of the central town of Sam Neua district:

> The first real raid against the population center itself was launched on February 19, 1965. Very serious attacks were made on it quite recently on March 17 and 19, 1968.... The two ends of the town were razed to the ground. The old ruins of 1965 have disappeared, those of March 1968 were still "smoking" when we visited them. Branches of trees lay all along the length of the river, houses were totally burned out (phosphorus had been used). At the other end of Sam Neua, the sight was even more painful. Everywhere enormous craters; the church and many houses were demolished. In order to reach the people who might be living there, the Americans dropped their all-too-famous fragmentation bombs. Here lay a "mother bomb" disemboweled, by the side of the road. All round, over a dozen meters, the earth was covered with "daughter bombs," little machines that the Vietnamese know well, unexploded and hiding hundreds of steel splinters.... One of the officials of Sam Neua district told us that between February 1965 and March 1969, 65 villages had been destroyed. A number impossible to verify in a short report, but it is a fact that between Sam Neua and a place about 30 kilometers away where we stayed, no house in the villages and hamlets had been spared. Bridges had been destroyed, fields up to the rivers were holed with bomb craters.

Decornoy reports that "American raids on 'liberated Laos' began in May 1964, therefore well before the Gulf of Tonkin incident (August 1964) and the policy of escalation to North Vietnam (spring 1965). Under these circumstances, Laos has, in some ways, served as a testing ground or experimental site." He describes the amazing persistence of the Laotians in maintaining and advancing the social revolution in the face of this attack, their "virulent nationalism" and refusal to follow foreign models, the schools and factories in caves, the prosperity of the rare villages that have still, for unknown reasons, escaped destruction. Finally he quotes an American diplomat in Vientiane who says: "To make progress in this country, it is necessary to level everything. It is necessary to reduce the inhabitants to zero, to eliminate their traditional culture, for it blocks everything." And Decornoy comments: "The Americans accuse the North Vietnamese of intervening militarily in the country. But it is they who talk of reducing Laos to zero, while the Pathet Lao exalts the national culture and national independence."

No doubt Laos is still serving as a testing ground or experimental site, for the next stage of the Vietnam war, for our new long-haul, low-cost policy. If the American people will only trust their leaders, perhaps there is still a chance to crush the people's war in South Vietnam in ways that will be as well concealed as have been those of the Laotian war.

The secret can be kept. Americans know virtually nothing about the bombing of South Vietnam. To my knowledge, there has been only one pro-Western correspondent who has spent time in the liberated zones of South Vietnam, Katsuichi Honda—and I am sure that his reports in *Asahi Shimbun* in the fall of 1967 are known to very few Americans.[14] He describes, for example, the incessant attacks on undefended villages by gunboats in the Mekong River and by helicopter gunships "firing away at random at farmhouses":

> They seemed to fire whimsically and in passing even though they were not being shot at from the ground nor could they identify the people as NLF. They did it impulsively for fun, using the farmers for targets as if in a hunting mood. They are hunting Asians... This whimsical firing would explain the reason why the surgical wards in every hospital in the towns of the Mekong delta were full of wounded.

He is speaking, notice, of the Mekong Delta, where few North Vietnamese soldiers were identified until several months after the Tet offensive; where, according to American intelligence, there were 800 North Vietnamese troops before last summer;[15] and, which contained some 40 percent of the population of South Vietnam prior to the American assault.

Occasionally such material finds its way to the American press. Consider again the Mekong Delta. "In March [1969] alone, the United States Ninth Infantry Division reported that it killed 3,504 Vietcong troops and sympathizers in the northern delta [and] senior officers confidently forecast that they will continue to kill at least 100 a day well into the summer." The "conflagration ... is tearing the social fabric apart." In "free-fire zones, the Americans could bring to bear at any time the enormous firepower available from helicopter gunships, bombers and artillery ... fighter-bombers and artillery pound the enemy positions into the gray porridge that the green delta land becomes when pulverized by high explosives."[16]

Apparently the performance of the Ninth Division was not entirely satisfactory, however. "[I]n the Mekong Delta, United States military advisers at My Tho told a UPI correspondent, Robert Kaylor, that the government's pacification program was still being hampered by the effects of indiscriminate killing of civilians by United States Ninth Infantry Division troops recently withdrawn from the area. 'You can't exactly expect people who have had parts of their family blown away by the Ninth to be wholeheartedly on our side,' said the United States source, a member of a pacification team."[17]

In the *Christian Science Monitor*, October 14, 1969, there is a front-page story reviewing such efforts. It explains that "the proportion of the country 'pacified' has risen with the flow of peasants to resettlement and refugee areas," although the Viet Cong "currently are intensifying their campaign to drive peasants back to their home areas where [they] have a better chance of controlling them." The picture is clear. We, in our magnanimity, are using our modernizing instruments, bombs, and artillery, to lead the suffering peasants to the promised land of resettlement and refugee areas, while the ferocious Viet Cong—mere "village thugs," as the MIT political scientist, Ithiel Pool, explains in the journal of the Gandhi Peace Foundation—cruelly drive them back to their homes. The *Monitor* article also notes that "Despite years of thought and effort, officials here are still not agreed on how best to pacify a troubled land. In those years, pacification has advanced from being a theoretical ideal—though inconvenient—to the more important but second-class status of being 'the other war'"—and a proper theoretical exercise for American scientists and scholars.

The New York Times, September 24, 1969, presented an example of how pacification proceeds. Northwest of Saigon, seven hundred soldiers encircled a village, killing twenty-two and arresting fifty-three. It was the fourth such operation in this village in fifteen months. As for the villagers: "The Vietcong are everywhere, they say, and will be back when the Americans leave." An American junior officer, looking at the deserted central market, had this to say: "They say this village is 80 per cent VC supporters. By the time we finish this it will be 95 per cent." Such reports are hardly more newsworthy than a small item of September 27 which notes "that United States Army helicopter gunships mistakenly attacked a group of Vietnamese civilians 25 miles west of Tamky Tuesday, killing 14 civilians.... United States helicopter gunships killed 7 unarmed civilians and wounded 17 others in a similar incident Sept. 16 in the Mekong delta." It is not easy to avoid such accidents as we try to ensure that the Viet Cong constituency ceases to exist.

In *Look* magazine, November 18, 1969, Foreign Editor Robert Moskin describes his visit to a refugee camp, which "tells part of the story of Vietnam's hopelessness." Its 3,125 refugees (240 men) were transferred to this "desolate sand-dune camp" in a military sweep last summer from an island that was regarded as a VC stronghold: "The rest of the men are still hiding with the VC in the tall grass." This is in Quang Nam Province, where even the American officials in charge admit that the battle was lost "to Viet-Cong forces recruited for the most part from within the province."[18] With an honesty that others would do well to emulate, Moskin states that in Vietnam "America's historic westward-driving wave has crested."

With justice, "a staff major [of the American Division in Chulai] said: 'We are at war with the 10-year-old children. It may not be humanitarian, but that's what it's like.'"[19]

And now there is Song My—"Pinkville." More than two decades of indoctrination and counterrevolutionary interventions have created the possibility of a name like "Pinkville"—and the acts that may be done in a place so named. Orville and Jonathan Schell have pointed out[20] what any literate person should realize, that this was no isolated atrocity but the logical consequence of a virtual war of extermination directed against helpless peasants: "enemies," "reds," "dinks." But there are, perhaps, still deeper roots. Some time ago, I read with a slight shock the statement by Eqbal Ahmad that "America has institutionalized even its genocide," referring to the fact that the extermination of the Indians "has become the object of public entertainment and children's games."[21] Shortly after, I was thumbing through my daughter's fourth-grade social science reader.[22] The protagonist, Robert, is told the story of the extermination of the Pequot tribe by Captain John Mason:

> His little army attacked in the morning before it was light and took the Pequots by surprise. The soldiers broke down the stockade with their axes, rushed inside, and set fire to the wigwams. They killed nearly all the braves, squaws, and children, and burned their corn and other food. There were no Pequots left to make more trouble. When the other Indian tribes saw what good fighters the white men were, they kept the peace for many years.
> "I wish I were a man and had been there," thought Robert.

Nowhere does Robert express, or hear, second thoughts about the matter. The text omits some other pertinent remarks: for example, by Cotton Mather, who said that "It was supposed that no less than six hundred Pequot souls were brought down to hell that day."[23] Is it an exaggeration to suggest that our history of extermination and racism is reaching its climax in Vietnam today? It is not a question that Americans can easily put aside.

The revelation of the Song My atrocity to a wide public appears to have been a by-product of the November mobilization. As Richard L. Strout wrote in the *Christian Science Monitor*:[24]

> American press self-censorship thwarted Mr. Ridenhour's disclosures for a year. "No one wanted to go into it," his agent said of telegrams sent to Life, Look, and Newsweek magazines outlining allegations.... Except for the recent antiwar march in Washington the event might not have been publicized. In connection with the march a news offshoot (Dispatch News Service) of the left-wing Institute of Policy Studies of this city aggressively told and marketed the story to approximately 30 United States and Canadian newspapers.

Apart from this, it probably would have disappeared from history, along with who knows what else.

The first investigation by the Pentagon "reported that the carnage was due to artillery fire. Civilian casualties by artillery fire among hostile villages are so common that this explanation ended the inquiry."[25] But the murdered Vietnamese were not the victims of artillery fire. Since the soldiers looked into the faces of their victims, the inquiry must continue, despite the difficulties. Henry Kamm reported in *The New York Times* that:

> The task of the investigators is complicated by the fact that last January, most of the inhabitants of the peninsula were forcibly evacuated by American and South Vietnamese troops in the course of a drive to clear the area of Vietcong. More than 12,000 persons were removed from Bantangan Peninsula by helicopters and taken to a processing camp near this provincial capital. Heavy American bombing and artillery and naval shelling had destroyed many of the houses and forced them to live in caves and bunkers for many months before the evacuation…. An elaborate interrogation and screening procedure, in which American intelligence agents were said to have taken an important part, yielded only a hundred or so active Vietcong suspects. Most of the people were sent to a newly established refugee camp…. Despite the extensive movement of the population and the military operation, the Vietcong remain active in the area.[26]

On November 22, Kamm adds the further information that "the number of refugees 'generated'—the term for the people forcibly dislocated in this process—exceeded intelligence estimates four-fold." "The 12,000, instead of being scattered in many hamlets where it would be difficult to keep out the Vietcong, are now concentrated in six guarded, camp-like settlements."

It is perhaps remarkable that none of this appears to occasion much concern. It is only the acts of a company of half-crazed GIs that are regarded as a scandal, a disgrace to America. It will, indeed, be a still greater national scandal—if we assume that to be possible—if they alone are subjected to criminal prosecution, but not those who have created and accepted the long-term atrocity to which they contributed one detail—merely a few hundred more murdered Vietnamese.

Recently, a study of American public opinion about Vietnam concluded with this speculation: "... little reaction to the war is based on humanitarian or moral considerations. Americans are not now rejecting 'war,' they merely wish to see this current conflict ended. To achieve this goal, most Americans would pursue a more militant policy and ignore resultant atrocities."[27] We may soon discover whether this speculation is correct. Of course, there is sure to be a segment of American society that will not "ignore resultant atrocities"—namely, the irresponsible, loud-mouth vocal minority, or those who are described so nicely by Colonel Joseph Bellas, commanding officer of a hospital in Vietnam where soldiers boycotted Thanksgiving dinner in protest against the war: "They're young, they're idealistic and don't like man's inhumanity to man. As they get older they will become wiser and more tolerant."[28] If a majority of the American people will, indeed, ignore resultant atrocities and support Nixon's policy of pursuing a war without discernible end, then this segment of American society may be subjected to domestic repression of a sort that is not without precedent in American history; we seem to be seeing the early signs today with the savage repression of the Panthers, the conspiracy trial in Chicago, and other incidents.

The fact that repression may be attempted does not imply that it must succeed. Surely the possibility exists, today, of creating a broad-based movement of opposition to war and repression that might stave off such an attack. It is now even imaginable, as a few years ago it was not, that a significant American left may emerge that will be a voice in national affairs, and even, perhaps, a potential force for radical social change. There has been a remarkable shift in popular attitudes over the past months, an openness to radical political thinking of a sort that I do not recall for many years. To let these opportunities pass is to condemn many others to the fate of Vietnam.

Is there an "honorable" way out of Vietnam—meaning by that a way that might be tolerable to the present state of American opinion? The question is important, for if the answer is negative, it may well be that the threat of extinction that Fall recognized will in fact be realized. It is important to stress this possibility, in view of the present mood in certain "movement" circles where it is a criterion of one's radicalism to believe that America has been defeated and that the Vietnamese will win. On the contrary, a serious person will follow Gramsci's maxim: pessimism of the intelligence, optimism of the will. There is not much doubt that the United States has the power to deny victory, or even continued existence, to the people of Vietnam. No one knows whether the present strategy of capital-intensive war can reduce the level of organized social life in Vietnam to the point where an American-imposed solution may, in its terms, be successful.

There surely is an "honorable" way of ending the war. The PRG and DRV delegations in Paris have proposed such a way, repeatedly. It is a measure of the government's contempt for the American people that Nixon was willing to publish Ho Chi Minh's conciliatory letter, with the statement that it signified—in Nixon's phrase—"the other side's absolute refusal to show the least willingness to join in seeking peace." It seems that the intermediary in the Ho-Nixon exchange was Jean Sainteny. He was interviewed by Joseph Kraft, who writes:

> I saw Sainteny at the end of September, just after his return from the funeral of Ho Chi Minh in Hanoi. He had had a long talk with Premier Pham Van Dong. He was persuaded that the other side was prepared to accept a settlement that would include an independent and non-Communist South Vietnam set in a neutralist Southeast Asia. The obstacle to agreement in his view was that Hanoi did not have any faith in Mr. Nixon's claim that he wanted an agreement. On the contrary, the North Vietnamese thought the United States was still trying to impose in Saigon, by military means, a pro-American government hostile to Hanoi. M. Sainteny felt—and his feelings were made known to the President—that the United States could dispel Hanoi's doubts in two ways. One would be a formal statement that the United States recognized the principle of total withdrawal of American troops from South Vietnam at some unstipulated date. The other would be by broadening the present regime in Saigon to include some political figures who were not die-hard anti-Communists.[29]

Corroboratory evidence appears in an article by Philippe Devillers in *L'Actualité*, October 24, and Averell Harriman has publicly stated that Kraft's report is consistent with his understanding of the situation.[30]

Subsequent statements by Xuan Thuy and Mme. Binh in Paris provide further confirmation of the possibilities for a reasonable settlement.

Since 1960, the NLF has demanded that a neutralized South Vietnam be governed by a coalition in which they would have a fair representation. It is this demand that we have consistently opposed—not surprisingly, in view of the judgment of the American mission at the time, and since, on the political power of the NLF relative to that of the succession of puppets we have installed. When the full-scale American invasion began, Bernard Fall cited a remark to George Chaffard of *Le Monde* by a "high-ranking spokesman of the Front": "We have not fought all these years simply to end up by installing one set of dictators in place of the old." Fall added: "One does not fight for eight long years, under the crushing weight of American armor, napalm, jet bombers and, finally, vomiting gases, for the sheer joy of handing over what one fights for to some bureaucrat in Hanoi, merely on the say-so of a faraway party apparatus."[31] Despite the intensive American effort since 1965 to destroy social life in Vietnam, there is no reason to believe that the situation is fundamentally different today.

Nixon's speech of November 3 must be understood as a rejection of these possibilities for an "honorable" settlement, one that should be acceptable to a large, I should think overwhelming, segment of the American public. Nixon denied the existence of the PRG-DRV initiatives, and made it clear that we have no intention of withdrawing our expeditionary force or broadening the Saigon regime. The present Saigon regime, which exists solely by the force of American arms, is not an acceptable partner in a coalition with the PRG and would no doubt collapse were a realistic effort to resolve the conflict seriously contemplated.

Under these conditions, it is important to take note of recent political developments in Saigon. President Thieu has apparently abandoned any effort to construct a significant political base. Elizabeth Pond reports from Saigon that his new party "should be very similar to the Can Lao Party [virtually, a branch of Diem's secret police], as it is being directed by old Diemists, several of whom were Can Lao members." Thieu has been able to find no political base apart from the generals and the Northern Catholics—essentially a reconstruction of the Diem regime.[32]

One of the Hoa Hao factions recently left Thieu's party in protest "against the intensification of military control of the government in recent months—and the president's continuing refusal to deal seriously even with the member groups of his own alliance." Its leader asserted that the President's coalition "cannot do anything good for the country."[33] A report on the non-Communist opposition in South Vietnam quotes Pham Ba Cam, a Hoa Hao leader: "It's not very healthy to be in the opposition in Vietnam. If you want to learn about the status of the non-Communist opposition, go to Con Son [offshore prison island]. That's where you'll find the largest gathering."[34] As Pond reports, "President Thieu's decision to organize an Army/Catholic party—at this time and in this manner—sets the course for increasing isolation of the Saigon regime." It is a decision "to maintain the narrow interests and power of the existing military oligarchy as long as possible."

This narrowing of the base of the Saigon regime reflects the political realities of South Vietnam. It also reflects a rational political judgment on the part of General Thieu:

> As Vietnamese sources analyze President Thieu's thinking, he is calcu-
> lating that the United States cannot afford to lose the war and is there-
> fore stuck here almost no matter what Saigon does. The United States
> might dare, it is reasoned, to abandon the Thieu regime within a year
> or so, but it would never dare to destroy the South Vietnamese Army.
> If President Thieu links his destiny inextricably to that of the Army,
> then, he may figure that the United States cannot depose him.[35]

Thus current political developments confirm, once again, the failure of the American military to create a workable Quisling regime in the manner of the Russians in Czechoslovakia or the Germans in much of Occupied Europe. The consequences of this situation are summarized adequately by Jacques Decornoy: "Under these conditions, a military solution may be a task for several decades, supposing, that is, that there still remain Vietnamese to fight and Americans to accept a conflict without end and without hope."[36]

Twenty years ago the People's Republic of China was founded. Just a few months earlier, Dean Acheson had formed a committee to reassess

American policy in Asia, now that China was "lost." The committee was to operate under this instruction: "You will please take it as your assumption that it is a fundamental decision of American policy that the United States does not intend to permit further extension of Communist domination on the continent of Asia or in the Southeast Asia area...."[37] Acheson made his thoughts more precise, shortly afterward, when writing on the Soviet threat: "It is not only the threat of direct military attack which must be considered, but also that of conquest by default, by pressure, by persuasion, by subversion, by 'neutralism.' ..."[38]

In May 1950, Acheson announced that economic aid and military equipment would be sent to the French in Indochina "in order to assist them in restoring stability." Not long after, the State Department explained our support for French imperialism in Indochina in these terms: "... the fall of Indochina ... would be taken by many as a sign that the force of communism is irresistible and would lead to an attitude of defeatism.... Communist forces there must be decisively conquered down to the last pocket of resistance"—in the name of French imperialism.[39] The "much-needed rice, rubber, and tin" were also cited as a justification for our support for the French in their ill-fated effort to re-conquer their former colony. Upon their failure, we took over management of the enterprise directly.

In 1955 the Communist threat was defined in *The Political Economy of American Foreign Policy* (see Chapter 1, Section 1) as the economic transformation of the Communist powers "in ways which reduce their willingness and ability to complement the industrial economies of the West." Communism, in short, reduces the "willingness and ability" of underdeveloped countries to function in the world capitalist economy in the manner of the Philippines—to take a classic Asian example—where:

> Their economy has for nearly half a century been deliberately geared into that of the United States to an extent which caused Mr. McNutt, in testifying as High Commissioner, to say that "our businessmen and our statesmen in past years allowed the Philippines to become a complete economic dependency of the United States to a greater degree than any single State of the Union is economically dependent on the rest of the United States."[40]

Since then, there has been little substantive change in what United Nations Ambassador Salvador Lopez called the classic colonial economy of the Philippines. To be sure, we have bequeathed them the blessings of democracy. As Tillman Durdin accurately describes this legacy of half a century of colonial domination: "Filipinos view elections as a confirmation of the power of the wealthy business and landed interests who back both parties but usually pick the winners before Election Day and quietly give them the most support. In this case they picked President Marcos."[41] And in gratitude, the Filipinos have helped us in out war in Vietnam, in the manner explained in a recent report of the Symington subcommittee. William Selover summarized this report in a recent *Christian Science Monitor.*

> The hearings showed, for example, that the United States taxpayer has been paying for the Philippine troop commitment in Vietnam. It has also shown that, without this payment, the Philippines would not have sent a single man to help the United States in Vietnam.... Administration officials admitted paying the Philippines some $40 million to send the troops to Vietnam.[42]

Still more revealing is the stated purpose of the United States military commitment to the Philippines. Selover reports Lieutenant General Robert H. Warren's admission that the commitment was designed partly "to maintain internal security and stability and, thereby, make our own activities over there more secure." Senator Symington put it succinctly, with General Warren's reluctant assent: "In other words we are paying the Philippine Government to protect us from the Philippine people who do not agree with the policies of the government or do not like Americans." Pentagon Officials admitted in the hearings that "the only real threat that the Philippines faces ... [is] ... internal subversion." The threat is related, perhaps, to the fact that for most of the population, living standards have not materially changed since the Spanish occupation.

It is this "Communist threat" that we have been combating in Vietnam, where, as has frequently been noted, Vietnamese Communism threatens the new order that we have been trying to construct in Asia with Japan as junior partner, linked to Asia by essentially colonial relationships. As President Eisenhower expressed it:

One of Japan's greatest opportunities for increased trade lies in a free and developing Southeast Asia.... The great need in one country is for raw materials, in the other country for manufactured goods. The two regions complement each other markedly. By strengthening of Vietnam and helping insure the safety of the South Pacific and Southeast Asia, we gradually develop the great trade potential between this region ... and highly industrialized Japan to the benefit of both. In this way freedom in the Western Pacific will be greatly strengthened.[43]

It remains to be seen how long Japan will be able to fend off economic intervention of a sort that is increasingly turning Western Europe into a dependency of American-based multinational corporations, those "United States enterprises abroad [which] in the aggregate comprise the third largest country ... in the world—with a gross product greater than that of any country except the United States and the Soviet Union."[44]

It is not likely that the population of the empire—the "integrated world economy" dominated by American capital, to use the technical euphemism—will remain quiescent, willing indefinitely to complement the industrial economics of the West. Seventy-five years ago, shortly before the American invasion of the Philippines in a war that was, apart from scale, rather like our present war in Vietnam, the Philippine nationalist José Rizal castigated his countrymen because they were "like a slave who asked only for a bandage to wrap the chain so that it may rattle less and not ulcerate the skin." Those days are past. Those whom Marx called "the slaves and drudges of [the bourgeois] order" are no longer satisfied with a bandage to wrap their chains, and their discontent will lead to turmoil and violent repression, so long as we consent.

What can we do to affect the events that are to come? First, we must not make the mistake of placing trust in the government. The large upsurge of antiwar sentiment can be an effective device for changing national policy if it is sustained in continuing mass actions across the country. Otherwise the administration can ride out the storm and continue as before to systematically demolish the society of South Vietnam and Laos. It is difficult week after week, month after month, to sustain a high level of protest against the war. As American society becomes more polarized and the true, familiar Nixon emerges in the person of Mitchell or Agnew, as the threat of repression becomes more real, it will be hard to maintain the kinds of resistance and protest that the Vietnam catastrophe demands. As the reports of massacres and automated murder become routine, the impulse to respond by violence may become more difficult to stifle, despite the realization that this can only have the effect of bringing the mass of the population to "ignore resultant atrocities." Continued mass actions, patient explanation, principled resistance can be boring, depressing. But those who program the B-52 attacks and the "pacification" exercises are not bored, and as long as they continue in their work, so must we.

Notes

1 Assistant Secretary of Defense Paul Warnke, as quoted by Townsend Hoopes; see *New York Times*, September 28, 1969.

2 Richard M. Pfeffer, ed., *No More Vietnams?: The War and the Future of American Foreign Policy* (New York, Harper & Row, 1968), p. 107.

3 For detailed analysis based largely on Defense Department sources, see Gabriel Kolko, *London Bulletin*, August 1969.

4 *No More Vietnams?*, p. 212. For further discussion, see Chapter 1, Section III, and my article in *The New York Review*, January 2, 1969.

5 Elizabeth Pond, *Christian Science Monitor*, November 9, 1969.

6 On December 10, 1969, Reston returned to the question of Cam Ranh Bay, stating that it was now "an air and naval base which is the best in Asia," and that it has been a "fundamental question throughout the Paris negotiations" whether the United States is willing to abandon it "and many other modern military bases." He raises the question whether the United States would withdraw all troops or only all "combat forces," a plan which "could leave a couple of hundred thousand Americans in Vietnam to maintain and fly the planes and helicopter gunships and continue to train and supply and help direct the Vietnamese." There is no indication of any serious intention to withdraw all forces or to abandon the bases. As Joseph Kraft has reported (see page 78) the American refusal to commit itself to the principle of complete withdrawal is one of the factors blocking progress in Paris.

7 In the apt phrase of E. Herman and R. Duboff, "How To Coo Like a Dove While Fighting To Win," pamphlet of Philadelphia SANE, 20 South 12th Street, Philadelphia 19107.

8 *Congressional Record*, August 8, 1969, F 9589. Cited in the *Bulletin of Concerned Asian Scholars*, Vol. 2, No. 1 (October 1969), 1737 Cambridge Street, Cambridge, Mass—an important journal for those concerned with Asian affairs.

9 *War, Peace, and the Viet Cong* (Cambridge, Mass., The M.I.T. Press, 1969). He estimates that in 1963 "perhaps half the population of South Vietnam at least tacitly supported the NLF." The same estimate was given by the United States Mission in 1962. Elsewhere, he has explained that in late 1964 it was impossible to consider an apparently genuine offer of a coalition government, because there was no force that could compete politically with the Viet Cong, with the possible exception of the Buddhists, who were, not long after, suppressed as a political force by Marshall Ky's American-backed storm troopers. The same difficulty has been noted, repeatedly, by spokesmen for the American and Saigon governments and reporters. For some examples, see Herman and Duboff, *op. cit.*, or my "The Logic of Withdrawal," *American Power and the New Mandarins* (New York, Pantheon Books, 1969), pp. 221–94.

10 *New York Times*, June 11, 1968.

11 *New York Times Magazine*, November 23, 1969.

12 See *Washington Post*, October 31, 1969; *Los Angeles Times*, October 31; *New York Post*, November 4; *Science*, November 7. A Vietnamese student in the United States, Ngo Vinh Long, has summarized much of what is known, including his personal experience from 1959 to 1963 when he visited "virtually every hamlet and village in the country" as a military-map maker, in *Thôi-Báo Gà*, November 1969, 76a Pleasant Street, Cambridge, Mass., a monthly publication of Vietnamese students in the United States. He describes how defoliation has been used since 1961 to drive peasants into government-controlled camps, and from his own experience and published records in Vietnam, he records some of the effects: starvation, death, hideously deformed babies. He quotes the head of the Agronomy Section of the Japan Science Council who claims that by 1967 about half the arable land had been seriously affected. For American estimates, see the report of the Daddario subcommittee of the House

Committee on Science and Astronautics, August 8, 1969. They estimate the total area sprayed through 1968 as 6,600 square miles (extrapolating through 1969 the figure would reach about 8,600 square miles, about 60 percent of this respraying—over 10 percent of it crop destruction).

13 *Le Monde Weekly Selection*, October 1, 1969.

14 They have appeared in English, and can be obtained from the Committee for the English Publication of "Vietnam—A Voice from the Villages," c/o Mrs. Reiko Ishida, 2-13-7, Nishikata, Bunyo-ku, Tokyo.

15 "Before this summer, the enemy in the delta consisted mostly of indigenous Vietcong units and guerrillas, many of whom worked during the day in the rice fields and fought at night. The only North Vietnamese were troops and officers who led some of the guerrilla units. They numbered about 800 as against an estimated total of 49,000 Vietcong soldiers and support troops," *New York Times*, September 15, 1969. On September 16, the *Times* reports that "for the first time in the war, a regular North Vietnamese army unit, the 18B Regiment, had attacked in the delta."

16 *New York Times*, Peter Arnett, April 15, 1969. Arnett claims that only 90 percent of the enemy forces of 40,000 are recruited locally, giving a far higher estimate of North Vietnamese than the intelligence reports cited above, or others: e.g., *Christian Science Monitor*, September 16, which reports that in the early fall of 1969 "North Vietnamese troops in the delta doubled in number, to between 2,000 and 3,000 men."

17 *Boston Globe*, December 1, 1969.

18 William Nighswonger, *Rural Pacification in Vietnam* (Praeger Special Studies; New York, Frederick A. Praeger, 1967), p. 116.

19 Henry Kamm, *New York Times*, December 1, 1969.

20 *New York Times*, November 26, 1969.

21 Pfeffer, ed., *No More Vietnams?*, p. 18. On the widely noted analogy between Vietnam and the Indian wars see my *American Power and the New Mandarins*, pp. 279–80, n. 42.

22 Harold B. Clifford, *Exploring New England* (New Unified Social Studies; Chicago, Follett Publishing Co., 1961).

23 See Howard Zinn, "Violence and Social Change," Boston University *Graduate Journal*, Fall, 1968. When disease decimated the Indians, Mather said: "The woods were almost cleared of those pernicious creatures, to make room for a better growth."

24 On November 24, 1969. Attention, Mr. Agnew.

25 *Christian Science Monitor*, November 29, 1969.

26 Henry Kamm, *New York Times*, November 15, 1969.

27 J. Robinson and S. G. Jacobson. in Walter Isard, ed., *Vietnam: Some Basic Issues and Alternatives* (Cambridge, Mass., Schenkman Publishing Company, 1968), a symposium of the Peace Research Society (International). This organization, following a script by Orwell, is concerned with a special kind of peace research: the question of "how pacification can be achieved in turbulent village societies," along lines that we have been pioneering in Vietnam, for example. But even the Peace Research Society (International) is not monolithic. it would be unfair to assume that the conclusion of the cited study is mere wishful thinking. It has to be taken seriously.

28 Reuters, *Boston Globe*, November 27, 1969.

29 *Boston Globe*, November 10, 1969.

30 In a panel at Johns Hopkins University, November 14, 1969.

31 *New Society*, April 22, 1965, reprinted in Bernard B. Fall and Marcus G. Raskin, eds., *The Viet-Nam Reader* (New York, Vintage Books, 1965). Those who speak so glibly of "blood-

baths" might note the casualty figures that Fall cites: for example, 89,000 Viet Cong killed between 1961 and April 1965 (United States sources); 66,000 Viet Cong killed between 1957 and 1961 (AFP); 160,000 South Vietnamese (presumably NLF) killed thus far in the war (NLF sources).

32 *Christian Science Monitor*, November 6, November 8, November 14, 1969. Miss Pond has been one of the few correspondents, over the years, to give any serious attention to Vietnamese political and social life. In the past, her analyses have proved quite accurate. For additional corroboratory information, see D. Gareth Porter, "The Diemist Restoration," *Commonweal*, July 11, 1969.

33 John Woodruff, *Baltimore Sun*, October 25, 1969.

34 Terence Smith, *New York Times*, dateline October 24, 1969. The scale and character of forceful repression of dissent in South Vietnam have been amply reported. See, for example, Herman and Duboff, *op. cit.*, and references therein.

35 Pond, *Christian Science Monitor*, November 6, 1969.

36 *Le Monde diplomatique*, November 1969.

37 Memorandum from Acheson to Philip Jessup, cited by Gabriel Kolko, *The Roots of American Foreign Policy* (Boston, Beacon Press, 1969), p. 95.

38 Cited by Walter LaFeber, *America, Russia and the Cold War 1945–1966* (Ithaca, N.Y., Cornell University Press, 1967), p. 102.

39 *Ibid.*, p. 116.

40 Rupert Emerson, in J.C. Vincent, ed., *America's Future in the Pacific* (New Brunswick, N.J., Rutgers University Press, 1947), p. 87.

41 Commenting on the recent elections, *New York Times*, November 16, 1969. For some discussion of Philippine politics, see Onofre D. Corpuz, *The Philippines* (Englewood Cliffs, N.J., Prentice-Hall, 1965).

42 November 28, 1969: "From the hearings it is learned that the United States paid South Korea and Thailand as well to send their troops to Vietnam in a show of solidarity." This was somewhat more expensive. According to the *Times*, December 1, the bribe to Thailand amounted to a billion dollars.

43 April 4, 1959, quoted in Harry Magdoff, *The Age of Imperialism* (New York, Monthly Review Press, 1969). See Chapter 1, pages 20–22.

44 Leo Model, *Foreign Affairs*, July 1967, quoted in Magdoff, *op. cit.*

Chapter 3
Cambodia

I

THE INVASION of Cambodia by the United States and its Saigon subsidiary comes as no surprise, in the light of recent events in Southeast Asia.
Since 1968, the United States has steadily escalated the war in Laos, both
on the ground, as the CIA-sponsored Clandestine Army swept through
the Plain of Jars in late 1969, and from the air. When the report of the
Symington subcommittee on Laos was finally released on April 20, the
Washington Post carried the front-page headline: U.S. ESCALATES WAR
IN LAOS, HILL DISCLOSES. The headline was accurate; other evidence, to which I shall return in the next chapter, shows that the subcom-
mittee hearings seriously understate the scale, and the grim effects, of the
American escalation. This American escalation provoked a response by the
Pathet Lao and North Vietnamese, who now control more of Laos than
ever before, and led to devastation and population removal on a vast scale.

The destabilizing event in Cambodia—assiduously ignored by
President Nixon in his speech of April 30 announcing the American invasion[1]—was the right-wing coup of March 18 which overthrew Prince
Sihanouk and drove him into an alliance with the Cambodian left and the
mass popular movements of Laos and Vietnam, which are dominated by
left-wing forces. The coup, and the events that followed, must be understood as a further step in the internationalization of the Vietnam war.
However, the coup should also be seen in the context of developments
internal to Cambodia over the past several years. These factors are, of
course, interrelated.

Since early 1964 the United States has been conducting its war in
Indochina from sanctuaries scattered from Thailand to Okinawa. The
bombardment of Laos, which appears to have begun in May 1964, and the
intensive bombardment of North and South Vietnam that followed in

February 1965, make use of bases in Thailand, South Vietnam, Okinawa, the Philippines, and Guam, not to speak of the naval units that control the surrounding oceans. The control center for the bombing of North Vietnam and northern Laos is in Thailand, presumably, at Udorn Air Base. In 1968, the bombing of Laos greatly increased in intensity, when aircraft formerly employed against North Vietnam were shifted to the bombardment of Laos. In 1969, the bombing of northern Laos was again greatly intensified as infiltration fell off on the so-called "Ho Chi Minh Trail." Most of this area has long been under Pathet Lao control.

As a glance at the map makes clear, the bombing of northern Laos takes place in a region far removed from the "Ho Chi Minh Trail" and has no direct connection to the war in South Vietnam. It is, in fact, directed against civilian targets and has resulted in almost total destruction of most settled areas and forced evacuation of much of the population. Where people remain, they live, for the most part, in caves and tunnels. According to American Embassy figures, the population remaining in the Pathet Lao zones is over a million, well over a third of the population of Laos. There may be as many as three-quarters of a million refugees in the government-controlled areas. The planes that attack northern Laos are based in Thailand, whereas the bombing of southern Laos (including the "Ho Chi Minh Trail") originates from Danang, Pleiku, and the Seventh Fleet. Now the Thai bases are also being used to bomb Cambodia.[2]

The American escalation of the war in Laos provoked a response by the Communist forces, which now control more of Laos than ever before. Since this result was predictable, the question naturally arises: What was the American government hoping to accomplish by the 1968–69 escalation? Some regard this escalation as merely another major error of the Pentagon and the CIA, but there are grounds for skepticism. The objective of the bombing seems to be to destroy the civil society administered by the Pathet Lao. Quite possibly, the United States is pursuing in Laos the dual policy of massive destruction in areas that are beyond the reach of American-controlled armies, and removal of the population to refugee camps and urban slums wherever this is feasible. This has been the effect of the American escalation, and it is likely that it was the intended effect, as in Vietnam.

To facilitate the all-weather bombardment of North Vietnam, advanced navigational facilities were established in northern Laos. One of these, at Phou Pha Thi, became known to the American public when it was overrun on March 11, 1968. It was seventeen miles from the border of North Vietnam, on a mountain peak. There were American casualties, but the number remains classified. The base had been established in 1966. Other such facilities were established, but information is classified. The CIA has also endeavored to maintain guerrilla bases in these territories, long administered by the Pathet Lao.[3]

The United States also has employed extensive mercenary forces—the term is precise—from South Korea, Thailand, and the Philippines, as well as Chinese and Cambodian mercenaries. The number of these forces, taken together with the troops from Australia and New Zealand, over the years, has been about the same as that of the North Vietnamese claimed by the Americans to be in South Vietnam. Of course, all of these forces and their fire power are quite small as compared with the American occupying army, even apart from the Pacific Naval and Air Command operating from its privileged sanctuaries.

During the 1960s, Prince Sihanouk tried, with much success, to save Cambodia from the spreading Indochina war. Nevertheless, the war has spilled over into eastern Cambodia. Those whose information is restricted to American government propaganda may have visions of an invasion of Cambodia by great North Vietnamese armies. The truth is rather different. As American ground sweeps and aerial bombardment devastated much of the Vietnamese countryside, Vietnamese resistance forces have taken refuge in sparsely inhabited areas of eastern Cambodia, which have increasingly been used as rest-and-recreation areas and, conceivably, command posts. At the same time, the armed forces of the United States and its allies and collaborators have carried out substantial military attacks against Cambodia. Evidence is meager, but what there is supports these general conclusions.

The earlier stages are described as follows by the British scholar Michael Leifer:

From the early 1960's charges had been levelled from Saigon and later from Washington that Cambodian territory was being used as an active sanctuary for Viet Cong insurgents. Prince Sihanouk had denied the charges consistently and the denials had always been substantiated as a result of inquiries by the International Control Commission for Cambodia, by Western journalists, and even by Western military attachés stationed in Phnom Penh.[4]

In July 1966, an American study team investigated specific charges by the United States government on the scene and found them to be entirely without substance.[5] However, the team happened to be present immediately after an American helicopter attack on the Cambodian village of Thlok Trach, and its published report, relying on information supplied by Cambodian officials, also mentions other specific attacks on villages. The Thlok Trach attack was at first denied by the United States, but was then conceded, since eyewitnesses (including a CBS television team) were present. (This, incidentally, is the usual pattern. To cite only the most recent case, the bombing of North Vietnam on May 1, 1970, was admitted by the United States government, but, it appears, only after a report was filed by an American newsman, Robert Boyd, who happened to be present near the site of the bombing.[6])

The Cambodians report many other such incidents. For example, on February 24, 1967, "a large number of armed forces elements consisting of Americans, South Vietnamese and South Koreans entered Cambodian territory and fired heavily on the Khmer defenders of the village of Duan Roth.... On the same day ... aircraft of the same armed forces heavily bombed the Khmer village of Chrak Kranh ... [which] was then invaded and burnt by the United States-South Vietnamese troops" who occupied the village until March 3.[7]

According to official Cambodian statistics, up to May 1969, the United States and its allies were responsible for 1,864 border violations, 165 sea violations, 5,149 air violations, 293 Cambodian deaths, and 690 Cambodians wounded.[8]

In a review of events of 1967, Roger Smith writes that relations between Cambodia and the United States "were strained because of periodic South Vietnamese and American bombing of Cambodian villages along the South Vietnamese frontier, armed incursions from Thailand, and, late in the year, a reported South Vietnamese-imposed blockade of shipping to Phnom Penh via the Mekong River."[9] Additional problems were caused by the activities of the Khmer Serei (Free Khmers), which, in the beginning of 1966, "declared war on Cambodia and claimed responsibility for incursions across the border."[10]

The Khmer Serei are reported to be led by an adventurer named Songsak, who fled Cambodia by bribing a pilot of an aviation club (taking with him all its funds), and the "fascist" Son Ngoc Thanh, who was the head of the Cambodian government under the Japanese, after spending most of World War II in Tokyo, and later switched his allegiance to the CIA—not an unfamiliar pattern.[11] This group is made up of Cambodians who were trained by the American Special Forces in South Vietnam and have carried out operations against Cambodia from bases in South Vietnam and Thailand.[12] We shall return to this interesting organization and its recent activities in a moment.

The Cambodian Government White Paper of January 1970 (see note 8) covers events up until May 1969. Since then, there have been many further incidents. The American biologist Arthur Westing, who was investigating American defoliation in Cambodia (see note 8), inspected the site of one such incident shortly after it occurred last November. He describes this as a "particularly vicious" case. A village was attacked, and houses, a school, livestock, a hospital marked with a giant red cross on its roof, and a well-marked ambulance trying to retrieve wounded were all destroyed by bombs, rockets, and napalm. The ICC reported no evidence of the presence of Viet Cong, nor could the United States produce any photographic (or other) evidence, despite daily reconnaissance flights. The United States chargé suggested that "our pilots must have lost their cool"—for about forty-eight hours.

Westing speculates that the attack may have been "a punitive or retaliatory measure following the destruction of a United States helicopter last October 24 and particularly of a U.S. F-105 on November 14, both shot down in the course of attacking Dak Dam in casual and callous disregard of Cambodian neutrality."[13] The American government apologized and paid $11,400 in reparations. I shall return below to other recent incidents reported by Americans present at the scene.

As in the case of Laos, it may be asked what the United States hoped to achieve by these repeated attacks on Cambodia, in which, so far as is known, no Viet Cong or North Vietnamese was ever killed and no damage was done to any Vietnamese military site. Again, it is possible that "faulty intelligence" is to blame. I suspect, however, that the aerial, naval, and ground attacks were for the most part capricious or vengeful, as appears to have been the case in the incident that Westing reported. The American military does not recognize the right of others to defend their own territory from American attack or overflight, or to interfere with American plans by inhabiting areas that the United States government feels should be cratered or defoliated. And when such people aggressively insist on these rights, the United States authorities feel free to react as they choose. Where we have evidence at all, it appears that the American attacks on Cambodia were governed by such assumptions, though it is possible that in some cases it was believed (apparently falsely) that Vietnamese military targets were being attacked.

A European resident of Phnom Penh described to a reporter a visit, before the recent coup, to Svay Rieng town in the "Parrot's Beak" area, five kilometers from the closest border point:

> During lunch, an American plane came over and looped the loop over the governor's house. The plane kept diving at a Cambodian flag which was flying in the front garden. A policeman took out his pistol and fired a few shots at the plane. I suppose if he had hit it, the Americans would have come in and napalmed the whole town.[14]

An exaggeration or a joke? One can hardly say so, given what evidence we have regarding American military actions.[15] Very likely something of the sort accounts for many, perhaps most, of the attacks on Cambodia.

The first attested case of a Viet Cong installation within Cambodia was in November 1967, when American journalists claimed to have found a Viet Cong campsite four miles within Cambodian territory.[16] Since that time, Viet Cong and NVA forces have taken refuge in eastern Cambodia after intensive bombardment and American ground sweeps in South Vietnam, using these territories much as the United States makes use of Thailand, Vietnam, the Philippines, Taiwan, Japan, Okinawa, Guam, Hawaii, and the oceans of Asia and the Pacific. (The analogy is, of course, inexact, since the Vietnamese obviously do not dispose of anything like the resources that the United States employs for its war against the people of Vietnam, Laos, and now Cambodia.) T. D. Allman, one of the most knowledgeable and enterprising of the American correspondents now in Cambodia, describes the situation as follows:

> ... although tens of thousands of Vietnamese Communist troops have been for long on Cambodian soil, they have been lying low in the border regions and causing little trouble.... The arrangement has meant the presence of foreign troops on Cambodian soil, but it has also allowed Cambodia, alone among its neighbors, to pass through the dangers of the Vietnam war without having its countryside ravaged and its population brutalized.[17]

I will not take the space to comment on the hypocrisy of the reference to "sanctuaries" by the American government and its propagandists and apologists. Perhaps the most appropriate remark, in this connection, was made by Prince Sihanouk after the coup:

> The cynicism of the United States executive reached its peak when he demanded that the resistance forces of our three peoples [i.e., of Vietnam, Laos, and Cambodia] evacuate their own countries in response to the withdrawal of a part of the United States forces, and especially when our resistance has become "foreign intervention" on our own soil. Where then should our liberation armies go? To the United States?[18]

Sihanouk is quite correct. When President Nixon refers to the lack of sincerity on the part of the "North Vietnamese" (an expression now used by American propaganda as a cover term for Cambodians, Laotians, South Vietnamese, and North Vietnamese who obstinately refuse to obey American orders) in Laos, Cambodia, and South Vietnam, to their continued aggression in the face of American withdrawals which now leave in South Vietnam a force considerably larger than the entire North Vietnamese army, the meaning of his words is, plainly, that these "aggressors" have refused to surrender to the right-wing governments that the United States has installed and the native military forces that it organizes, trains, supplies, pays, and "advises." With equal justice, Hitler might have spoken of the aggressiveness of the French *maquis*, who were of course supplied and advised by the Anglo-Saxons, and Tojo of the lack of sincerity of the Chinese bandits, who refused to accept the rule of Wang Ching-wei, whom the Japanese installed as a puppet ruler in 1940.

But Wang Ching-wei had at least been a leading Chinese nationalist, not a General Thieu. Nor did the Germans deploy an expeditionary force on anything remotely approaching the American scale to ensure the rule of the Vichy government. It cannot be stressed too strongly that what is remarkable about the Indochina war is the inability of the American invaders to establish indigenous governments that can rule effectively and control their societies with their own means. In this respect, the United States in Indochina still falls short of its distinguished predecessors, though the American White House easily matches them in cynicism and mendacity, and surpasses all current competitors in its reliance on violence and terror.

II

TO RETURN to Cambodia: the country was, then, partially drawn into the Indochina war, though Prince Sihanouk managed to maintain neutrality by a delicate balancing act and to save it from the terror that ravaged Vietnam and Laos. The contrast between Cambodia and its immediate neighbors was described by T. D. Allman, just a few months ago, as follows:

> A few days later, in a commercial plane, I flew over Svay Rieng province. From the air the frontier is now clearly defined: beyond the parrot's beak peninsula of neat Cambodian rice fields and villages the land is pitted by literally hundreds of thousands of bomb and shell craters. In some cases the years of day-and-night bombing have changed the contours of the land and little streams form into lakes as they fill up mile after square mile of craters. Above this desolation and along and just across the Cambodian frontier, the American helicopters and planes whirr continually, firing their guns and cannon, dropping their bombs.[19]

The March 18 coup against Sihanouk marked the end of this period of fairly effective neutrality. It is safe to predict that the frontier will no longer be so clearly defined.

Evidently, it was the coup of March 18 that destabilized the Cambodian situation. It created an entirely new situation within

Cambodia, and may also prove to have affected significantly the long-term relations among the peoples of Indochina. Cambodia, like the other states of the region, is a mélange of ethnic groups. The large majority of its population of about seven million is Khmer (the term is often used as synonymous with "Cambodian"), but there are substantial Chinese and Vietnamese minorities of perhaps about half a million each, in addition to mountain tribes. Many Vietnamese were brought to Cambodia (as to Laos) by the French to work in rubber plantations (in Laos, in the mines), but also to serve as administrators for the colonial government and private businesses. They also succeeded in taking over a large share of local commerce.

The French capitalized on feelings of inferiority toward the Vietnamese among the native Khmer and Lao, and by so doing, no doubt intensified these feelings, which remain an important factor in current politics. They adopted the standard colonialist policy of using minorities or outsiders to help control native populations. Jean Lacouture describes the French colonial system as one of "double domination: that of the [French] administration over the three Vietnamese regions and that of the Vietnamese cadres over the two small countries of the west [Laos and Cambodia]."[20] The French scholar Jean Chesneaux writes:

> If the popular movements of Cambodia were repressed by "Annamite riflemen," it was the "Cambodian riflemen" who were brought in to restore order among the Vietnamese of the lower Mekong. [21]

(The Americans do much the same, relying on Khmer mercenaries in South Vietnam—see note 31—and using the Saigon Army to restore order in Cambodia.)

At the same time, there is a Khmer minority of about 700,000 in the western part of South Vietnam. According to Chesneaux, the Khmer minority, oppressed by Saigon's policies of racial discrimination, gave "massive support" to the NLF.[22] He also reports that the Khmer peasants in Cambodia took no part in the recent pogroms initiated by the Lon Nol government against the Vietnamese minority in Cambodia.

Such observations suggest that there has always been a possibility of peaceful cooperation among the peoples of Indochina—the Viet, the Lao, the Khmer, the Chinese, and the mountain tribesmen—if the Western imperialists, whose presence has exacerbated all potential conflicts, were to depart. It is interesting, in this connection, that the 1962 Congress of the NLF of South Vietnam called for a neutralist bloc including South Vietnam, Laos, and Cambodia. The United States, hoping to convert South Vietnam into a permanent base for its colonial operations, showed no interest in this idea (if, indeed, it even took official notice of it).

In 1965 Prince Sihanouk convened a "Conference of the Indochinese People" in Phnom Penh. It brought together representatives of the Democratic Republic of Vietnam (North Vietnam), the NLF of South Vietnam, the Pathet Lao, the ruling Sangkum party of Cambodia, and other South Vietnamese "opposed to American hegemony."[23] It was able to achieve very little, coming as it did immediately after the initiation of the intensive and regular bombardment of South and North Vietnam in early February 1965.

As the Vietnam war expanded, tensions began to develop between Sihanouk and the Viet Cong. Sihanouk's press began to speak of Viet Cong support for the small local guerrilla groups, the so-called "Red Khmer" or "Khmer Viet Minh." T. D. Allman, reviewing these developments just a few months ago,[24] described the conflicts as more potential than real, if only because Sihanouk's "enormous popularity continues undiminished in the countryside."

Immediately after the March 18 coup, the leadership of the "Red Khmers" approached Sihanouk and offered to join him in opposition to American imperialism.[25] Sihanouk accepted this offer and called for guerrilla war. In his speech to the closing session of the April 1970 Summit Conference of Indochinese Peoples in China (see note 18), Sihanouk said that United States imperialist aggression has created a new unity among the peoples of Indochina:

> This process of union and cooperation is in the line of history, in the same way as decolonization and liberation of oppressed peoples in the Third World. Only yesterday the colonial powers divided these peoples in order to "rule" them, and they did not accept decolonization until forced to do so by armed resistance. Today the old colonialists have been replaced by imperialists and neo-colonialists, and there is no hope, through diplomacy, negotiations, conferences or even friendly neutrality, of avoiding the mortal danger that they represent.

> Wherever this danger appears, armed struggle alone is the only way to eliminate it.

His closing words were: "Long live the united peoples of Indochina."

Whether real unity among the Indochinese peoples will be achieved remains to be seen. Some of the best-informed observers are optimistic in this regard. Jean Chesneaux writes:

> The history of Viet-Lao-Khmer relations has not bequeathed these peoples a burden of territorial conflicts: the frontiers fixed by colonization have not been placed in question. The moral relations among them are also disentangled from the frictions of the past.... Cambodia today is plunged directly into the war by an external initiative, the promoters of which doubtless did not gauge all of the consequences: in particular, the development of solidarity among the Vietnamese, Laotians, and Cambodians.[26]

In the past, Sihanouk hoped, with much reason, that China would in the long run be the guarantor of Cambodian neutrality against possible Vietnamese incursions. China has no reason to want a powerful bloc of unified states to its south controlled either from the outside or by one dominant member, any more than the U.S.S.R. in the postwar world looked with favor on a Balkan alliance dominated by Tito.[27] Hence it is opposed to American domination of Indochina, as it would no doubt oppose Thai or Vietnamese domination were either to appear likely. American propaganda naturally insists that China hopes to rule the region itself, or to do so through its "puppet" in Hanoi, but these claims are supported by no evidence or serious argument. Sihanouk, though himself strongly anti-Communist in the past, appears to have had faith in China's intentions, in part for the general reasons just mentioned, but in part also because of China's attitude since his regime was established. Michael Field comments:

> ... as he [Sihanouk] frequently remarks, China has behaved in an exemplary fashion towards Cambodia; its independence and territorial integrity have been harassed, not by the Chinese colossus but by South Viet Nam and Thailand, camp-followers of the West.[28]

Now, of course, Sihanouk has formed a direct alliance with the Cambodian left and with China. It remains to be seen how the situation will develop under these changed circumstances, though it would appear that China's long-term goals should remain unaltered, even after Cambodia's most popular political personality, the formerly anti-Communist spokesman for Cambodian nationalism, has been driven into an alliance with the Communists.

The immediate background for the Cambodian coup of March 18 is described as follows by T. D. Allman:

> The underlying cause for Sihanouk's fall probably lay in the fact that although he revolutionised Cambodia's foreign policy, and his own relations with the peasants and workers, he left the traditional Khmer elite free to occupy office and eventually use their traditional power against him.[29]

The report notes that "the common people continued to revere Sihanouk," but a "tiny minority brought Sihanouk down." However,

> The new rulers, as they busy themselves taking back in power and financial opportunities what Sihanouk took away from them, doubtlessly will have a much harder time retaining the loyalty of the countryside—where all real Asian revolutions begin and are won. By biting off the hand which fed them, the tiny group of aristocrats, army officers and businessmen which toppled Sihanouk may have insured its own doom.

The coup, Allman writes elsewhere,[30] was not only shortsighted, in that it upset the delicate balance that Sihanouk had maintained, but also selfish. The main complaint of the tiny elite that staged the coup is that Sihanouk "had deprived the aristocracy, the bourgeoisie and the army of their traditional slice of the financial action and of their accustomed place in the sun. It was an upper-class coup, not a revolution."

This fact must be appreciated. It goes a long way toward explaining the American invasion of Cambodia.

The March 18 coup was the culmination of a carefully prepared series of actions taken over the past several years that slowly eroded the position of the Cambodian left—tenuous at best—within the government. In the elections of 1966, Sihanouk departed from his usual practice of endorsing candidates. Under the conditions of Cambodian society, the result was a general victory for the most corrupt and the wealthiest candidates, those who could freely distribute bribes, patronage, and promises. As Jean Lacouture put it: "Khmer society received the kind of representation, manipulated by money and feudal conditions, which was natural to it in this period of its history."

The only exceptions were three left-wing delegates—Hu Nim, Hu Yuon, and Khieu Samphan—who won easily. At the time, Sihanouk was warned by the leftist minister Chan Seng that a right-wing coup led by Lon Nol might be in preparation, but he apparently felt that he could keep the right under control, relying on the loyalty and support of the people. Step by step, he succumbed to right-wing pressures that were directed as much against his economic reforms as against his personal power, with its extensive and unique popular base among the peasantry and the small urban proletariat. By the end of 1969, much of Sihanouk's "Khmer socialism" had been dismantled,[31] and the few left-wing members of the government had been removed. To a large extent, these developments must be seen as an internal struggle for power among the Cambodian elite.

While this shift to the right was taking place within the government, the radical left took on a more activist policy in the cities, with demonstrations and popular agitation, and rebel groups were formed in rural areas. The intensification of the Vietnam war, with the spillover into Cambodia, also served to increase the polarization within Cambodia that was held in check by Sihanouk's personal popular strength.

Several months before the coup, members of the Khmer Serei began crossing into Cambodia and "rallying" to the Cambodian army with their arms and equipment. In retrospect, it appears that the Khmer Serei may have been a "Trojan horse" infiltrated into the Cambodian forces, perhaps by the CIA, to stiffen the right-wing elements that were readying the anti-Sihanouk coup.[32]

On March 4, General Lon Nol, then President of the Council of Ministers and Minister of Defense, took on in addition the post of Minister of Information, thereby gaining control of the press, radio, and television. A few days later the army organized anti-Vietnamese demonstrations in Svay Rieng Province, and staged a demonstration in Phnom Penh, where soldiers in civilian dress sacked the PRG and DRV embassies.

Sihanouk, who was then visiting Paris, noted the rising threat to his rule, and he commented:

> If I do not obtain satisfaction that the Communists will respect Cambodia's neutrality, then I will resign. A showdown between the extreme right wing and myself is most probable.

He went on to speak of the possibility of a *coup d'état*, led perhaps by General Lon Nol. He observed that many army officers are naturally right wing and "are nostalgic about American aid, which would enable them to lead an easy life." "The Americans are inside the castle walls—that is, inside our homes." He expressed certainty that right-wing leaders in the government were in contact with the United States, "whether through the embassy, the CIA or any such like organization, I do not know.[33]

On March 18, the coup took place, led by General Lon Nol and Sirik Matak. A tiny Cambodian elite, hoping to win for itself a larger share of control in the economy and political life and resentful of Sihanouk's personal authority and prestige, plunged the country into civil war and set the stage for the American invasion that now threatens to turn Cambodia into another Laos or Vietnam.

The role of outside governments in the March 18 coup can only be guessed, and will probably never be known in any detail. Most observers take for granted that the Americans played a role. Chesneaux, for example, states that "the taking of power by the Lon Nol group is the result of a long series of attempts by the Cambodian right, supported by the United States."[34] As already noted, the actions of the Khmer Serei provide evidence for this view. The role of the French government is also open to some speculation. There are those who feel that the French government may have been directly implicated in the coup. Certainly, it gave little support to Sihanouk when the coup took place. Jean Lacouture describes the behavior of the French government as follows:

> It now seems established that Prince Sihanouk, upon learning of the Lon Nol coup, telephoned directly to the Elysée—where, six days earlier, he had been the guest of M. Pompidou—to determine whether Paris would support him: if assurance would have been given him, he would have attempted, come what may, to land the next day in Phnom Penh. The response was so evasive, we have been told, that the

prince turned towards Moscow and Peking. One might judge that this was one of the moments when the elimination of General de Gaulle has played a role in international politics."[35]

Elsewhere, Lacouture notes that "in private circles, many Vietnamese and Khmers who support Prince Sihanouk are asking if one must not see, in this 'neutrality' of France face to face with the destruction of the policy of neutrality, one of the results of M. Pompidou's trip to the United States."[36] An interesting speculation indeed.

Immediately after the coup pro-Sihanouk demonstrations broke out in many places. About eighty to one hundred Cambodians, all unarmed, were killed in the repression of these demonstrations. ("Significantly," notes Allman, "no Vietnamese was killed.") Jean-Claude Pomonti of *Le Monde* reports:

> Repression of pro-Sihanouk demonstrations among the peasants toward the end of March in the wake of the coup could only have served to swell the small bands of insurgents generally referred to, rightly or wrongly, as "Red Khmers." Many peasants, fearful of arrest after the demonstrations, took to the jungle rather than return to their homes. And today the Red Khmers are in a position to exploit the discontent in the country areas where the army opened fire on the peasants. The conditions for an active rebellion have been fulfilled one by one.[37]

Pomonti continues:

> Information coming in from the provinces early last week seems to confirm that Khmer peasants in Viet Cong areas are now armed and trained. The nucleus of a "liberation army" is very probably being constituted, and the Phnom Penh government could find itself in a more precarious position before long, particularly if it fails to reassert its authority in the areas abandoned for more than two weeks by the central government.

He quotes a diplomat who says:

> It did not surprise me in the least to hear announcements of liberated zones being established … or of a "liberation army" being formed. It would not surprise me either if the Viet Cong should say they are pulling out of certain zones and that from now on dealings should be with the "new Khmer authorities." Then they might well announce

the return of Prince Sihanouk to one of these zones—armed with a powerful radio transmitter.

Within days after the coup, elite troops of the Saigon Army, with American air and logistic support, entered Cambodian territory for extensive attacks on Viet Cong positions. American advisers accompanied these troops and also took part in planning meetings with military officers of the ARVN and Cambodian armies. Air strikes and large-scale attacks continued through late March and early April. The Viet Cong response was predictable. Viet Cong and North Vietnamese troops simply moved away from the sparsely inhabited border regions and deeper into Cambodia, and, for the first time, began to take an active part in creating a Cambodian guerrilla army. They also, for the first time, conducted military operations against Cambodian troops. Shortly before the full American-ARVN invasion began in late April, the situation was described as follows by T. D. Allman:

> Under Sihanouk, areas of Vietcong control were measured in kilometres—even metres—from the border. Now they are measured in districts or whole provinces. In Takeo, Kampot and Kandal provinces, south of Phnom Penh, villages have been taken over by mixed bands of armed Cambodians and Vietnamese calling themselves "Sihanouk's Army."[38]

Le Monde comments editorially that "the 'Red Khmer' movement is led by able men, and now that it has some support in the countryside, it can no longer be dismissed—as Washington tends to do—as a mere appendage of the North Vietnamese Communist Party." The new government in exile announced by Sihanouk from Peking will probably include the three delegates to the Cambodian parliament mentioned earlier, who were elected with "overwhelming majorities" in the last (1966) elections and "can hardly be considered 'Vietnamese agents.'"[39] They are generally regarded as the only delegates elected who represented something other than the feudal and wealthy elements in Cambodian society (see Roy, *op. cit.*), and they appear to have a reputation for honesty and integrity that is rare among Cambodian politicians.

Among those who have joined Sihanouk in China are Huot Sambath, Cambodian delegate to the United Nations, Penn Nouth, one of his long-term associates and advisers (Field describes him as "a close collaborator of Sihanouk and with him an architect of Cambodian neutrality"), and Chan Seng, formerly Minister of Education and Minister of National Economy and editor of the leading left-wing journal, one of the outstanding personalities and political figures of Cambodia until his exile, to Paris, in 1967, during the early stages of preparation for the takeover by the right.

On departing from Paris to join Sihanouk, Chan Seng said that the coup has advanced the revolutionary cause by five years. Commenting, Lacouture writes:

> Has anyone ever seen such incompetent sorcerer's apprentices as the plotters of Phnom Penh who, in less than a month, will have thrown their country into a civil war and brought it to the edge of an international war, and made the most important and prestigious personality of their country the unconditional ally of the revolutionary movement?[40]

Lacouture, who sees the hand of the Americans behind the coup, describes it as "a suicide operation for the American party, which offers their enemies an opportunity to deploy themselves, with a popular base, over the whole Indochina theater."

As already noted, the view that the perpetrators of the coup "may have ensured their own doom" is shared by Allman. Henry Kamm of *The New York Times* notes further that, among foreign observers in Phnom Penh, disenchantment with the new regime "has set in with a vengeance":

> The uncharitable feelings of most observers toward the Lon Nol government are compounded of evidence of their military futility, revulsion over atrocities and callousness toward the large Vietnamese minority, scorn for the political *naïveté* that led the leaders to put real faith in the possibility of help from the International Control Commission or the United Nations to drive out the Vietcong, and impatience with a cacophony of blusterous and chauvinistic talk and empty mock-martial gestures such as putting high school girls in khaki shirts to cover an air of feckless irresolution.[41]

He also notes that the United States government seems to share this contempt, as one must conclude from the manner in which it has carried out the invasion, hardly bothering even to inform the Cambodians:

Whatever the reason, America seems clearly to have decided to make war in Cambodia without the Cambodians. And it is a measure of the low morale of Cambodia that she accepted this without immediate outcry as though, like the Vietnamese Communist incursion, it is a fact of life beyond her control.

A diplomat in Phnom Penh stated recently that "We probably shall look back on these days as the opening phases of the Cambodian civil war." Citing this observation, T. D. Allman writes:

> … for the first time since independence in 1953, Cambodians were killing Cambodians … the Phnom Penh government's hold on the rural population was in doubt. The average Cambodian wants most of all to live in peace, but already he is being urged to choose sides. On the government side are the army, most of the business class, the aristocracy, the intellectuals and government functionaries. Ranged against the new government are some 40,000 Vietnamese troops [i.e. NLF and North Vietnamese]—who so far have taken only a small role in the anti-government movement—the tiny Khmer Rouge guerrilla movement, and most importantly, a sizable but unknown proportion of Cambodia's six million peasants who still see Sihanouk as a god-king and the nation's only leader.[42]

Speculating a year ago about the prospects of the Cambodian rebels for success, Michael Leifer wrote that these prospects "will depend (discounting external factors) not only on the exploitation of genuine grievance but also on an ability to identify with the nationalist cause for which Prince Sihanouk has been the most ardent and passionate advocate. This would seem unlikely."[43] Before March 18, this was a reasonable assessment. Now, however, Sihanouk, the "most ardent and passionate advocate" of the national cause, the person whom one American expert described as being "a significant expression of the Cambodian people's will,"[44] has identified himself with the rebels. It is doubtful that the right-wing Lon Nol government, with its narrow urban base, can counter this popular force or win it over.

The March 18 coup reflects a split within the Cambodian elite, the exact nature of which is not entirely clear. However, two things do seem clear. First, the best-known members of the Cambodian left are now aligned with Sihanouk. Second, the Cambodian left is now in a position to mobilize the peasantry, capitalizing on Sihanouk's personal prestige and with the backing of the Vietnamese resistance forces; while the Lon Nol government, isolated from the peasantry, will increasingly be driven into an alliance with the extreme right-wing forces in Indochina, the Saigon authorities, and the Americans.

The bankruptcy of the elite that managed the coup is reflected clearly by its resort to terror against the Vietnamese minority, reported in ample detail in the press. The reports of Cambodian military operations fortify this impression of weakness and ineptitude. We know what to expect when we read the description of the commanding officer who sent Cambodian civilians, ethnically Vietnamese, who were described as "volunteers," to be mowed down by crossfire, in a well-publicized story.[45]

> The Cambodian commandant, an elegant youngish man, shirtless and wearing a heavy gold necklace, lay like a sultan on an army bed in a clearing among the bamboo trees.... [He] lounged on his bed, coolly talking into the field telephone. Then he asked whether there was news in Phnom Penh of help from the Americans.[46]

It is interesting to observe the Viet Cong strategy in the same incident. According to a detailed report by Allman,[47] the Viet Cong captured the village of Saang, killed eight soldiers, and then "distributed arms and ammunition to the villagers in the name of the 'Sihanouk' army." Three Cambodian spies reported that "the Viet Cong were backed by local Khmer and Cham villagers, who had joined the Communist forces."

More generally, *Le Monde* reports that "the NLF in Cambodia is not trying to capture the capital, but to establish 'free zones' where the 'Red Khmers' can build up their own armies ... [the North Vietnamese] would rather arm the peasantry than establish a puppet regime."[48] Jean-Claude Pomonti reports, after the American invasion, that the aim of the war

> ... is no longer to push [the Viet Cong] out of Cambodia but to prevent their gaining enough local support and power to sooner or later threaten General Lon Nol's government. On one side, an embryonic Khmer Communist Party, backed by active and vital support from the Viet Cong, has temporarily allied with Prince Sihanouk to organize a liberation army. On the other, a large segment of the upper class has called for foreign aid in order to build up its authority throughout the country.[49]

Pomonti's report has a familiar ring to it.

III

THE VIET CONG strategy of establishing freed zones in which the Red Khmers can build up their own armies, based on the peasantry, no doubt explains Stanley Karnow's observation that "the Communists have carefully refrained from moving against towns they could probably capture without firing a shot."[50] As he also notes, they have not even attempted "to prompt uprisings in areas like western Battambang Province, where a local left-wing dissident movement has been implanted for years." They appear fully confident that, without the commitment of major forces,[51] they can create a peasant-based guerrilla force loyal to Sihanouk that will restore him to power, this time in a firm alliance with the Cambodian left and a peasant-based popular movement. Reports from the field support this judgment. No doubt the Americans agree as well. This is surely one major reason for the invasion of Cambodia during the last week of April.

There were, no doubt, other supporting reasons. Nixon implied in his April 30 speech announcing the invasion that the alternatives were escalation or defeat. That seems a not unreasonable assessment. The invasion may indicate that "Vietnamization" is so fragile that even reduction of American forces to a quarter of a million men is regarded as unfeasible in Washington—that it is feared that to secure this immense army of occupation much wider areas of Indochina must be turned into free-fire zones, empty and desolate.

However, it is hardly clear that there are "reasons," in any serious sense, for the new escalation, any more than one can hope to construct a sensible and reliable explanation for the thinking, such as it was, that led to the unprovoked bombardment of North Vietnam in 1965. Shortly after the anti-Sihanouk coup in 1959, the Saigon government diplomatic representative in Phnom Penh (later a minister under Diem), who appears to have been implicated in the coup, told a reporter:

> You must understand that we in Saigon are desperate men. We are a government of desperadoes.[52]

An accurate description, which applies with equal force to those who design American policy. These men have enormous power at their command and can do very much as they wish, with few restrictions. As recent events once more reveal, the Constitution and unorganized public opinion serve as no serious constraint, and international law and our "solemn treaty obligations"—to the United Nations Charter, for example, which remains, if anyone cares, "the supreme law of the land"[53]—have long faded from consciousness. Reference to them has become "moralistic" or "naive," as it no doubt is.

More seriously, the victims have absolutely no way of striking back at the United States, the source of aggression, and it is unlikely that their allies will risk the fury of American nuclear attack by threatening the United States with retaliation. Therefore, the American government can "experiment" with one technique of destruction after another—"population-control methods" and other police-state tactics, assassination teams to destroy the enemy "infrastructure," defoliation, forced evacuation, concentration of the population in camps and urban slums, bombardment on a scale unknown in human history,[54] invasion of other countries, and whatever other ideas happen to occur to them. The disparity of force between the American government and its victims is so enormous that American planners can pretty much do as they wish, without fear of serious retaliation. In such a situation, it is quite pointless to try to explain the actions of these frightened and limited men on rational grounds. They have the force at their command, and can use it with impunity. Further explanations are in a sense superfluous.

President Nixon wishes us to believe that after a right-wing coup in Cambodia, the Viet Cong and North Vietnamese have become a more serious military threat to South Vietnam. This is as convincing as his fantasies about North Vietnam surrounding the South with its awesome military might. He also alluded ominously to the sanctuaries in Svay Rieng Province ("Parrot's Beak"), "as close to Saigon as Baltimore is to Washington," and spoke of the rapid NVA buildup in Cambodia in April. As to the latter, military sources in Saigon report that they know of no Communist buildup in Cambodia.[55] What of the prior situation in the densely populated flat riceland of Svay Rieng Province? The province was visited by T. D. Allman a few months ago.[56] Four things, he wrote, seem evident as a result of his investigation. I quote:

1. The Vietcong use Cambodian territory much less than the Americans in Saigon claim.

2. United States aircraft violate Cambodian air space and bomb and strafe Cambodian territory in violation of the United States guidelines, frequently with no cause at all, and much more often than the United States admits.

3. In fairness to all sides, it is obvious that the Americans, South Vietnamese, Vietcong and North Vietnamese, are all making some degree of effort to keep the war out of Cambodia.

4. The Cambodian effort to hold ground against all comers belies any reports that they have an "agreement" with the communists—or for that matter with the Americans.

He describes this dangerous "sanctuary" as "an absolutely flat country—rice paddies, villages, occasionally a small grove of trees … scanning the open horizon, broken only by Cambodian villages and mango groves, there seemed no place the Vietcong could hide, let alone establish a permanent sanctuary." Allman spent a day in the border district of Chantrea. The evening before, American planes had bombed and strafed a village "2,300 metres inside Cambodia and clearly visible across a rice field," killing two farmers and destroying a hectare of paddy. The district officer stated:

There are no Vietcong in Chantrea district. They never enter our territory more than 500 metres, even at night. Mostly they are passing, There are no camps here. No sanctuaries.

During 1969 [the district officer added], in this one district of Svay Rieng province, nine Cambodians were killed by American bombs or guns; 20 Cambodians were wounded; 100 hectares of rice paddy was damaged; and more than 100 farm animals were killed; no Vietcong were killed by Americans, and no Cambodians were killed by Vietcong.

As they spoke, a policeman entered to report bombing and strafing 200 meters inside Cambodia: "Incidentally, there is no one there [the policeman reported]. No Vietcong, no Cambodian. But one rice field and a grove of mango trees are being destroyed."

From these accounts, it is not difficult to predict the character of the invasion of Svay Rieng Province, now in its initial stages. It will lead to the destruction of villages and the displacement of population, but probably little else. Early reports indicate that this is exactly what is being achieved. James Sterba reports that "few people were to be seen in the Parrot's Beak ... but animals were everywhere," water buffalo and herds of cattle near abandoned houses.[57] The ARVN soldiers as usual were stealing chickens. "Dozens of houses were burned by South Vietnamese troops in the Parrot's Beak. Their charred frames dotted the landscape."

American troops will be unable to match the ARVN accomplishments, since the "Fishhook" area that they are invading is more thinly settled. But at least they are trying:

> ... troops of the United States 11th Armored Cavalry Regiment burned down at least five villages, each with 30 to 40 houses. Officers said they were told to burn the villages because they could be of use to North Vietnamese and Viet Cong troops. The Americans met no resistance. Villagers fled.[58]

Peter Arnett is quoted as reporting that American troops entering Snoul were ordered to "blow the town away."[59]

Returning to our comrades in arms, Gloria Emerson reports from Prasaut, totally abandoned before the South Vietnamese troops entered. French-speaking General Do Cao Tri ("smoking a pipe and holding a swaggerstick") did not discourage his troops from writing anti-Cambodian slogans on the walls of buildings, for example: "Now is the time for the killers to pay in blood," a reference to the Cambodian massacre of eighty-nine Vietnamese in Prasaut on April 10, when the Lon Nol government was desperately attempting to hold its authority by brutally fanning ethnic hostilities:

> If this was a triumphant day for the South Vietnamese, it was a bewildering, frightening one for the Cambodians who hid inside their houses near Route 1 or fled their homes. Close to the Vietnamese border at Godauha, only a few men watched the South Vietnamese troops pass. They stared with tight, sullen faces. Just outside Prasaut,

the doors of the wooden houses that stand on stilts were empty and silent. There were thick locks on the doors of the better houses, and portraits of Prince Sihanouk, the deposed Chief of State of Cambodia, still hung on the walls of one porch.[60]

The Observer (London), May 3, 1970, cites

… reports that seem to carry a grimmer significance. Apart from the Viet Cong casualties, the Americans have announced that scores of "persons" have been detained by the allied forces. They have been led out of the area under guard, blindfolded with their hands tied behind their backs, suspected of being North Vietnamese soldiers. The area is inhabited by many civilians, both Vietnamese and Cambodians, families of rubber plantation workers and woodcutters.

This lends a fearful emphasis to the remarks of American officers on the spot that American observation and gunship helicopters have been given clearance "to fire on anything that moves" in an area extending about three miles north and west of the ground operations.

What of the Cambodian troops? Jack Foisie, reporting from Svay Rieng, describes "the churlishness of Cambodian army troopers who appeared dismayed that the Saigon government army was occupying their town, even though at the moment they were allies"[61]—a fact too subtle, apparently, for the simple peasant mind to comprehend.

And so we proceed to save the people of Cambodia from Vietnamese aggression, just as we have been saving the Laotians and the Vietnamese themselves.

It is difficult to believe that American strategists expect to find the highly mobile Viet Cong and North Vietnamese troops sitting and waiting after several days of obvious preparations for an invasion, any more than they expect to find Pathet Lao and North Vietnamese troops strolling through the market place when they wipe out a Laotian village from the air. The experience of earlier sweeps within South Vietnam has been that there was little contact with Communist forces, and virtually no correlation between contact and prior intelligence. This is a story in itself, still largely untold. For example, a map of Operation Junction City in the 1966–67 Yearbook of the 25th Infantry Division shows extensive "objective" areas that were devastated prior to the sweep, but virtually no "contact"—sniper fire or soldiers, dead or alive—within the objective areas, several of which were heavily settled.[62]

It is a virtual certainty that great victories will be claimed in the Cambodian invasion, and that the military will release reports of arms caches and rice destroyed, military bases demolished, and much killing of "North Vietnamese," i.e., people who find themselves in the way of an American tank or in an area bombed or strafed. So many reputations and careers are at stake that glorious victories are guaranteed.

Furthermore, some of these reports may even be correct. On probabilistic grounds alone, one would expect that American military intelligence can't always be wrong about everything. The headquarters of the Vietnamese resistance forces and the bases that they use for R-and-R must be somewhere, and they may well be found and destroyed during the American-Saigon sweep. Whether the invading troops will withdraw remains to be seen. That the countryside will be devastated and its population removed or destroyed is reasonably certain. Very probably, if these territories are abandoned by the invading forces, some, at least, will be joined to the area on the South Vietnamese side of the border as an extended free-fire zone.

IV

THE AMAZING, unanticipated popular revulsion against the American invasion of Cambodia indicates that it will be very difficult, in the short run at least, for the government to make use of American ground troops to ensure its control of those who remain refractory. The Pentagon will therefore have to learn to rely more effectively on the technology of destruction. Chances are that a ring of fire and devastation will surround the outposts of the "free world" in South Vietnam, protecting the American army of a quarter of a million men and its permanent bases from attack. If eastern Cambodia must be sacrificed to this end, neither General Thieu nor his employers can be expected to shed many tears.

As in Laos and Vietnam, the United States is intervening—whatever its immediate reasons—to support reactionary, even feudalistic elements, and to suppress an emerging peasant-based movement of national independence. As I have already noted, there is some evidence that the CIA had a finger, and perhaps a hand, in the March 18 coup. In any event, when Sihanouk refused to retire to France like a well-behaved Bao Dai, as the Viet Cong strategy of arming the peasants and encouraging the formation of a pro-Sihanouk Cambodian liberation army became evident, American intervention became essential. Tad Szulc reported from Washington that "The Khmer Rouges, the Cambodian equivalent of the South Vietnamese Vietcong guerrillas, may become an important political element in Cambodia, in the opinion of United States Government experts on Indochina."[63] The Khmer liberation forces, if they continue to expand, can be expected to link up with the NLF (now the Provisional Revolutionary Government of South Vietnam), the Pathet Lao, and the North Vietnamese in a general Indochina war against the right-wing elements backed by the United States.

It is widely admitted that the revolutionary groups we confront in Laos and Vietnam—and soon, very likely, in Cambodia—are the only indigenous forces that have any immediate prospect of mobilizing mass support in Indochina. For example, a recently published RAND Corporation study concedes that apart from the Neo Lao Hak Sat (the political party of the revolutionary movement in Laos), there is no "broadly based political organization" in Laos, a country run by an "extremely small elite,"[64] to be more precise, hardly more than a façade for the Americans. Similarly, the Council on Vietnamese Studies of SEADAG (the Southeast Asia Development Advisory Group) in its meetings of May 3, 1969, struggles with the fact that the NLF is the "best organized political group," the "strongest political group in South Vietnam."[65] The same conclusions are reached in scholarly literature. For example, the Vietnam scholar Allen Goodman concludes:

> Indeed, it would appear that the organization of a cadre structure and the nurturing of strong local governments will continue to be the forte of the Viet Cong as South Vietnam approaches peaceful conditions. The ultimate victor in South Vietnam will not be that party which necessarily wins the war, but rather that party which organizes for peace.[66]

Thus the United States is forced to resort to the Phoenix program to destroy the Viet Cong "infrastructure," and to the other means of annihilation and population control with which it experiments throughout Indochina. In Cambodia too it is likely that the United States will have to undertake intensive bombardment of civilian targets, as in Laos, or direct occupation, as in South Vietnam, to maintain in power the right-wing elements to which it is committed.

Nor is this likely to be the end. The *Far Eastern Economic Review* comments editorially that there are grounds for "claiming that the revolutionary situation in the region is excellent." Extending their "gloomy speculations" about Indochina, they proceed:

> ... to envisage a people's war, supplied and supported from Laos, engulfing the northeast and north of Thailand, eventually linking up with dissidents in the south fomented by Ching Peng and the rump of the Malayan Communist Party, and spreading across the country to join hands with the numerous factions in open revolt within Burma. From here the revolutionary line leads via the Nagas and other minorities to the Naxalites and West Bengal .[67]

It is not difficult to imagine other reasons, in each of the countries named, for the expansion of "people's war." The American involvement alone is a contributing factor. The United States can hardly expect to turn Thailand into a military base for its Southeast Asian wars without calling forth a response by "Communists" who refuse to follow the rules.[68] Domestic reasons are also not difficult to conjure up. The editorial comment in the *Far Eastern Economic Review* also notes that "China would probably be much happier with a neutralist Laos and a neutralist Cambodia." This is no doubt true. Sihanouk, for one, continually emphasized this point, as noted earlier. The United States, however, is unlikely to permit this option.

By its insistence on imposing right-wing governments with virtually no popular support on the people of Indochina, the United States may ultimately succeed in bringing about a Pacific or even a global war. Though this may not appear likely at the moment, it is easy to imagine a sequence of events that would lead to this consequence. In any event, the future for the people of Southeast Asia is dim. The United States is using its incomparable technological resources and its internationally based military forces to occupy and destroy vast territories, to uproot and demoralize the population, to disrupt social life in the areas it cannot physically control. So long as the American people tolerate these atrocities, the people of Southeast Asia can look forward only to continued misery.

One can, of course, trace the policy of expansion into Asia far back in American history. The postwar American effort to dominate Southeast Asia has an element of "rationality," according to the perceived interests of many of those who manage American society—unfortunately for the people of Indochina and the United States, who will pay the price. It is not unlikely that the price will be that described by Professor Fairbank, in the remarks quoted at the beginning of Chapter 1: a war against the people of Asia and a growing totalitarian menace in the United States.

None the less, the grim game is far from ended. So long as the war continues, it may be impossible to reduce inflation and unemployment to "tolerable" limits without imposing the kinds of controls that are unacceptable to the business community. If so, American workers may refuse to continue to sacrifice their jobs and livelihood in the cause of American domination of Southeast Asia. Perhaps much wider circles can be drawn into the movement against the war. There is no doubt that many, many people are confused and troubled. With serious work, they might be brought to join those great numbers who actively oppose the war. There is resistance in the military and continuing resistance to military conscription—according to a recent report, "The Oakland induction center, which processes draftees for all of Northern California and a portion of Nevada, says more than half of the young men ordered to report fail to show up—and 11 percent of those who do show up refuse to serve."[69]

Many more people are refusing to support criminal acts by payment of war taxes. As I write, there is an unprecedented student strike. Acts of sabotage directed against the military are on the increase. An underground is developing, as such "criminals" as Daniel Berrigan refuse to accept the legitimacy of the authority that has sentenced them to prison for trying to impede the war machine. Congress is seething, and state legislatures are registering opposition in surprisingly strong ways. In short, those who still hope to subdue and hold their Southeast Asian colonies have plenty of trouble in store for them, here as well as there.

To pursue the war, the government will have to subdue dissent and protest, which is sure to take more militant forms as the war expands and its character becomes continually more clear. It may have to make a choice between abandoning this war, with long-term and unforeseeable consequences for American imperial policy, and jettisoning what remains of the structure of American democracy. The choice might arise fairly soon. Consider, for example, the legislation introduced by Senators Hatfield, McGovern, and others to cut off funds for continuation of the war. This was a courageous move on their part. It establishes a sharp criterion by which it can be determined whether any congressman is for war or for peace in Indochina. Suppose that it becomes law. Then the choice will be posed quite clearly. I would hesitate to predict the outcome.

Postscript

Just over a month has passed since the preceding article on Cambodia was submitted for publication, in the first week of May. In the interim, there have been several interesting developments. Our man in Saigon, Vice-President Ky, has officially rejected the "silly argument of silly people" that "if some day the Americans leave Cambodia then the South Vietnamese will have to follow them out of Cambodia too."[70] On the same day that the Marshall spoke so frankly in Saigon, a spokesman for the Lon Nol government, Major Am Rong, declared that "we will never be dominated by the Vietnamese—that is why the population is rising against them." He noted explicitly that he referred to all Vietnamese.[71] There are other, confirmatory indications. Henry Kamm reports "deep uneasiness among the sectors of the population that most enthusiastically supported the Government of … Lon Nol and … Sirik Matak," a result of the occupation by ARVN troops of a major part of Cambodia east of the Mekong, and the presence of South Vietnamese troops in Phnom Penh:

> In the university and high schools, reports of killings, rapes and plundering by South Vietnamese troops circulate and find an eager hearing. Faculty members reported today that a delegation of student leaders has called on General Sirik Matak to express concern over the takeover of much of Cambodia by South Vietnamese and over the conduct of these troops.[72]

In Phnom Penh,

> Posters appeared on the glass walls of the government department store in the capital asking South Vietnamese troops to withdraw from Cambodian soil. The posters charged that the troops from Saigon had ill-treated Cambodian villagers, violated Cambodian women, and destroyed Cambodian property. These charges had been known to correspondents ever since South Vietnamese units moved into Cambodia, but no one quite expected that the Phnom Penh government would come out with open accusations so soon.[73]

The same correspondent reports that "territorial occupation of parts of Cambodia is Saigon's aim in the deal it has apparently struck with America to make Cambodia safe for democracy."

General Do Cao Tri, the top ARVN commander in Cambodia, explained the difficulty of determining whether the Cambodians in the villages being occupied "are for Sihanouk, Lon Nol or the Vietcong."[74] He also complained of the unwillingness of the Cambodian army to fight. He announced that "if the Cambodians should continue to mistreat our compatriots [referring to the massacres perpetrated by the Cambodian army], then our army will have an appropriate reaction," details unspecified.[75] Marshall Ky also explained: "We will continue to maintain our military presence in Cambodia, not only to destroy the Communists but also to provide protection for the lives and property of 600,000 resident Vietnamese in Cambodia."[76] The Vietnamese minister in charge of the problem of ethnic Vietnamese in Cambodia suggested that they be resettled in the Cambodian border provinces of Svay Rieng, Takeo and Kampot, where "they would live in the security of the South Vietnamese units operating there and could earn their living in large part by working for and trading with those units."[77] Obviously, then, it is anticipated that ARVN troops will remain in these regions in substantial force.

Speaking in the Cambodian town of Neak Luong, Marshall Ky announced that eleven airfields are being constructed in Cambodia by the South Vietnamese army to facilitate air operations.[78] President Thieu has also chimed in, predicting "that his forces would be engaged in a long war in Cambodia"—"we must help Cambodia as we must help ourselves," he added, and make sure that neither Sihanouk nor "another Communist chief" returns to power.[79] Terence Smith reports from Saigon that President Thieu expects ARVN troops to "operate in Cambodia for an indefinite period after United States units are withdrawn," with "continued American logistical and combat support to sustain those operations."[80] President Thieu seems to share some of the uneasiness of the Cambodians over the behavior of Marshall Ky and General Tri in Cambodia. Henry Kamm reports from Saigon that Marshall Ky "was reported to be seeking powers that would make him something akin to a viceroy of eastern Cambodia," and there is concern as well over "the imperious conduct" of General Tri, which may suggest possible political ambitions.[81]

Saigon's intention "to maintain its troops indefinitely on Cambodian territory" is reported from Washington to be "apparently enjoying full

United States blessing."[82] Szulc also notes that the administration admits "the possibility that the United States would provide tactical air support to the South Vietnamese troops in Cambodia after the Americans had left." More interestingly, he observes that now administration officials speak freely "of the changing mission of the Saigon troops—from the initial attack on the sanctuaries to the support of the Lon Nol Government." He explains the basic reason in another report from Washington:

> … the Lon Nol regime will need assistance to deal with guerrilla and subversive activities. Officials said that in some ways the situation developing in Cambodia was beginning to resemble South Vietnam in 1960, when the Vietcong began their rebellion against the Saigon regime.[83]

It is reassuring that senior American officials are now beginning to comprehend (or at least admit) what has been fairly obvious to readers of the world press since the end of March.

In fact, it is likely that one of the original motives for the American-ARVN invasion was to support the Lon Nol government against the mounting threat of "guerrilla and subversive activities." Congressman Hamilton Fish summarized a private briefing by Under-Secretary of State Richardson for selected members of Congress in a letter to constituents.[84] The congressmen were told:

> Following the fall of Sihanouk, the new anti-Communist government cut all supply lines [of the North Vietnamese Army and Viet Cong] except the Ho Chi Minh trail.[85] To re-secure their severed supply routes, VC and NVA began moving out of the enclaves, thereby threatening the overthrow of the Cambodian government…. [It is] against this background that the American-South Vietnamese strikes into Cambodia were ordered.

A fuller briefing would have explained that the American-ARVN military strikes across the border, beginning directly after the Lon Nol coup, were also a factor in impelling the Communist troops to move out of the enclaves and threaten the overthrow of the coup regime.

Nixon's original claim was that the American-ARVN invasion was motivated by increased North Vietnamese military activity which threatened the American military position in Vietnam. As noted earlier, this is plainly absurd; an anti-Communist coup in Phnom Penh could hardly increase the North Vietnamese threat to American troops in South Vietnam, and, as noted above, American military sources in Saigon denied knowledge of any such increased threat. Further information has since appeared. A staff report of the Senate Foreign Relations Committee states that United States military authorities in Saigon and Washington do not support Nixon's claim; the commonly expressed intelligence estimate was that the Communist forces had moved into a defensive position and were dispersing westward in Cambodia away from the South Vietnamese border.[86] The staff was informed that the American invasion was directed against the enemy sanctuaries and "against the main COSVN [Central Office, South Vietnam] control headquarters for South Vietnam," though nine days after the invasion, "COSVN had disappeared from military briefings." (See page 125.)

Tad Szulc reports from Washington[87] that "The United States is known to favor a long-range pacification program in Cambodia" under South Vietnamese and Thai supervision. As in Vietnam, B-52 raids will continue "on enemy supply lines," a phrase which will no doubt signify in Cambodia what it has come to mean in Vietnam. The reason for this long-range pacification program is that Prince Sihanouk "still enjoys widespread popularity in the Cambodian countryside and that this popularity provides fertile ground for the insurgency," which is proceeding apace, as revolutionary cells are being established in villages. A further problem is the Cambodian economy. As Szulc discreetly puts it, the economy was "badly hurt by the destruction of rubber plantations during Allied thrusts into Cambodia"—"by Allied thrusts," to be more exact. Cambodia's largest rubber plantation, the Chup plantation, was attacked by 10,000 ARVN troops and armored vehicles on May 23. On the first day of the assault, according to an AP report,[88] "A dozen men identified as members of the Khmer Rouge, a Cambodian Communist guerrilla force, were reported killed on the plantation's southern edge and 15 were reported captured." Twenty-five more of "the enemy," nationality unidentified, were reported slain. Henry Kamm adds from Phnom Penh that according to witnesses, South Vietnamese Air Force planes bombed and strafed the rubber-processing plant, "leaving it aflame and causing at least 15 deaths among the

550 workers" and 80 wounded. The witnesses report that "no Vietcong or North Vietnamese forces had been in the plant at the time of the attack or had ever been there." Less than an hour later, a second raid dropped napalm on the plant area, wounding a number of persons who were trying to aid those hurt in the first attack. Shortly after, "planes were reported to have attacked the villages scattered around the southern half of the vast plantation, as well as the central market and the principal school."

Another headline in the same issue of the *Times* reads: "Cambodian Drive Called Success by U.S. Commanders." It reports, for example, the shelling of "North Vietnamese troops" who were dug in around a "small bamboo hut village"; the shelling and aerial attacks "bombed into ruins every structure including the Buddhist pagoda.... The fate of the 35 Cambodian inhabitants was not known." The same report notes that B-52 strikes have been called in "even in areas known to contain Cambodian villages." South Vietnamese troops "reported finding 33 dead civilians, apparently killed by United States bombs" in these attacks.[89] The 43,000 South Vietnamese troops have "fought well, in the judgment of United States commanders." American pilots have also performed with authority, as the report makes clear.

An American biologist, Arthur Westing, visited the Chup rubber plantation last December with the study group investigating American defoliation in Cambodia (see note 8). On reading the reports describing "in harrowing detail the rape of the rubber plantations in Kompong Cham province and the pillage by RVN forces (equipped with U.S. arms, supplied with U.S. ammunition, and protected by U.S. air cover) of the rubber processing factories," he wrote a letter to *The New York Times* (dated May 25, not accepted for publication) in which he observed:

> Rubber has been Cambodia's most important source of international solvency. In December I examined in some detail the plantations now being laid waste. The endless acres of carefully tended plantings represented the most productive rubber to be found anywhere in the world; they were a horticultural joy to behold. The processing plant at Chap, just plundered and destroyed (with the loss of numerous innocent Cambodian lives), was a showplace of automation and gleaming stainless steel—the pride of that poor country.

And so the American forces and their allies, with their newfound aggressiveness, march on to even more glorious victories.

A correspondent for the *Far Eastern Economic Review*[90] suggests that one purpose of the American-ARVN invasion was "to boost the morale of South Vietnam's army." These troops, he goes on to point out, "have been provided with what amounts to a paper victory (because they have never actually encountered the communists in any strength in Cambodia)." Destroying Cambodian villages is much easier than fighting the Viet Cong at home. Joseph Kraft comments:

> As Gen. Do Cao Tri, the South Vietnamese Patton, put it: "There are no booby traps here. And no political infrastructure."[91]

For the time being, at least. And there are other rewards as well, Henry Kamm reports: "Witnesses in Chup said that troops of the South Vietnamese task force had driven off all usable vehicles, loading some with air conditioners, refrigerators and other appliances taken from the houses of the French managers."[92] AFP reports that the Cambodian mercenary troops are also performing nobly.[93] Thus "two battalions of a contingent that formerly served with the United States Special Forces in South Vietnam entered the town" of Tonle Bet, meeting little resistance from the "North Vietnamese" who "appeared to have left a few hours earlier." The town

> had been pounded by Cambodian artillery and mortars for a week. The main street is piled five feet high with rubble. Walls and roofs have collapsed. Not a pane of glass was left unbroken. No building in the center of town escaped the shelling. There are gaping holes everywhere, and thousands of spent cartridge cases and jagged pieces of shrapnel lie in the still-smoking rubble.

Several days before, Gloria Emerson visited the "ruined town" of Snoul in the Fishhook area, destroyed by American fire, tanks, and artillery.[94] No one reported having seen North Vietnamese "in the town or on the rubber plantation, also called Snoul, which is about 6 by 10 miles in size." She speculates that the reason for the denials is that the people are afraid, though it is hard to see what they have to gain by denying the presence of North Vietnamese troops after the town has been destroyed by the Americans. "Are they mad?" one of the rubber workers asked, referring to the attack: "Why destroy the whole town when there was no resistance and no shots from the ground? Just to kill Chinese merchants?" This witness, who had left before the fighting started, "did not believe, as civilian American witnesses have reported, that the North Vietnamese opened fire on American tank forces." The report continues:

> No one seems to know how many deaths were caused by the fighting and by the United States air strike. There are freshly dug graves, but children were buried together.

The reporter adds: "United States military commanders in Cambodia believe that too much attention has been paid to the damage to Snoul." Let us drop the subject, therefore, and turn to other places.

Peter Arnett reports[95] that the American troops are facing a "political problem." American foot soldiers are forced to operate in the midst of the civilian population in Cambodia. "The Americans, who in Vietnam have difficulties in separating 'friend' and 'enemy' among the civilian population, must now try to distinguish 'good' from 'bad' Cambodians."

> So, the Vietnamese story is being renewed. The tactic of scorched earth leads the Americans to set fire to houses because they may be used by the communists. Cattle are killed for the same reason. Spirals of smoke rose on Sunday above the area. Groups of houses were transformed to heaps of reddening embers.

Arnett quotes an American commander who says, "My orders are to burn everything," and reports that air raids have partially destroyed the town of Memot, villages have been burned, and thousands of civilians have fled. An observer comments:

> Such actions may drive the Vietnamese population of the rubber plantations into the ranks of the Viet Cong, and the Cambodian population into the arms of the "Khmer Rouges," if we are not careful.

An American briefing officer explained the "rules of engagement" to a group of helicopter pilots:

> There are beaucoup villages down there. Don't shoot at the villages unless you take fire from them. A dink in the open is fair game, but we don't want to kill innocent civilians. Any questions?[96]

Only one. How do you distinguish a dink in the open from an innocent civilian? And what difference does it make anyway, when the other air and ground units are leaving a trail of devastated villages as they march from success to success?

So far, the only failure has been the inability to discover any of the main targets. The original goal of the American invasion, as President Nixon grandly announced at the outset, was to destroy the legendary COSVN, the Communist Pentagon, to which he pointed on the map as he spoke. References to COSVN have now disappeared from briefings. "Despite periodic reports to the contrary, knowledgeable military sources say that no part of COSVN has been captured."[97] A writer for the *Far Eastern Economic Review* defines COSVN as "a hypothetical structure in the minds of frustrated American military planners in Saigon."[98] An NLF officer captured in Cholon, South Vietnam, in late May, who believes that the loss of arms and matériel may set the Communist forces back by three months (American and South Vietnamese military sources believe it may be as long as six months), expressed amazement that the Americans expected to capture the Viet Cong headquarters, pointing out "that after a full month of operations the Americans and South Vietnamese had not even been able to locate a single one of the many prisoner-of-war camps along both sides of the border."[99] Jean-Claude Pomonti observes that the series of attacks in Cambodia by ARVN and ethnic Cambodian Special Forces units from March 20 gave the Viet Cong plenty of warning, ample time to fall back deeper into Cambodia. Other reports indicate that the Viet Cong were forewarned by their agents in the ARVN General Staff.[100] Pomonti does not believe that the ARVN will be able to keep its forces outside of the Parrot's Beak and Fishhook areas because of growing Viet Cong strength. Even in the Parrot's Beak, "It's hard to say who's the hunter," General Tri remarked. Moving back into evacuated areas of Cambodia may not be too easy: "Next time around there will be mantraps and mines. It's bad for the troops' morale," a South Vietnamese officer explained as he departed from Chup. General Tri complained:

> The Cambodians refuse to take over. As soon as we pull out of an area the Vietcong will move right back in after us. The Cambodian admin-

istration and the army have fallen apart. Outside of Phnom Penh they are virtually non-existent.

Furthermore, he added, the ethnic Cambodians from Vietnam, trained by the Americans and brought into Cambodia to serve as the nucleus of a new Cambodian army, "are gradually turning into bandits." Morale has collapsed, and it appears that they will filter back to South Vietnam.

Pomonti observes that one goal of the American intervention was to strengthen the Lon Nol government, "which was starting to flounder and by the end of April controlled only the capital and a few other towns." But this goal has not been achieved. "The only relatively secure areas are those occupied by the South Vietnamese Army." In fact, he comments:

> One of the ironies of the Cambodia operation is that documents captured by American troops reveal that Prince Sihanouk's United Liberation Front is more solidly organized than was originally suspected. The goal is to build a solid organization rooted among the peasants and based on close cooperation between the Cambodian and the Vietnamese Communists. The Red Khmers have been assigned a leading role in the movement, which is already at work in strategically important provinces such as Battambang.

If the ARVN attempts to re-invade Cambodia, the South Vietnamese Patton will find both booby traps and a political infrastructure, not merely lightly defended villages to be razed.

American reports affirm that "North Vietnamese troops are reportedly conducting an intensive recruiting and proselytizing campaign among the rural population of Cambodia in what official sources here see as an attempt to create a broadly based Communist guerrilla organization similar to the Vietcong in South Vietnam."[101] This is a "major shift from the North Vietnamese policy during the last five years of remaining relatively isolated in their border sanctuaries and away from rural Cambodians." Prospects for the new policy are good, the report continues:

> Traditional rural support for the former Cambodian Chief of State is still believed to be strong, and some sources and independent observers believe that a local guerrilla and political apparatus can be formed far more quickly in Cambodia than it took in South Vietnam.

Large parts of Cambodia are under Communist control, which has greatly expanded since the American-ARVN invasion. Prisoners and defectors report that North Vietnamese units have been broken into teams to recruit Cambodian villagers, "forming Communist governing groups and training guerrillas." The native Red Khmers form the nucleus of the organization. The sources on which this report is based released this analysis with the apparent intention "to justify the Allied thrusts into Cambodia." The idea is to show that the invasion followed the "North Vietnamese" steps to recruit a pro-Sihanouk army and to organize a popular-based guerrilla movement. The "sources," however, failed to note that American-ARVN incursions followed immediately upon the Lon Nol coup of March 18, and thus made it impossible for the Viet Cong and NVA forces to remain in the isolated border regions that they had been using for refuge ever since the ground sweeps and aerial attacks of 1966–1967 made the areas of Vietnam where they had been based entirely unlivable. These military actions initiated by the United States also eliminated any possibility that the Lon Nol government might reach an accommodation that would have permitted it to continue Sihanouk's neutralist policies, as some specialists believe it intended.[102]

Other reports from Washington confirm this assessment. Tad Szulc cites intelligence estimates in Washington which "depict the Chinese-backed Sihanouk government in exile as coordinating its operations with the North Vietnamese command in Cambodia…. The Khmer Rouge guerrillas are part of what officials in Washington see as a growing body of support for the Sihanouk regime in outlying areas of Cambodia."[103]

> Fragmentary information reaching here suggests that Sihanouk supporters are busily building a political structure in northeast Cambodia and taking over villages. Experts here have noted that Prince Sihanouk has appealed for support to traditional groups in Cambodia, including "our beloved Buddhist monks." … In the words of an American specialist, a "scenario is being written for a civil war."

French sources, in general far better informed, tend to agree. An analyst in *Le Monde diplomatique* writes:

> Henceforth the situation is clear. On one side, the "reactionaries": the government of General Lon Nol; on the other, the "revolutionaries":

the Cambodian Government and National Union Front of Kampuchea of Peking. The former hold the cities, the latter hold the countryside. The former survive only thanks to the military aid of the imperialists, the latter enjoy all popular support. This is a simple schema, clear-cut, irrefutable: one knows who are the friends and who are the enemies.[104]

Communist efforts to build a popular guerrilla force rely on more than Sihanouk's unquestioned popularity among the peasantry. In some areas Red Khmer forces already existed in some strength, even during Sihanouk's rule. In 1967 a peasant rebellion in Battambang was suppressed by Lon Nol's army, and peasant forces took to the jungle, allegedly under the leadership of the popular left-wing delegates from that region.[105] Some scholars trace the rebellion to an attempt by Lon Nol's army to expel peasants from their land in favor of military leaders and their civilian collaborators.[106] It is interesting that documents of the insurgents from that time speak of the "men of the party of treason, with Lon Nol at their head, [who] have compromised with American imperialism [and its] valets": the Thai and South Vietnamese governments and the American-trained and American-led Khmer Serei—a perceptive prediction, in December 1967.[107] Insurgency has continued in that area since, as American sources also report. Melvin Gurtov, a RAND Corporation scholar, notes that "the Khmer Viet Minh [Red Khmers] have been active in central and western Cambodia no less than in the provinces bordering Vietnam."[108] Similarly, in the northeastern mountain areas of Ratanakiri Province insurgency has been reported in strength for the past several years. As Jacques Decornoy notes,[109] Communist forces there were so strong that an American effort to penetrate the area during the recent invasion (after intensive B-52 raids, in waves of up to 40 aircraft, dropping 1,000 tons of bombs) was quickly turned back, with admitted losses almost equal to the "estimated" enemy losses. It is expected that these guerrilla units can be rapidly expanded now that Sihanouk, with his popular prestige, has lent his support, and as the Lon Nol government is forced by events toward authoritarianism and repression.

The political program of the guerrillas is based on "democratization"; reforms in favor of the peasantry concerning such matters as the right to private plots and "an equitable solution of unjust debts"; educational reforms, with an emphasis on Khmer language and culture; and so on, along the lines that have proved so successful in Vietnam and Laos.[110] Military tactics also seem to be based on a sophisticated effort to achieve political goals, in part by the "judo" techniques of the other Indochinese revolutions. T. D. Allman gives a striking example.[111] He points out that when the guerrillas took Ang Tassom in the south, "as at every other Vietcong halt in Cambodia, the communist troops seemed more interested in giving political lectures than taking anything from the inhabitants." They left rice untouched and, one villager reported, even refused a chicken that was offered to them.

> Thus the contrast was between small and well-disciplined bands of Vietnamese soldiers humiliating the Phnom Penh government at virtually no cost in civilian lives and property, and much larger Cambodian forces milling around the country-side, killing Vietnamese civilians deliberately—and many Cambodians by indiscriminate firepower—while their packs bulged with stolen food. The lack of Cambodian military skill, even simple courage or respect for civilian lives and property, seemed more to undercut than support Cambodian claims that the real reason for the uninspiring performance on the battlefield was a lack of foreign military aid.

Communist tactics were particularly likely to be effective in towns such as Ang Tassom, where 84 peasants were killed on March 29 by government forces in suppressing a spontaneous pro-Sihanouk demonstration.[112]

Cambodian military forces have repeatedly behaved in such a way as to antagonize the peasantry, exactly as occurred in South Vietnam. Lightly defended towns have been blasted by artillery barrages and air attacks, and soldiers have often been seen looting after recapture of the towns. Furthermore, popular demonstrations have been harshly repressed, not merely the pro-Sihanouk outbreaks that followed the coup, when 200 Cambodians were killed by Cambodian army units, according to T. D. Allman.[113] Thus after government MIGs bombed several villages in Svay Rieng Province in an effort to stop the Viet Cong, a group of outraged people marched toward the provincial capital of Svay Rieng…. The Vietcong attacks were not stopped but the column of demonstrators was. Cambodian army units fired on it with 75 millimetre recoilless rifles; the crowd of civilians fled, carrying their dead, into nearby ricefields which until last week were peaceful, and which now are fields of battle.[114]

The vicious pogroms launched by the Lon Nol government against Vietnamese in an apparent effort to stir up chauvinist sentiments among the peasants failed in that purpose. "In general the people took no part in the misdeeds committed by the army and the police. The orders came from above."[115]

Most observers think that the Communists' chances of success in their effort to create a popular resistance movement are high. The Lon Nol government has largely lost control of the country, and is buttressed only by foreign force. Allman comments:

> Certainly, as the military defeats continue and as the economy declines and as more of Cambodia is ravaged by war, the communists—who, thanks to Sihanouk's still significant popularity in the country, have been able to win support among the population—will gain more adherents, and government popularity will decline correspondingly.
>
> "They will wait until the fruit is ripe, and then let it fall by itself," said one disillusioned Cambodian last week.[116]

T. J. S. George, who replaced Allman as *Far Eastern Economic Review* correspondent in Cambodia,[117] essentially agrees:

> [The Communist forces] may be trusted to go on quietly building up their strength in the countryside. It is Vietnam all over again—heavy military support from outside keeping the capital relatively safe for the government and the Vietcong biding their time around it.[118]

Jean-François Kahn reports that "thousands of peasants have joined the armed resistance during May."[119] The American intervention, he comments, has temporarily harmed the revolutionary forces, but has not really weakened them. On the contrary, "it has accelerated the engagement in the battle of a new force which was neglected by the Saigon General Staff: the indigenous Khmer guerrillas." It is ironic that the American intervention, which was presumably undertaken, in part at least, in an effort to prop up the Lon Nol regime, may have administered the *coup de grâce* to the Lon Nol government. T. J. S. George[120] quotes "a perceptive diplomat," who believes that "before the American intervention the present Cambodian government had a sporting chance to consolidate its position," but that the surrender of neutrality and the war losses have changed the perspective. Jacques Decornoy reports that even in the urban centers the Lon Nol regime has not succeeded "in organizing truly popular meetings in its favor."[121] Jean-Claude Pomonti, who seems better acquainted with Cambodian society than any other current commentator, reports that even among the segments of the Khmer elite that were initially quite favorable to the Lon Nol regime, support seems to be fading:

> Among the political clans who were opposed to Prince Sihanouk, only those belonging to the extreme right-wing have, for the moment, been willing to rally to the new government. The others are hesitating or, like the "Red Khmers," are already fighting it openly…. [Many] began gradually to make up their minds, and finally came out for the United Front [of Sihanouk].[122]

Only a few days before the American-ARVN invasion, Ton That Thien wrote in the *Far Eastern Economic Review* that "Cambodia's plight will be worse if the South Vietnamese Government decides to come to the rescue of Lon Nol and Sirit Matak. Only Saigon's realisation that it would embarrass rather than help Lon Nol has so far kept its soldiers from crossing into Cambodia."[123] A reasonable observation, although the deterioration of the position of the Lon Nol government, after the American-ARVN attacks on Viet Cong "sanctuaries" in late March and April and the Viet Cong-NVA reaction—taking over the countryside and initiating a popular armed revolt—might in any event have made this impossible.

As the situation continued to deteriorate, the United States was forced to call on its Thai allies. For twenty years, since the Thai postwar experiment in parliamentary democracy was brought to an end by a military coup immediately backed by the United States,[124] the Thai dictatorship has provided the main support for American military efforts in Indochina. At first, the United States hoped to be able to uphold the coup regime in Cambodia with the Khmer Serei and Khmer Khrom, ethnic Cambodians trained by the Special Forces in Vietnam and directed by the CIA,[125] and through the use of ARVN troops in eastern Cambodia. By the beginning of June, Thai "volunteers" were also reported on their way.[126] Thai planes are also to be sent to Cambodia, it is reported.[127] A report from Bangkok adds an interesting twist to this request for assistance from the Thai, traditionally the enemy of Cambodia:

> According to well-informed sources, Cambodia's Premier, Lieut. Gen. Lon Nol, has asked the Thais for regular troops to defend Phnom Penh because he suspects that Cambodian commanders now guarding the capital may be sympathetic to Prince Norodom Sihanouk....[128]

Prince Sihanouk once wrote, apropos of the tenuous neutrality of Cambodia in the midst of hostile neighbors:

> China is in fact synonymous with the survival of Cambodia ... in independence, peace, and with its territorial integrity. If we keep distant from China, we will be devoured by the vultures who eternally prey upon Khmer territory.[129]

This was a constant theme of the Prince. Years earlier, he remarked:

> Westerners are always astonished that we Cambodians are not disturbed by our future in which China will play such a powerful role. But one should try to put himself in our place: in this jungle which is the real world, should we, simple deer, interest ourselves in a dinosaur like China when we are more directly menaced, and have been for centuries, by the wolf and the tiger, who are Vietnam and Thailand?[130]

The wolf and the tiger, the vultures who seek to devour Khmer territory, have now been given carte blanche—in fact, dispatched directly—by the United States. And some of its other clients may also be called upon for help. Henry Kamm reports:

> Sources whose thinking reflects that of President Nguyen Van Thieu expressed a hope that current exchanges of visits between officials of Cambodia and those of Nationalist China and South Korea will result in the speedy dispatch to Cambodia of troops from those countries. They advocate this even in the awareness that such action might provoke counteraction from Communist China and North Korea.[131]

Of course, Chinese Nationalist troops have long been used by the United States in Laos, and formerly (perhaps still today) in Thailand and Burma, while the South Koreans have been compiling a brilliant record for themselves in South Vietnam.[132] It is, unfortunately, no exaggeration to say that the United States is creating a clique of gangster states on the fringes of Asia, hoping to enlist them in its anti-Communist jihad.

Present prospects are for a "Balkanization" of Cambodia, with a central area held by the Lon Nol government or its successor, a region held by the ARVN forces that will "consider Phnom Penh its military protectorate," a region controlled by Thailand, a northeast region linked to Communist-held areas of Laos and Vietnam,[133] and the unpredictable countryside, where the Red Khmer guerrillas, backed by the Viet Cong, will be busy organizing the peasants. With justice, a resident of "the gloomy majority" of Phnom Penh told a reporter:

> I'm not hopeful about the future of Cambodia as an independent state. I can't see South Vietnam removing their military presence until the end of their war. Now, when is the end of their war going to be?[134]

The South Vietnamese now reportedly intend to maintain a bridgehead at Neak Luong on the Mekong with three battalions of marines stationed permanently and an airfield nearby, and also a permanent intervention corridor on the Cambodian side of the frontier that may penetrate almost twenty miles into the interior.[135] And the intentions of the Saigon authorities are only a part of the story, as has already been noted.

I have discussed so far only the immediate situation in Cambodia, but of course the effects of the American invasion are far broader. The North Vietnamese and the Pathet Lao immediately responded by extending their control of southern Laos, capturing several towns that had long been left under the control of the Royal Lao Government and moving onto the Boloven Plateau.[136] This may prompt a further American response, perhaps a further escalation of the war in southern Laos, even an attempt to cut the Ho Chi Minh Trail west of Quang Tri. The pro-government Senator Nguyen Gai Hien, one of the leaders of the Catholic refugees from the North, said in Saigon:

> One can now perceive the early signs of an American-South Vietnamese offensive in the region of southern Laos and the installa-

tion of a rightist government in Vientiane. A military plan is now being put into action. In the very near future, American-South Vietnamese forces will attack the region of southern Laos and the menaced sector of the Thai frontier. This military plan was conceived as encompassing all of Indochina and requiring all the countries concerned to find a final and global solution.[137]

This "final and global solution" will, of course, also involve Thailand, where one may expect guerrilla warfare to intensify. Sooner or later, it may involve China as well. Chan Seng, a minister in the Sihanouk government, stated in an interview in Paris:

> The direct intervention of our Chinese friends as volunteers in Cambodia is not excluded if the United States and its valets cross a certain threshold in their aggression by putting our resistance movement in grave difficulties. China cannot accept its defeat.[138]

This is surely more than bravado. China has identified itself closely, though so far only in an undertone, with the newly combined Viet-Khmer-Lao resistance forces; and having made this commitment, is unlikely to watch silently if American escalation puts their future in danger. American observers also finally seem to comprehend this simple fact. United States specialists now realize that:

> What faces the United States now in Southeast Asia ... is protracted war with virtually no possibility of arriving at a settlement in Vietnam unless there is a settlement covering Laos and Cambodia at the same time [and perhaps Thailand as well].... Prior to the United States entry into Cambodia ... it was possible to envisage a settlement embracing only North Vietnam and South Vietnam, with Cambodia and Laos left to one side, presumably continuing in their theoretically neutral status. Now ... there is no question of such an approach.[139]

Many government officials now admit that "the outlines of a far-ranging civil war are swiftly emerging in Cambodia" and that the situation there is "fluid" and "dangerous."[140] Many officials expect this civil war to "erupt in a major way" at the end of the rainy season in the autumn of 1970,[141] and it will be a great surprise if it does not involve all the countries of Indochina, and perhaps Thailand as well. How the Soviet Union will react to this quite serious blow to its prestige and influence—as the Indochinese revolutionary movement, now unified, seems for the moment to be settling into the lap of China—remains to be seen. Russia, of course, has the capacity to respond in many parts of the world.

It is interesting that even America's Asian allies are showing some reluctance to participate in the latest, and to date most perverse, of the American ventures in Indochina. At the Jakarta conference in mid-May, attended only by pro-Western governments including some, like Japan, that are directly involved in the American war in Indochina, the participants refused to allow the Foreign Minister of the Lon Nol government to attend as a regular delegate or to put forth formal requests for aid.[142] Saville Davis summarizes this "remarkable event,"[143] noting that the participants rejected "the plea for aid to Cambodia" and "the American concept of a defensive alliance," and "refused even to send an inspection team to Cambodia." Declining to accept the American government position on Asian security, these powers "distributed their blame impartially among the big powers" and tried to lay the basis for a much broader, less military grouping. Considering the composition of the conference, this was indeed a "remarkable event," a further testimony to the triumph of American diplomacy and arms in Cambodia.

The Cambodian events are arousing some recriminations within the highest circles of the government. According to Tad Szulc,[144] high officials are complaining, "with some bitterness," that the White House disregarded intelligence estimates and analyses by the State Department and the CIA, and "completely misjudged the communist political and military response." Unless one assumes a White House plot to strengthen China at the expense of the Soviet Union, one must also assume that the White House revealed an abysmal misunderstanding of international affairs in its latest maneuvers.[145]

President Nixon, in Cambodia, has succeeded in demonstrating to the world that the United States is exactly what he claimed it is not: a helpless (though hardly pitiful) giant, flailing about wildly in an effort to extricate itself from the morass it has created, thundering new threats—who knows whether they are empty? If the United States does not gradually escalate to war with China, perhaps through an undisciplined, provocative act of the military or perhaps in a desperate move by the civilian authorities, then the architects of this new disaster in Cambodia will not pay the costs of their blundering aggressiveness. Perhaps someday they will acknowledge their "honest errors" in their memoirs, speaking of the burdens of world leadership and the tragic irony of history. Their victims, the peasants of Indochina, will write no memoirs and will be forgotten, They will join the countless millions of earlier victims of tyrants and oppressors.

Notes

1   I will not discuss the content of this speech, which was an insult to the intelligence and an expression of contempt for Congress and the American people.

2   Sidney Schanberg, *New York Times*, May 7, 1970.

3   Much of this information is presented in the report of the Symington subcommittee: Hearings before the Subcommittee on United States Security Agreements and Commitments Abroad of the Committee on Foreign Relations, United States Senate, 91st Congress, 1st Session, October 20–28, 1969. Other details come from interviews with refugees and on-the-scene reports by journalists and other visitors to the bombed areas.

4   Michael Leifer, "Rebellion or Subversion in Cambodia," *Current History*, February 1969.

5   *Is Cambodia Next?* (Washington, D.C., Russell Press, 1967). An ABC television crew had also been unable to substantiate the American charges. Both groups were free to travel anywhere in Cambodia and checked locations specifically alleged to be base camps and transit routes. See also footnote 9. The Australian journalist Maslyn Williams investigated specific allegations of the American military on a recent trip and found them to be without substance, though he did hear reports of a Viet Cong camp "in an area that has only a nomadic local population" (*The Land in Between* [New York, William Morrow & Co., 1970], p. 221). He reports a Cambodian view that the reason American allegations generally prove false may be that the Americans rely on local agents who "feel that they should provide good stories in exchange for their pay." This may be true, though it is small consolation for the villagers who are bombed.

6   Details are still obscure, but this appears to be the order of events, as well as I can reconstruct from the information in the *Boston Globe* and *New York Times*, May 3, 1970. In his statement of May 2, in which he discussed the possibility of a resumption of the bombing of North Vietnam, Secretary Laird made no mention of the attack that had already taken place. Later, the Pentagon admitted the raid (presumably after Boyd's story was intercepted), but claimed that it was a "protective reaction" against anti-aircraft guns. Boyd reports that he heard several dozen explosions but heard no defensive fire and saw no smoke from anti-aircraft.

7   United Nations Document S/7820 15/3/67, quoted in *Is Cambodia Next?*

8   T. D. Allman, *Far Eastern Economic Review*, February 26, 1970. Cited in an informative discussion of the Cambodian situation in *Vietnam International*, April 1970, 6 Endsleigh Street, London, WC1. Allman noted that the number has continued to rise, and that not all such incidents are reported. More details are given in a Cambodian Government White Paper, January 3, 1970. The report also notes that not a single Viet Cong body has ever been found after United States-Saigon bombardments or ground attacks. For evidence on American defoliation in Cambodia, see "Report on Herbicidal Damage by the United States in Southeastern Cambodia," A. H. Westing, E. W. Pfeiffer, J. Lavorel, and L. Matarasso, December 31, 1969, Phnom Penh, in T. Whiteside, ed., *Defoliation* (New York, Ballantine Books, 1970). They note, incidentally, that "despite a week of free and unhampered travel by automobile, on foot, and by low-lying aircraft along hundreds of kilometers of the border, we could find no evidence of Viet Cong activity in Cambodia; nor did our repeated conversations with Cambodians and Europeans living along the border suggest any such activity." But they do report extensive damage from defoliants, in direct and apparently deliberate overflights.

9   "Cambodia: Between Scylla and Charybdis," *Asian Survey*, January 1968.

10 Michael Leifer, "Cambodia," *Asian Survey*, January 1967.

11 For example, the dictator of Thailand under the Japanese, who had in fact declared war against the United States, was reinstalled by an American-backed military coup in 1948; the liberal Pridi Phanomyong, who had worked with the OSS against the Japanese during the war

and later won easily in the only relatively free election in Thailand in 1946, soon found his way to Communist China, where at last report he still remains. It should, incidentally, be noted that the involvement of a Southeast Asian political leader with the Japanese in itself proves very little, since there were many possible motivations, including opposition to Western colonialism.

12   This characterization of Son Ngoc Thanh and Songsak is given by Daniel Roy, "Le Coup de Phnom-Penh," *Le Monde diplomatique*, April 1970. Other sources indicate that Songsak was a millionaire who did not need to resort to petty theft, and that Son Ngoc Thanh is essentially an apolitical opportunist. For example, the English journalist Michael Field suggests in his book *The Prevailing Wind* (London, Methuen, 1965) that Thanh gravitated toward the South Vietnamese and the Thais (i.e., the American-supported right-wing dictatorships) only when he could receive no other support in his effort to oppose the far more popular Sihanouk. Those familiar with internal Cambodian politics regard the information that is available to Westerners as being of highly uncertain quality, and any effort at detailed interpretation must surely be taken with caution. CIA involvement with the Khmer Serei is not in doubt, however. Some details were publicly revealed during the recent appeal of Green Beret officer John J. McCarthy, Jr., who had been convicted for killing a member of Khmer Serei. See *New York Times*, January 28, 1970.

13   Letter, *New Republic*, March 28, 1970.

14   Allman, *Far Eastern Economic Review*, February 26, 1970.

15   For innumerable examples taken from the press see *In the Name of America* (Annandale, Va., Turnpike Press, 1968), published by Clergy and Laymen Concerned About Vietnam. Capricious terror bombing of civilians has been reported even from sources highly sympathetic to the Pentagon, for many years. See, for example, Richard Tregaskis, *Vietnam Diary* (New York, Holt, Rinehart & Winston, 1963).

16   See Leifer, "Rebellion or Subversion in Cambodia."

17   "Anatomy of a Coup," *Far Eastern Economic Review*, April 9, 1970, an excellent analysis of the immediate background of the March 18 coup. A more far-reaching analysis of the events leading up to the coup appears in the cited article by Daniel Roy. These events are placed in the relevant historical context by Jean Lacouture, "Opération-suicide," *Le Nouvel Observateur*, April 20, 1970. For additional background, see the articles cited by Michael Leifer, and also Roger M. Smith, "Prince Norodom Sihanouk," *Asian Survey*, June 1967, and the articles already cited.

18   Speech to the closing session of the Summit Conference of Indochinese Peoples, which took place at an unidentified location in south China on April 25, 1970, translated and slightly shortened by Maria Jolas. I use her translation, and a few sentences quoted by Stanley Karnow, *Washington Post*, May 1. Prince Sihanouk goes on to ask: "Have the United States aggressors, through some operation of the Holy Ghost, become pure-blooded Indochinese? Who escalated the war in Laos and Cambodia? From which airfield (certainly not from Gia Lâm) do the one thousand daily air-raids over Laos take off? Do the 'Columbia Eagle' and the 'Caribou' planes that are flying an entire arsenal of weapons for Lon Nol and Sirik Matak and their mercenaries come from General Giap? And the hundreds of CIA 'special advisers' who have arrived in Vientiane, are they a 'present' from Premier Pham Van Dong?"

19   *Far Eastern Economic Review*, February 26, 1970.

20   Lacouture, *op. cit.*

21   *Le Monde diplomatique*, May 1970.

22   One of the vice-presidents of the NLF is a Buddhist monk of the Cambodian minority, who joined the NLF after a destructive Saigon Army sweep through his province in 1961. See

George M. Kahin and John W. Lewis, *The United States in Vietnam* (New York, Dial Press, 1967).

23 Lacouture, *op. cit.*

24 *Far Eastern Economic Review*, February 26, 1970.

25 Lacouture, *op. cit.*

26 Chesneaux, *op. cit.*

27 As has been frequently observed, this was probably one reason why Stalin did not support the Greek Communist guerrillas in the 1940s, contrary to American propaganda claims which continue to this day.

28 Field, *op. cit.*

29 *Far Eastern Economic Review*, April 2, 1970.

30 *Ibid.*, April 9, 1970.

31 On the actual character of "Khmer socialism," see Field, *op. cit.* Some observers see the conflict between the "socialists" and those in favor of "liberalization of the economy" as essentially a struggle between elements of the Cambodian elite. Others regard "Khmer socialism" as being a step toward an egalitarian and modern society, within the specific context of Cambodian history and culture. I do not have enough information to attempt a judgment.

32 Cf. Roy, *op. cit.*, for this and other details. Among the current American allies in Cambodia are also several thousand "semi-pirates, semi-mercenaries" of the Khmer minority in South Vietnam, organized in the "National Liberation Front of the Khmers of Kampuchea Khrom" (K.K.K.). Their history is interesting. They were "formed under the Japanese occupation, then mercenaries for the French during the first Indochina war, and of the Americans during the second...." The leader, Kim Keth, formerly a French parachutist, explained that they "like to eat the flesh of Vietnamese, particularly the liver, which is the best." See Jean-Claude Pomonti, *Le Monde*, April 25, 1970. Their presence was noted by the American press a week later. *The New York Times*, May 3, states that 2,000 well-armed members were flown into Phnom Penh the preceding night (in fact, Kim Keth, who claims that the K.K.K. has 4,500 armed members, arrived in Cambodia in 1956, and claims to have been an interpreter for the American Embassy in Phnom Penh until it was closed, when he became an actor). Kim Keth states that they detested Sihanouk. Other sources report that Sihanouk always permitted a pro-K.K.K. paper to operate, though left-wing papers were suppressed in recent years. One would like to learn more about their activities in Cambodia and South Vietnam in the past fifteen years. It is interesting that Premier Lon Nol requested the use of these troops from President Nixon directly. Obviously, he understands very well who runs Indochina. It is perhaps relevant that an anti-Sihanouk coup attempted in 1959 is widely assumed to have been inspired by the CIA. See Field, *op. cit.*, for a brief (and somewhat skeptical) account.

33 John L. Hess, *New York Times*, March 13, 1970.

34 Chesneaux, *op. cit.* In the same issue of *Le Monde diplomatique* François Honti comments: "It is now certain that those who took it upon themselves to abandon [Sihanouk's policy of neutralism] received serious encouragement from American military circles hopeful of being able to count on Phnom Penh for a friendly government and to cut off the Viet Cong and North Vietnamese troops from their 'Cambodian sanctuary.' ... One might ask whether the United States, unable to win the war in Vietnam, is making a wise calculation in enlarging the field of battle...."

35 Lacouture, *op. cit.*

36 Lacouture, *Le Monde diplomatique*, May 1970.

37 *Le Monde Weekly Selection*, April 22, 1970. Pomonti is one of the very few correspondents to have reported in depth from Cambodia.

38 *Far Eastern Economic Review*, April 23, 1910. A detailed analysis of American press reports of ARVN and American military activities in Cambodia from mid-March is presented in an unpublished essay by Jeff Pearson and Jessica Smilowitz, "Biting the Fishhook: How the United States Raped Cambodia," Ann Arbor, Michigan. Some details are presented in the weekly reports of the Bay Area Institute, 9 Sutter Street, Suite 300, San Francisco.

39 *Le Monde Weekly Selection*, April 22, 1970. Assuming, that is, that they are alive. After their disappearance, during the general purge of the left several years ago, they were rumored to have been assassinated. Recently, the Cambodian and French press have stated that they are alive and with the guerrillas, and I was given the same information in Hanoi, but I do not know how firm the evidence is. Added in proof: the new government has since been formed and the three are listed with major ministerial posts (national defense, information and propaganda, and interior communal reforms and cooperatives). Tillman Durdin, *New York Times*, May 6, 1970.

40 Lacouture, *Le Nouvel Observateur*, April 20, 1970.

41 *New York Times*, May 3, 1970. A former American teacher in Cambodia informs me that such "mock-martial gestures" involving students were common practice under Sihanouk.

42 *Far Eastern Economic Review*, April 9, 1970.

43 *Current History*, February 1969.

44 Roger Smith, "Prince Norodom Sihanouk," *Asian Survey*, June 1967.

45 See *Le Monde*, April 23, 1970.

46 Victoria Brittain, "Cambodia's Grim Lesson," *New Statesman*, May 1, 1970.

47 *Washington Post*, April 22, 1970.

48 *Le Monde Weekly Selection*, April 29, 1970.

49 *Ibid.*, May 6, 1970.

50 *Washington Post*, April 24, 1970.

51 "According to well-informed sources there are about 24,000 Communist troops in Cambodia or on the border." (Ian Wright, *Guardian* (London), April 27, 1970). Other estimates go as high as 50,000. As noted earlier, prior to the coup they remained in uninhabited areas. Wright reports that American military sources give little credence to Cambodian army reports of VC and NVA military action. Actually, official American government statements are almost worthless unless subject to independent check. I shall return to this matter, in connection with Laos, in Chapter 4.

52 Field, *op. cit.*

53 A fact that leads to some weird contortions. For example, Ambassador William Sullivan, now Deputy Assistant Secretary of State for East Asian and Pacific Affairs, makes the absurd claim that the Truman Doctrine is a "parsing" of the United Nations Charter (Symington subcommittee hearings).

54 According to Pentagon sources, aerial bombardment of Indochina from 1965 through 1969 reached 4.5 million tons, nine times the total tonnage in the entire Pacific theater in World War II. This is about half of the total ordnance expended.

55 Robert G. Kaiser, *Washington Post-Boston Globe*, May 3, 1970.

56 See *Far Eastern Economic Review*, February 26, 1970.

57 *New York Times*, May 3, 1970.

58 AP, *Boston Globe*, May 4, 1970.

59 CBS radio news, May 5, 1970. They did: "Front line reports said American tanks and aircraft strikes that included napalm drops against Communist defenders destroyed the town of Snoul inside Cambodia on Tuesday. UPI correspondent Leon Daniel reported some of the

GIs looted goods from deserted shops Wednesday as they swept through the town of 10,000 in the heart of rubber plantation country." Henry Huet reports from Snout that it was reduced to rubble with tank guns and air attacks the day before it was assaulted. The French manager of a rubber plantation informed him that between fifty and sixty North Vietnamese had driven off a 500-man Cambodian garrison on April 22. They armed the 1,600 workers, 95 percent of whom are Cambodians, and took them along as they fled from United States tank and air attacks. "They gave guns to the people and now they are fighting with the Viet Cong," the plantation manager reports. (*Boston Globe*, May 7.) Daniel reports that the only dead he saw were Cambodian civilians, including "a little girl horribly maimed by what must have been napalm." The United States Army claimed to have killed 88 Communist troops in the area. Daniel doubts it. (*Boston Globe*, May 8, 1970.)

60 Gloria Emerson, *New York Times*, May 3, 1970.

61 *Los Angeles Times-Boston Globe*, May 5, 1970.

62 Further evidence of major war crimes, as hardly need be stressed. These facts were brought out at a press conference held in Boston, May 7, 1970, under the auspices of the National Committee for a Citizens Commission of Inquiry on United States War Crimes, 156 Fifth Avenue, Room 1005, New York 10010. I might add that they desperately need funds to continue the important work of permitting former soldiers, many of whom are eager to cooperate, to testify concerning their experiences. It is difficult to overestimate the importance of bringing out this kind of information about the nature of the war.

63 *New York Times*, April 19, 1970.

64 Paul F. Langer and Joseph J. Zasloff, *Revolution in Laos: The North Vietnamese and the Pathet Lao*, RM-5935, September 1969. They claim, however, that the Pathet Lao could not function without North Vietnamese control. Their evidence, and other evidence that is available, does not seem to me to support this conclusion.

65 In a letter to *The New York Review*, February 26, 1970, I naively accepted Samuel Huntington's statement that the Council is primarily concerned with fund-raising for scholarly research on Vietnam. Having read the report of this meeting, which is concerned to find a proper strategy for ensuring control at the national level for "our side," given the insistence of the public on scaling down the United States military role, I would like to retract my acquiescence.

66 "South Vietnam: Neither War nor Peace," *Asian Survey*, February 1970.

67 April 9, 1970.

68 On the American role in creating guerrilla activity in Thailand, see some interesting comments by George Kahin in Richard M. Pfeffer, ed., *No More Vietnams?* (New York, Harper & Row, 1968), with the assent of Chester Cooper of the State Department.

69 *New York Times*, May 5, 1970.

70 *New York Times*, May 22, 1970.

71 *Boston Globe, New York Times*, May 22, 1970.

72 *New York Times*, May 25, 1970.

73 T. J. S. George, *Far Eastern Economic Review*, May 28, 1970.

74 Daniel Southerland, *Christian Science Monitor*, May 20, 1970.

75 *New York Times*, May 23, 1970.

76 *New York Times*, May 22, 1970.

77 Reported by Henry Kamm, *New York Times*, June 6, 1970.

78 François Nivolon, *Figaro*, May 13, 1970.

79 John Hess, *New York Times*, June 14, 1970.

80 *New York Times*, May 28, 1970.

81 *New York Times*, June 2, 1970.

82 Tad Szulc, *New York Times*, May 26, 1970.

83 *New York Times*, May 21, 1970.

84 May 13. I quote from *I. F. Stone's Bi-Weekly*, May 18, 1970.

85 Which, of course, is largely outside Cambodian territory.

86 John Finney, *New York Times*, June 7, 1970.

87 *New York Times*, June 7, 1970.

88 *New York Times*, May 24, 1970.

89 Three days earlier (*New York Times*, May 21, 1970) the same reporter, Ralph Blumenthal, reported that American troops had found the bodies of 33 Cambodian civilians—presumably the same unfortunates—"who were apparently killed by an American B-52 bombing strike last night."

90 May 28, 1970.

91 *Boston Globe*, June 8, 1970.

92 *New York Times*, May 25, 1970. American troops have also joined in. See note 94.

93 *Ibid.*

94 *New York Times*, May 23, 1970.

95 *Le Monde*, May 6, 1970, retranslated. It is an interesting question what has happened to the reports by Peter Arnett, one of the outstanding war correspondents in the area. I have seen very few of them. *Newsweek* reports (May 18) that the AP deleted references to looting by American soldiers from one Arnett story on the domestic (but not foreign) wires. The AP admitted the "error in judgment" (motivated by the political situation in the United States) and said, "The episode is over." It might be useful to investigate further.

96 *New York Times*, May 21, 1970.

97 Ralph Blumenthal, *New York Times*, June 9, 1970.

98 Carl Strock, May 14, 1970.

99 Jean-Claude Pomonti, *Le Monde Weekly Selection*, June 10, 1970.

100 Jean-François Kahn, *L'Express*, June 8–14, 1970.

101 James Sterba, *New York Times*, May 29, 1970.

102 See, for example, Milton Osborne, "Cambodia: Runaway Coup d'état," *The Nation*, June 8, 1970.

103 *New York Times*, May 18, 1970.

104 François Joyaux, June 1970. This is the situation as seen by the Sihanouk forces—correctly, this anti-Communist commentator suggests.

105 See pages 103–104.

106 Léon Boramy and Malcolm Caldwell, *Cambodia, Peace Press*, March/April 1970. 6 Endsleigh Street, London, W.C.1. Jean-François Kahn (*op. cit*) states that the insurrection was "provoked by the corruption of the [government] officials." Prince Sihanouk, at the time attributed it to Maoist Thai intruders (*Le Monde*, March 7, 1968, cited by François Joyaux, *op. cit.*), and claimed that captured brochures support this interpretation.

107 Cited by Jacques Decornoy, *Le Monde diplomatique*, June 1970.

108 *Southeast Asia Tomorrow* (Baltimore, The Johns Hopkins Press, 1970). Gurtov seems to interpret this as an indication that North Vietnam is not concerned solely with Vietnam but has designs on Cambodia as well. A more rational interpretation is that Khmer insurgency is not

directed by the North Vietnamese, there being no evidence at all that the Khmer Viet Minh in areas such as Battambang Province was created or directed by North Vietnam.

109   *Op. cit.* See also *Le Monde*, May 6 and June 10, 1970.

110   See Decornoy, *op. cit.*

111   *Far Eastern Economic Review*, May 7, 1970.

112   See Jean-Claude Pomonti, *Le Monde Weekly Selection*, June 3, 1970.

113   *Far Eastern Economic Review*, April 23, 1970.

114   *Ibid.*

115   Jean-Claude Pomonti, *Le Monde Weekly Selection*, June 3, 1970. T.D. Allman estimates that probably more than 5,000 Vietnamese were killed in these pogroms (*Far Eastern Economic Review*, May 7). Ninety percent of the Cambodian Catholic population was Vietnamese. Lon Nol announced: "The war now taking place, in accordance with predictions, is a war of religions" (*Le Monde*, June 3), Buddhism versus Communism. Apparently, the peasantry of Cambodia did not rise to the bait.

116   *Far Eastern Economic Review*, May 7, 1970.

117 The circumstances of Allman's departure have not been publicly discussed, to my knowledge. It may be that he was expelled from Cambodia, as was Jean-Claude Pomonti of *Le Monde*.

118   May 21, 1970.

119   *Op. cit.*

120   *Far Eastern Economic Review*, May 21, 1970.

121   *Op. cit.*

122   *Le Monde Weekly Selection*, June 3, 1970.

123   April 23, 1970. I assume that the commentator in the *Review* is the same person as the former Minister of Information in Saigon, a Saigon publisher.

124   The coup reinstalled the former dictator who had collaborated with the Japanese during World War II.

125   See notes 12 and 31 above. See also Ralph Blumenthal, *New York Times*, May 28, 1970. He reports that Green Berets and a Khmer Serei leader are recruiting ethnic Cambodians in the Mekong Delta to fight in Cambodia, much to the annoyance of the local officials of the Saigon government.

126   See *New York Times*, June 2, 1970 (Reuters). On June 3, Robert Semple reported from Washington in the *New York Times* that the United States would provide arms and equipment. These forces too were to be ethnic Cambodians, but later reports indicate that all Thai are being accepted as recruits. See Ralph Blumenthal, *New York Times*, June 16, 1970.

127   *Boston Globe*, June 10, 1970.

128   Blumenthal, *ibid.*

129   *Réalités Cambodgiennes*, June 24, 1966. Quoted by Michael Leifer, *Cambodia: The Search for Security* (New York, Frederick A. Praeger, 1967), p. 190.

130   Quoted by Cynthia Frederick, "Cambodia: Operation Total Victory No. 43," *Bulletin of Concerned Asian Scholars*, Vol. 2, No. 3 (April-July 1970).

131   *New York Times*, June 16, 1970.

132   Reports from South Vietnam indicate that the Koreans are the most vicious and brutal of the Allied forces. For some account of their exploits, see *New York Times*, January 10, February 1, 1970; *Boston Globe*, January 11, 1970. Professor Frank Baldwin of the Columbia East Asian Institute, commenting on the South Korean tactics in South Vietnam (and the admiration shown for them by Americans, who wish that the ARVN could be equally aggressive), wrote in a letter to the *New York Times*, January 25, 1970: "The silence of American Asian

specialists, who know the realities of the war in Vietnam, is a national disgrace. If timidity is not replaced by candor, there will be little Asian culture and few Asians left to study."

133 See Robert C. Toth, *Los Angeles Times-Boston Globe*, June 7, 1970.

134 Sidney Schanberg, *New York Times*, June 8, 1970.

135 Jean-Claude Pomonti, *Le Monde*, June 6, 1970, on the basis of a source close to President Thieu. Also Henry Kamm, *New York Times*, June 16, 1970.

136 See Sidney Schanberg, *New York Times*, June 11, 1970.

137 *Le Monde*, June 12, 1970.

138 *New York Times*, June 6, 1970.

139 These views are reported by Harrison Salisbury, *New York Times*, May 26, 1970.

140 Tad Szulc, *New York Times*, May 31, 1970.

141 *Ibid.*, May 24, 1970.

142 T. J. S. George, *Far Eastern Economic Review*, May 28, 1970.

143 *Christian Science Monitor*, May 21, 1970.

144 *New York Times*, June 14, 1970.

145 See the remarks by François Joyaux, *op. cit.*

Chapter 4
Laos

I ARRIVED IN VIENTIANE with two friends, Douglas Dowd and Richard Fernandez, expecting to take the International Control Commission plane to Hanoi the following day. Our trip to Hanoi was by invitation of the Committee for Solidarity with the American People of the Democratic Republic of Vietnam. I had received this invitation some time before, but was unable to arrange the trip until late March 1970. In fact, all of us were compelled to limit ourselves to an extremely short visit. The timing was tight, and it was with considerable disappointment that we learned from the Indian bureaucrat in charge of the weekly ICC flight that he would not be able to place us on the flight the following day. The previous flight had returned the North Vietnamese delegation from Phnom Penh to Hanoi after the sacking of their embassy by Cambodian troops (disguised as civilians), and the flight we intended to take was completely filled by passengers scheduled for the preceding week. Efforts by the North Vietnamese and American embassies were unavailing, and after exploring various far-fetched schemes, we decided, at first without much enthusiasm, to stay in Vientiane and try our luck a week later.

Vientiane is a rather small town, and within hours we had met quite a few members of the Western community—journalists, former workers with the International Voluntary Services in Laos and South Vietnam, and other residents. It quickly became clear that we would have more than enough to do to fill every waking moment. Through these contacts, we were able to meet urban Laotians of quite a range of sympathies and opinions, and with interesting personal histories on both sides of the civil war. We were also able to spend several days in the countryside near Vientiane, visiting a traditional Lao village and, several times, a refugee camp, in the company of a Lao-speaking American who is one of the outstanding specialists on contemporary Laos. Officials of the Laotian, American, North Vietnamese, and other governments were also available for discussion and helpful with information, and I was fortunate enough to obtain access to a large collection of documentary material accumulated by residents of Vientiane over the past few years. Many of the correspondents, both French and American, had a great deal to say, not only about Laos but also about their experiences in other parts of Southeast Asia. Unfortunately, most of the people with whom I spoke (and most forcefully, the Laotians) did not wish to be identified, and asked me to err on the side of caution in citing sources of information.

It doesn't take long to become aware of the CIA presence in Laos. The taxi from the airport to our hotel on the Mekong passed by the airfield of Air America, a theoretically private company that has an exclusive contract with the CIA.[1] Many of its pilots, said to be former Air Force personnel for the most part, were living in our hotel. If you happened to be up at 6 A.M. you could see them setting off for their day's work, presumably, flying supplies to the guerrilla forces of the CIA's army in Laos, the Clandestine Army led by the Meo General Vang Pao. These forces were at one time scattered throughout northern Laos, but a number of the CIA bases are reported to have been overrun. These bases were used not only for guerrilla actions in territory controlled by the Pathet Lao, but also as advanced navigational posts for the bombardment of North Vietnam and for rescue of downed American pilots. There are said to be hundreds of small dirt strips in northern Laos for Air America and other CIA operations.

After watching the Air America parade on my first morning in Vientiane, I decided to try to find out something about the town. Behind the hotel I came across the ramshackle building that houses the Laotian Ministry of Information, where one office was identified as the Bureau of Tourism. No one there spoke English or even French. However, I did find someone who could understand my bad French in another office of the Ministry. I explained that I wanted a map of Vientiane, but was told that I was in the wrong place—I should go to the American Embassy, where they might have such things. On my way out I walked through the reading room of the Ministry, where several people sat in the already intense heat, shooing off the flies and looking through the Lao and French newspapers scattered over the tables.

Across the street stands the seven-story modern building of the French Cultural Center. Its air-conditioned reading room is well stocked with the latest newspapers and magazines from Paris, and posters advertise French plays and lectures. On another corner is Vientiane's best bookstore, which sells French books and journals.

The striking contrast between the Laotian Ministry of Information and the French Cultural Center gives a certain insight into the nature of Laotian society. For a European resident or a member of the tiny Laotian elite, Vientiane has many attractions: plenty of commodities, a variety of good restaurants, some cultural activities (in our hotel a placard announced a reading of *Rosencrantz and Guildenstern Are Dead*), the resources of the French Cultural Center. An American can live in the sub-urbs, complete with well-tended lawns, or in a pleasant villa rented from a rich Laotian, and commute to the huge USAID compound with its PX and other facilities. For the Lao, however, there is nothing. Virtually everything is owned by outsiders: Thai, Chinese, Vietnamese. Apart from several cig-arette factories (Chinese owned), lumber, and tin mines, one of which is owned by the right-wing Prince Boun Oum, there seems to be little that is productive in the country. After decades of French colonialism and years of extensive American aid, "in 1960 the country had no railways, two doc-tors, three engineers and 700 telephones."[2] In 1963 imports were forty times the country's exports in terms of value:

> Economic development has been virtually non-existent and the attempts by the Americans to stabilise a right-wing and pro-Western regime by lavish aid programmes led merely to corruption, inflation and new gradients of wealth within the country and so played into the hands of the extreme left, the Pathet Lao.[3]

"From 1963 until June 1966 Laos exported some $3,000,000 worth while importing $108,000,000 worth of products."[4] A recent Laotian govern-ment economic report cites an import-export ratio of 14 to 1 from 1964 through 1968.[5] In 1968, 93 percent of the exports were tin, wood, and coffee, while 71 percent of the imports (by value) were food, gasoline, and vehicles. The dependence of the Lao economy on outside aid is also indi-cated by the Laotian budget, only about 40 percent of which is raised locally (83 percent of this by indirect taxes). Close to 60 percent of the budget goes to the military and police; about 2 percent, to development.[6]

The Laotian educational system presents a similar picture. It is estimated that only about half the children ever go to school. Of approximately 185,000 children in school in 1966–1967, 95 percent were in the first six grades, 70 percent in the first three grades. In 1969, a total of 6,669 students were enrolled in secondary schools. The American aid program has helped, but it too tends to perpetuate the distorted pattern of education for the elite. Funds for secondary education are about the same as the funds for primary education:

> The school is still training a minority of the youth, particularly at secondary levels, to take their place in administration. The biggest and best schools are still located in the cities. The values and attitudes communicated to children are still those of an urban-thinking, technocratic West. The curriculum is still a catch-all of often unrelated pieces of information. And the concept of responsibility to the nation is still not being taught forcefully anywhere in Laotian society.[7]

A sensible Education Reform Act of 1962 remains largely a paper program. Fred Branfman concludes that "the school system is training a class of consumers, not producers of wealth," a Western-oriented elite that might, at best, administer Laotian society in the interest of the domestic elite and its American backers.

Political life as well is limited to a tiny elite. The State Department *Background Notes* (March 1969) contend that "Only a few thousand individuals, many of them French-educated, participate in government and politics; the bulk of the population is illiterate and politically passive." Surely this is true of the government-controlled areas. I will return to the areas under Pathet Lao control later on.

The Laotian elite do not seem too popular among foreign observers in Vientiane, who comment repeatedly on their venality and corruption. They also do not receive a very good press. Not untypical is a report by two French journalists who were at the site of a short but brutal battle near Paksane, southeast of the Plain of Jars. They describe the arrival by helicopter of "the strongman of Vientiane, General Kouprasith ... the most powerful of the Lao generals," well after the battle was over:

A man with an enormous face and body, wearing heavily camouflaged clothing, he approaches one of the 7 wounded soldiers waiting to be evacuated, taps him on the shoulder, and turning toward us, cries, "You don't see any Americans here, nothing but Laos!" Behind him, someone brings over a case of Pepsi-Cola and ammunition. The General has himself photographed, arms akimbo, behind a cadaver presumed to be North Vietnamese. It has been searched for an identity card by a soldier, but in vain…. At the Paksane airport, we come across the American pilot who guided the T-28 bombing. He is dressed like a sheriff with sunglasses, a cartridge box, and a pistol in his belt. He says to General Kouprasith, "We did a good job today, General." He adds, "Don't forget to go see Colonel"—an Anglo-Saxon name—"he is waiting for you." Kouprasith makes an impatient gesture.[8]

A very well informed observer describes the Royal Lao Government in the following terms:

Its corruption, lethargy and indifference is as great if not greater than it ever was. Few people living under its rule actively support it. American officials have been unable to push for basic reforms due to the political necessity of getting on with the Lao civilian and military elite so that continued American bombing will be permitted.[9]

I discussed these matters with a middle-aged Lao intellectual, non-Communist but rather left-wing in his general outlook, a man who has had a great deal of experience with the Royal Lao Government and who also lived in a Pathet Lao area for some time. He seemed to feel that the only hope for Laos was a Pathet Lao victory, though he himself, as a Lao bourgeois, did not look forward to this with much enthusiasm. He felt, however, that nationalistic and uncorrupted bourgeois elements would find a place in a society organized by the Pathet Lao. For the Royal Lao Government he felt only contempt, and he expressed his belief that even the younger men, though less dedicated to total corruption, would be able to do very little. He recalled that while the Government of National Union was functioning, Prince Souphanouvong, the leading figure of the Pathet Lao, was widely regarded as its most capable and efficient member, and one of the few honest men in Laotian public life. He saw no sign that a productive economy could be developed or that control by foreigners could be overcome, given the nature of existing programs. He mentioned efforts to develop a "neutralist" organization based on younger, more nationalistic, and less corrupt segments of the elite, but with little hope. With some bitterness he gestured toward the street outside the room where we were talking, observing that every one of the stores that lined the street was owned by a non-Lao. The Laotian elite is busy building bowling alleys, running the prostitution and opium rackets,[10] renting villas to Americans, living at the exorbitant level permitted by the flow of American commodities and the ever-present corruption. He felt that the American aid program was essentially destructive in that it perpetuated a consumer-oriented society, benefiting while corrupting the elite, and did not even begin to lay the basis for development or modernization that would involve the Lao masses or create a productive society.

Other well-informed observers agreed in a general way with this analysis. One pointed to a large monument in the center of Vientiane referred to as the "vertical runway" because it was built by dictator Phoumi Nosavan with materials that were to be used for improving the Vientiane airport.[11]

A young Lao teacher, openly sympathetic to the Pathet Lao, gave a similar though more vehement account. Asked whether the Pathet Lao were attempting to build a clandestine organization within Vientiane to exploit such grievances and plan for an ultimate takeover, he said that to his knowledge they were not, but also that there was no necessity to do so. Many people, he reported, listen regularly to the Pathet Lao radio and have considerable, though hidden, sympathy for the Pathet Lao. He referred to the fact that the Neo Lao Hak Sat (NLHS), the political party of the Pathet Lao, had done very well in Vientiane in 1958 in the only real elections ever held in Laos, and asserted that these sympathies would once again be revealed if honest elections could be held. He claimed that similar sentiments are widely held among young urban intellectuals, though rarely expressed in the rather lax and inefficient police-state atmosphere of Vientiane.

I spoke at length with a refugee who had fled to Vientiane from Phonesavan, a town in the Plain of Jars, to escape the American bombardment which had wiped out the town by January 1969.[12] Few refugees will speak frankly to Americans, whom they naturally assume to be representatives of the American government.[13] However, I met this man under circumstances which encouraged him to believe we were quite neutral, perhaps even sympathetic to the Pathet Lao. He expressed a deep hatred for life in Vientiane. He was appalled by the widespread prostitution, fighting, gambling, and cheating, and the general atmosphere of hostility within the city. He described an incident he had witnessed when a policeman simply stole a pair of boots from a poor old man, who protested bitterly but could do nothing. Before the Pathet Lao came, he said, life was not too different even in the small town of Phonesavan where he grew up. The Pathet Lao tried to overcome these difficulties. They told people not to be afraid of "big men" or to use honorific terminology (*doi knoi*, the term used in speaking to superiors). They were scrupulously honest and tried to induce people to work out their disputes peaceably, through discussion. They respected traditional Lao culture and discouraged gambling and opium smoking,[14] as well as Western fashions and customs. There was no prostitution, and women were treated as equals.

> Here in Vientiane [he said], it is different. We can't speak freely like back with the Pathet Lao. There is freedom of speech there. If you don't do well, I can criticize you. Even big men. If a big man is no good, I can get a lot of my friends together and we get the big man sent away.

Other observers in Vientiane report that the Laotian elite live entirely beyond the reach of any law, free to do what they want, with few constraints. Corruption is so widespread that it is hardly even an interesting topic for gossip.

The Pathet Lao leadership speaks with great bitterness about the effects of the American involvement on life in Vientiane. Phoumi Vongvichit, Secretary-General of the Neo Lao Hak Sat Central Committee and Minister of Information for the National Union Government of 1962, writes:

> Together with military, political and diplomatic manoeuvres, the Yankees apply the so-called "counterpart aid" policy, flood Laos with their surplus goods and introduce American depraved culture to turn the Vientiane-controlled zone into a U.S. new-type colony. By

increasing the importation of surplus goods and luxury articles, they have seriously harmed the economy and finances of the country, driving Lao production into stagnation, wrecking handicraft and small industry, and in certain localities strangling whole branches of economy, such as hand-weaving and smithery in areas under Vientiane control…. As far as trade is concerned, with the system of "counterpart aid" the Americans want to gather and entertain a clique of valets and create a comprador bourgeoisie which will serve as a mainstay to their neo-colonialist policy. At present, import and export are entirely in the hands of those who control the ruling apparatus. Trade monopoly enriches lackeys of the U.S., while impoverishing the labouring masses.[15]

The head of the Pathet Lao Information Office in Hanoi[16] also deplores the situation in Vientiane. He claims that Vientiane gives the impression of a Thai town, so many Thai have entered it in recent years. Apparently, their role in the commercial life of the town is considerable.

Vientiane is a place of rumor and suspicion. Direct access to news is limited. Most of what appears in the press is simply based on American government handouts, and therefore lacks credibility. Little of the country is firmly under Royal Lao Government control. We were warned not to travel too far from Vientiane, and taxi drivers made much of the dangers of going more than a few miles from the city (in part, no doubt, so that they could demand higher fares). In a refugee camp about 35 miles from Vientiane along one of the few roads that can be freely traveled, the inhabitants refused to take us out to the forest where, they said, men were working, claiming that the Pathet Lao were there and the danger was too great. One man finally agreed to take us, but after leading us on a rather aimless path, said that it was quite impossible. Again, there may have been other reasons.

Parts of the nominally government-controlled areas are actually run by the CIA, and no one seems sure where the CIA ends and the civilian aid program, USAID, begins.[17] The CIA bases of Sam Thong and Long Cheng, north of Vientiane, are in an area designated as uninhabited on the detailed map that I purchased at the Service Géographique National du Laos, dated 1968 (supplied, I was told, by the United States). There are reported to be over 50,000 people in or near the two bases, and perhaps several hundred thousand in the vicinity, almost all refugees. According to the spokesman for the Pathet Lao Information Office in Hanoi (see note 16), these areas have been turned into "a second capital of Laos" since 1964. They serve as the headquarters for Vang Pao's Clandestine Army.

Sam Thong has been visited by correspondents and congressmen. Long Cheng is off limits. However, T. D. Allman made his way there on his own several months ago, and in a television interview with Bernard Kalb last February reported what he had found during a two-hour stay before he was picked up and shipped out.[18] He describes it as an immense intelligence-gathering and administrative logistics base, with a 3,000-foot runway, many planes, and rescue helicopters (one in the air constantly) to pick up American pilots shot down by Communist anti-aircraft. He estimates that ten to twelve Americans are lost each month in crashes of jets bombing in that area from their Thai bases. The Forward Air Control planes, which mark targets for the American jets, are also based in Long Cheng and flown by American pilots. He reports that there are CIA houses everywhere, identifiable by the fact that they have no windows but many antennas and air conditioners.

Sam Thong has been reported captured several times, most recently in mid-May 1970.[19] It was abandoned by the Vang Pao army in mid-March and occupied about two weeks later. "Allied sources said looting and vandalism by Laotian troops had reduced the base to 'a shambles.' The sources said looting had been going on since government forces retook the base earlier this week."[20] Most observers feel that the Communist forces can take these bases if they are willing to pay the cost, and that if they do the Vang Pao army, largely composed of Meo mountain tribesmen, may disintegrate, perhaps making an accommodation with the Pathet Lao or perhaps being moved to Thailand. This would be a major blow to the American effort, since the Clandestine Army is a more serious fighting force than the Royal Lao Army. While we were in Vientiane there were almost daily rumors of an attack on the bases, and North Vietnamese tanks were reported in the vicinity—surprising, it seemed to me, given the intensity of bombardment in northern Laos, though it was pointed out that jet bombing is quite ineffective against military targets in the mountainous jungle terrain.

The recent history of Laos contributes to the atmosphere of suspicion. The first Government of National Union of 1958 was overthrown by American subversion. As Ambassador Graham Parsons stated quite frankly in congressional hearings in 1959, "I struggled for 16 months to prevent a coalition." An American military mission was operating at the time, headed by an United States Army general in civilian guise. In the 1958 elections, of 21 seats contested for the National Assembly, 9 were won by the Neo Lao Hak Sat and 4 by the candidates of the Committee for Peace and Neutrality of Quinim Pholsena, a "left-leaning neutralist" allied with the NLHS. Five right-wing and 3 nonparty delegates were elected. The NLHS had put up only 13 candidates. Its leader, Souphanouvong, got the largest vote and was elected Chairman of the National Assembly. The United States withheld funds, thus impelling the Laotian elite to introduce a new government headed by "pro-Western neutralist" Phoui Sananikone. Shortly after, Phoui declared his intention to disband the NLHS as subversive, scrapping the earlier, quite successful agreements that had established the coalition. American aid was quickly resumed and Phoui pledged "to coexist with the Free World only." In December 1959, he was overthrown by the CIA favorite Phoumi Nosavan, something of a Lao equivalent to the military dictator of Thailand (a cousin, it happens), who was also receiving substantial United States support. Although the coup government did not last, Phoumi retained his powerful position as Minister of National Defense (controlling most of the budget), and the extreme right won the ridiculous 1960 elections, rigged so crudely by the CIA and its favorites that even conservative pro-United States observers were taken aback.

A coup by paratroop Captain Kong Le restored Prince Souvanna Phouma, and civil war broke out with these forces, supported by Russia and China, opposing the American-backed General Phoumi Nosavan and the government of the reactionary Prince Boun Oum. Recognizing that its policies were failing disastrously,[21] the American government agreed to participate in a new Geneva Conference which took place in 1961–62. The settlement reached at Geneva did not last long, however. After a series of assassinations in early 1963, the two most prominent Pathet Lao leaders, Prince Souphanouvong and Phoumi Vongvichit, departed from

Vientiane, "contending, not entirely without justification, that their security was threatened in the capital."[22] The two other NLHS cabinet members left soon after. The civil war was resumed with a somewhat different lineup. This time the Americans were supporting Souvanna Phouma and Kong Le, who joined forces with the Laotian right (Kong Le soon departed to French exile, where he remains), against the Pathet Lao and the "left-leaning neutralists" under Colonel Deuane.

Foreign troops were to depart after the Geneva agreements of 1962, along with all advisers, instructors, and foreign civilians "connected with the supply ... of war materials." The United States claims that North Vietnam never adhered to this agreement, leaving 6,000 soldiers in Laos. The Chinese claimed at the time that hundreds of American soldiers simply changed into civilian clothes, as in the late 1950s. The Pathet Lao maintain that "After the signing of the 1962 Geneva Agreements on Laos, the missions of military 'advisers'—P.E.O., M.A.A.G., P.A.G., U.S.O.M.—put on a common civilian cloak: USAID." They claim that there were 3,500 such military "advisers" in civilian camouflage by 1968 and that "the whole system is directly under the U.S. 'special forces' command, codenamed H.Q.333 and based in Oudone (northeast Thailand)."[23] Langer and Zasloff estimate that there are about 700 North Vietnamese military advisers with the Pathet Lao.[24]

The Chinese Nationalist troops supported by the United States remained after Geneva 1962, though some may have been evacuated. They were reported at one time to number in the thousands, and are said to be a fairly effective fighting force—the only Chinese fighting in Laos, incidentally. Vongvichit estimates their number at 600 by 1968, and reports that their activities were confirmed by an ICC investigation in December 1962. American-supported Thai and South Vietnamese troops are also reported to have remained.[25] Vongvichit asserts that "thousands of Thai soldiers and agents, especially those of Lao stock and coming from northeastern Thailand, have wormed their way into the royal army, police and administration, or have mingled with the population in strategic areas and economic centres." Similar reports of Thai soldiers in Laotian uniform are common, and generally believed, in Vientiane. No one has any idea how many CIA operatives remained, or what in detail they were up to, or to what extent they operate under civilian cover.[26]

Obviously, USAID attempts to implement American government policy in Laos and to build domestic support for the American-sponsored Royal Lao Government. A more interesting example of the difficulty of determining just how the United States is intervening in the internal affairs of Laos is the case of the International Voluntary Services (IVS). This is a private volunteer group that has attracted many idealistic young people who are eager to help with modernization and development in traditional societies without mixing in local politics. It has operated in Laos for about fifteen years. Beginning in 1962, IVS was offered a large USAID contract for work in Laos and grew to number about 100 members. The reasons for this sudden American interest seem clear. Prior to 1962, most American aid had gone to the urban areas. In fact, less than one-half of one percent of the extensive American aid funds[27] were spent on agriculture, the livelihood of over 90 percent of the population. This was, of course, a factor in the support for the Pathet Lao revealed by the 1958 elections and subsequent events. As Arthur Dommen points out, the Pathet Lao needed no propaganda to turn the rural population against the townspeople, and the enormous corruption and graft associated with the aid program sickened many city dwellers as well. In 1962 the United States therefore decided to channel more funds to the countryside and to do this through an American-controlled apparatus so as to reduce corruption. This required that there be Americans in the villages, and IVS filled the breach. As one volunteer puts it, "IVS became a private agency recruiting young, relatively idealistic Americans to engage in politically motivated counterinsurgency programs in Laos."

Many of the volunteers worked in the Forward Areas Program, which is described as follows in an IVS bulletin:

> Forward Area Team operations ... [are] ... composed of one or two IVS men. They move into areas recently secured from the Pathet Lao with basic tools and housing supplies and proceed with the "impact program." The idea is to help the people in these areas build what they need, whether it be a well, school or dispensary; giving them a

concrete example of the Royal Lao Government's and USAID's interest in their welfare.

Since there are no USAID personnel in Forward Area field stations, the IVSer, as a representative of USAID, works closely with the Chao Moung [village leader] and the local military commandant.

In later years IVS workers were the only Americans in many rural areas. Some were disturbed at the relation with the American government and felt that they were serving, in effect, as propaganda agents for the United States and the Royal Lao Government, by virtue of their control of USAID commodities. Some feel that they were inadvertently giving military information to the American government. Even in some urban centers there has been dissatisfaction among volunteers with USAID policy, administered in some cases by "retired" military officers.

Beginning in late 1969, IVS workers were withdrawn to provincial capitals for security reasons (several had been killed), and the scale of the operation was also reduced. Many volunteers then joined USAID. In many areas where IVSers formerly worked there is now no American or RLG presence.

It is difficult to avoid the conclusion that IVS is acting on behalf of the American government and the RLG in the midst of a civil war. An IVS handbook states:

IVS ... in Laos ... is working by virtue of government contracts and its activities must harmonize with US government policies in the broad sense. There is, therefore, an obligation on the part of IVS team members to endeavor to understand the nature of US policy and to avoid actions or statements to outsiders that might impair US policy objectives.

The situation is such that volunteers cannot help but appear to the villagers as representatives of the United States, conveying a benign image of the country that is in fact devastating Laos through intensive aerial bombardment and that is the sole support for the RLG in the civil war. Whether IVS efforts actually help the RLG is open to question; some feel that IVS activities simply reinforce the image of incompetence and corruption of the RLG, by showing that the rural assistance program must be implemented by Americans. Nevertheless, the IVS can hardly serve as anything other than an instrument of American foreign policy in Laos.[28]

Pathet Lao spokesmen have no illusions about the role of IVS. Phoumi Vongvichit writes:

> At present Americans of the "Rural Development Service" [of IVS] go to scores of provincial capitals and district centres, towns and villages, in eleven out of a total of sixteen provinces in Laos to supervise the implementation of that program, collect intelligence data and establish political bases in the countryside.[29]

It would appear that these suspicions are justified.

What is true of IVS holds, far more clearly, for the American aid program, and of course, for the direct involvement through the CIA and the military. From the information available, one must conclude that there has been a massive American intervention in the internal affairs of Laos in an effort to defeat the Pathet Lao insurgents and establish the rule of the RLG. This intervention involves heavy bombardment, support for guerrilla activity (by the CIA and its civilian air arm, Air America) in areas under Pathet Lao control, the operations of the CIA Clandestine Army, military operations of the United States-supported and advised Royal Lao Army, direct support to RLG administration and other programs, and aid and development programs administered by the Americans, sometimes through the medium of purportedly neutral organizations. To a significant extent, these activities are in violation of the Geneva agreements of 1962.

The scale of the American involvement is enormous. The gross national product of Laos is estimated at about $150 million a year. In the fiscal year ending in June 1969, USAID spending was about $52 million. In addition, $92 million was spent in direct military assistance. This is stated to be "much less" than the cost of the "American participation in the air war over the northern part of Laos," which is classified.[30] The costs of the air war in southern Laos and the funds expended in CIA operations are also unknown. In addition, there is the matter of support for the Thai troops in Laos. The Symington subcommittee hearings offer the following clarification on this matter:

Mr. Paul [of the Committee staff]. There have been reports in the press that have ranged as high as 5000 new Thai troops in Laos. Is this apocryphal?

Mr. Sullivan. Apocryphal?

Mr. Paul. Are there new Thais?

Mr. Sullivan. [Deleted.]

Mr. Paul. Do you know of any quid pro quo that was given by the Americans in return for the Thai contribution to the Laotian effort?

Mr. Sullivan. Well, I think, as we mentioned earlier, the question of these aircraft that were turned over to the Lao by the Thai, I believe I am correct [deleted] that the United States then replaced those aircraft in the Thai inventory. [Deleted.][31]

Information on the cost of the American intervention since 1962 is not available, but some indication is given in the following censored excerpt from the Symington subcommittee hearings:

Senator Fulbright. As I understand it, the military assistance to Laos has been [deleted] from 1962 to 1970, according to our figures. Nonmilitary, economic assistance to Laos from 1946 through 1968 ... was $591 million. This is over a billion dollars.[32]

Note that the reference is to the narrowest category of military assistance, the category which ran about $90 million in 1969.

The American involvement penetrates every phase of the existence (as well as the destruction) of Laos. To cite just one relatively innocuous case, consider the role of the United States Information Service (USIS) in "information dissemination" in Laos.[33] About half of the programming on the Laotian radio is music. Of the other half, USIS "prepared or participated in the preparation" of about two-thirds. USIS also participates in the publication of a bimonthly magazine with a circulation of 43,000 (the largest Laotian newspaper has a circulation of 3,300). In addition there are films and other printed material, pamphlets and posters, wall newspapers, leaflets for air drops. In most of this "there is not U.S. Government attribution"—that is, the impression is conveyed that these appear as documents or programs sponsored by the Royal Lao Government. But the government witness denied that any of this is done "covertly." When asked to explain, he answered:

> We do not hide our participation. It is not done secretly, and I believe that many people, I think that most people, in the Lao Government, for instance, or in the Lao bureaucracy are very aware of American participation in the preparation of these things.

Thus one could not accuse the United States government of any covert attempt to extend RLG influence over the population (or, as the more skeptical would say, to pretend that the RLG exists).

The official justification for this involvement is that it is necessary to defend Laos against North Vietnamese aggression. I will return to the details of the charges and such facts as have been presented to support them. However, a certain degree of skepticism arises even in advance of investigation. In part it derives from the record prior to 1962. There is no doubt that during this period, the outside intervention was overwhelmingly American. All sources agree that the Americans attempted to subvert the accommodation of 1958 (and succeeded, as noted earlier), and that the North Vietnamese played practically no role in Laotian affairs, nor did the Chinese or Russians, prior to the events of 1960 described earlier. In the 1960s, of course, the situation is complicated by the Vietnam war. The return of South Vietnamese cadres from the North is said to have begun in 1959 and involved sections of southern Laos (the so-called Ho Chi Minh Trail). The American use of Thailand as a base for the bombardment of northern Laos and later North Vietnam dates from early 1964, according to American government sources (American troops were sent to Thailand at the time of the Nam Tha incident[34] and have remained there under the United States Military Assistance Command—Thailand, established at the time of the landing).

A second source of skepticism was expressed, in a different connection, by Senator Symington in the subcommittee hearings:

> We have an over $800 billion gross national product; the Vietnamese [DRV] have practically none. We have 200 million people; the Vietnamese some 17 million. We have been escalating the fighting out there for over 4 years. We have had nearly 300,000 casualties, but

are now in the process of acknowledging a stalemate, or a passing over, or some kind of defeat.[35]

To accept the official American government position, one must believe that the Vietnamese are supermen, able to overthrow other governments with a flick of the wrist,[36] carrying out aggression throughout Indochina, successfully countering enormous American military and economic power—all of these exploits carried out by a small, poor nation that has been subjected to devastating bombardment which has destroyed virtually all of its meager industrial resources, not to speak of most of its cities, towns, and communications. It is not surprising that such ludicrous charges do not stand up very well when one seeks evidence. It is perhaps surprising that they are so widely believed by Americans. Thus even self-styled "doves" continually refer to the American war in Indochina as a war against Hanoi. I think it is fair to say that the propaganda achievement of the American government, in this regard, probably ranks higher than any use of the Big Lie since the technique was perfected a generation ago.

Since the civil war in Laos was resumed in earnest in 1963, American participation has been clouded in secrecy. The veil was lifted slightly by the Symington subcommittee hearings, but these still contain many lies that are not challenged in the published record. To select just the ugliest, William Sullivan, who presented the bulk of the administration case, stated that "it was the policy not to attack populated areas," referring to the period 1968–1969.[37] He also testified that as Ambassador (until 1969) he had approved each air strike. Thus he must surely have known that the policy was precisely to attack and destroy populated areas in the territory controlled by the Pathet Lao. The evidence that the bombing has been directed against farms, villages, and towns, most of which have been totally destroyed in these territories, is incontrovertible.

The extent of government deceit has been such that virtually no government statement is, or should be, believed. Consider, for example, President Nixon's speech on Laos on March 6, 1970.[38] The key paragraph is this:

> Hanoi's most recent military build-up in Laos has been particularly escalatory. They have poured over 13,000 additional troops into Laos during the past few months, raising their total in Laos to over 67,000.

Thirty North Vietnamese battalions from regular division units participated in the current campaign in the Plain of Jars with tanks,
armored cars and long-range artillery. The indigenous Laotian communists, the Pathet Lao, are playing an insignificant role.

These claims are presumably intended to justify the American escalation of
the air war, for example, with the first B-52 raids in northern Laos in early
1970.

When I arrived in Vientiane a few weeks after, I discovered that
Nixon's speech was a favorite topic of conversation—and ridicule. Every
reporter in Vientiane was aware that only a few days before the President's
speech, the American military attaché in Vientiane had given the figure of
50,000 North Vietnamese, approximately the same figure that had been
reported by the United States for the preceding year. This interesting fact
was reported by D. S. Greenway, head of the *Time-Life* bureau in
Bangkok, who wrote that "The President's estimate of North Vietnamese
troop strength in Laos was at least 17,000 higher than the highest reliable
estimate in Vientiane, including the estimates of the Americans themselves."[39]

Furthermore, all were aware of how misleading these figures are. The
North Vietnamese invasion that Nixon attempted to conjure up was in the
Plain of Jars, recaptured by Communist forces in February in a five-day
battle that reconstituted the territorial division that had existed from 1964
until August 1969, when the Clandestine Army of the CIA swept through
the area. Nixon's figure of "67,000" North Vietnamese does not distinguish between those in southern Laos—really an extension of the
Vietnamese war—and those with the Pathet Lao in northern Laos where
the "invasion" had taken place. It also does not distinguish combat troops
from support and communications units, which, according to military
observers in Vientiane, constitute about three-quarters of the North
Vietnamese forces, hardly a surprise when one realizes that they bring all
of their supplies, including food, through a heavily bombed area. In fact,
it is likely that this percentage is now an underestimate. The effect, and presumably the purpose, of the American bombardment in northern Laos has
been to destroy the civil society administered by the Pathet Lao and to

drive as much of the population as possible into government-controlled areas. As Tammy Arbuckle reports:

> Well-informed sources said the United States is pursuing a "scorched earth" policy to force the people to move into government areas—and thus deprive the Reds of information, recruits and porters.[40]

When the population is forced into government areas or driven into caves and tunnels, it can no longer provide support for the Pathet Lao and North Vietnamese troops, which are therefore forced to rely increasingly on supplies from North Vietnam. Hence it stands to reason that the percentage of combat troops must have decreased. Furthermore, the support and communications "troops" are said to include a large percentage of women and old men.

It has been widely reported, and is confirmed by American military sources, that the largest attacks in the recent "invasion"—namely, the attack on Moung Soui and the Xieng Khouang airfield—involved about 400 Communist troops, apparently shock troops. As to prisoners, 8 North Vietnamese were reported captured in the "invasion" which recaptured the Plain of Jars. In fact, since 1964, about 80 North Vietnamese have been captured, a figure which may be compared to the 200 Americans listed as missing in action or prisoners of war, in addition to "something under 200" listed as killed in military actions in Laos.[41]

These numbers must be taken with a large grain of salt. According to all reports, the Pathet Lao and particularly the North Vietnamese keep to isolated, heavily forested, and often mountainous areas. Few refugees report contacts with Vietnamese. Despite the vast intelligence-gathering effort of the United States, it is doubtful that any significant information is available concerning the number of North Vietnamese troops.

It is no doubt correct that there are North Vietnamese combat troops in northern Laos. This hardly comes as a surprise, given the American record of subversion and armed intervention reviewed above. In particular, it would have been remarkable had North Vietnam not involved itself directly in the fighting in northern Laos after the American bombardment of Laos and North Vietnam began.

As for southern Laos, according to American government sources South Vietnamese cadres of the former Viet Minh began to return to

South Vietnam in 1959 to take part in the fighting then underway against the American-installed Diem government. (By 1962 there were 10,000 American troops in South Vietnam, many involved directly in combat operations, for example, helicopter gunship attacks.) The South Vietnamese "infiltrators" had been regrouped to the North in 1954, in accordance with the Geneva agreements, with the expectation that they would return to their homes after the scheduled 1956 elections, blocked by the United States. They remained in the North, consistently with the North Vietnamese policy of attempting to reach a solution through negotiations and diplomatic initiatives. By 1959 it was clear that the United States would never agree to implement the Geneva Accords or permit any peaceful settlement, and under pressure from southerners who were being subjected to severe repression and direct military attack, South Vietnamese cadres began to return to the South. According to the Mansfield Report of 1966, before 1965 infiltration "was confined primarily to political cadres and military leadership," but when United States combat troops arrived "in strength" in early 1965, the "Vietcong counter-response was to increase their military activity with forces strengthened by intensified local recruitment and infiltration of regular North Vietnamese forces." Senator Mansfield himself stated on June 16, 1966:

> When the sharp increase in the American military effort began in early 1965, it was estimated that only about 400 North Vietnamese soldiers were among the enemy forces in the South which totaled 140,000 at that time.

This statement was confirmed as accurate by the Pentagon. The 400 North Vietnamese soldiers to whom Mansfield referred are presumably those identified by Secretary of Defense McNamara on April 27, 1965, as constituting a battalion of the 325th Division, the first confirmed report by the United States government of North Vietnamese troops in the South—eight months after the bombing of strategic targets in North Vietnam at the time of the fabricated Tonkin Gulf incident and two and a half months after the regular bombardment of North Vietnam was initiated. American Marines were landed in Vietnam in March 1965, and the American force level passed 53,000 by mid-year (not including the unknown thousands of troops involved in air and naval operations). By

February 1966, the American force level passed 200,000 and it was alleged that 11,000 North Vietnamese troops were in South Vietnam. By December 1967 the American force level was approaching half a million and it was alleged that 50,000 to 60,000 North Vietnamese troops were in the South (about the same number as the force of South Koreans fighting for the United States). The infiltration and supply of these troops made use of the so-called Ho Chi Minh Trail, most of which is in southern Laos.

On the "infiltration" from south to north, see note 36.

All of this is conceded even by those who are hardly more than propagandists for the American government. For example, Douglas Pike states that "Dispatch of [North Vietnamese] troops in numbers began in late 1964, and they began arriving in the South in early 1965; at that time the trip took three to four months" (*War, Peace and the Viet Cong*, p. 121n.). Recall, again, that the bombing of North Vietnam began on August 4, 1964, and the regular bombing on February 8, 1965.

I need hardly emphasize that the outrage expressed by the American government over "North Vietnamese aggression" is a bit farcical, given the actual historical record. It can be justified only on the assumption that the United States had a perfect right to undermine the Geneva agreements and carry out the forceful repression of dissidents in the South, to engage in large-scale combat operations in the early 1960s, to dispatch a huge army of occupation beginning in 1965, and to carry out extensive bombardment in Vietnam and Laos; while the South Vietnamese cadres in the North had no right to return to their homes, the southern resistance forces had no right to react to the repression or the subversion of the Geneva Accords, and the North Vietnamese had no right to react to the bombardment of their territory or the American attack on Laos and South Vietnam. In any event, whatever one may think about these assumptions, there is no doubt that by the early 1960s southern Laos was involved in an extension of the Vietnamese war and by the mid-1960s a civil war was underway, with substantial outside support for both sides, in northern Laos as well.

Consider Nixon's claim that in the recent offensive in the Plain of Jars area in early 1970 the Pathet Lao played only an insignificant role. In support of this claim, American military sources in Vientiane cite only one bit of evidence, namely, captured prisoners. As noted, 8 North Vietnamese were reported captured (according to the Lao officers in charge of prisoners). The American military claims that no Pathet Lao prisoners were taken. However, Americans who have spoken to soldiers of the Royal Lao Army on the spot in Sam Thong say they report that Pathet Lao prisoners were taken. There is also a report, attributed to a source within the United States Embassy, that 20 to 30 Pathet Lao prisoners were taken but were inducted at once into the CIA Clandestine Army. From such numbers (8, 20 to 30) one can conclude very little. However the proportions seem reasonable, given that American military sources speak of 40,000–50,000 Pathet Lao troops, about half in northern Laos.

Informed observers who have attempted to sift through what information is available speculate that there may be at most 5,000 North Vietnamese combat troops involved in the fighting in Laos—a figure which may be compared with the 5,000 Thai combat troops reported (see page 159), the unknown thousands of Americans involved directly in bombing and ground operations, and the other forces reported to be involved in the American operations.

The Pathet Lao claim that there are 1,200 American Green Berets fighting in Laos. This is denied by the Americans. The Pathet Lao also claim that the CIA Clandestine Army includes tribesmen brought in from Burma and Thailand as well as the Chinese Nationalist troops that remain in northern Laos.[42] Such reports are taken seriously by informed observers in Laos, some of whom note that the multi-ethnic character of the Vang Pao Clandestine Army must require American coordination and control down to the field level.

Interviews with defectors give some further information on the respective military forces. One, a soldier with the Deuane ("left-leaning") neutralists who defected in early January 1970 in the Plain of Jars, reports that there were five Vietnamese advisers in his battalions, none at the company level. The five spoke very good Lao because they were born in Laos or Thailand. He reports 2,000 to 3,000 Pathet Lao troops in the Plain of Jars, of whom only two or three defected, and about the same number of North Vietnamese. In the elite sapper units there were more Vietnamese than Laotians. The Vietnamese advisers, he reports, had no special privi-

leges, but lived just like the Laotian soldiers. He describes the Deuane and
Pathet Lao soldiers as dedicated nationalists, with excellent fighting spirit:

> But, you know, the Pathet Lao soldiers have a large point of view.
> They think about their country, they love their country, and they
> want progress for the whole nation. They do not think about them-
> selves personally until their country has been freed. Everyone must
> have his freedom before they can think about their own personal
> desires.

Asked about money, he said that the Pathet Lao soldiers don't care too
much about the fact that they are so poor:

> You see, they are fighting for their freedom and progress, and the free-
> dom and progress of their country. They don't care if they have much
> money, or little money, or even whether they die or not. They only
> care about their country.

Asked whether they understand why they are fighting, he replied:

> Oh yes, you see there are classes all the time. Also, the officers are
> always supposed to talk with their troops and explain to them what the
> war is all about. Every soldier in the Pathet Lao army understands
> very clearly what he is fighting for.

The Lao colonel in charge of the camp had a somewhat different view of
the matter. He believed that a Pathet Lao defector would fight just as well
for the Royal Lao Army, for one reason:

> [He] defects with his family. In this case we keep the family on our side
> and send the husband to be a soldier. He can't do any mischief
> because we have his family.
>
> They will fight all right. You see, first we have their families. Also
> we give them a lot of money. This encourages them to fight. Then,
> also, there is one important thing you must understand. These sol-
> diers have no education. They don't know what they're fighting for.
> They are with the Pathet Lao, and the Pathet Lao give them a gun and
> tell them to fight the enemy. So they do. On our side, it is the same.
> We tell them they must go to combat the Pathet Lao, and they do.
>
> To tell the truth, really, it's all a question of force. Whichever side
> is stronger, they will fight for it. If you force them to fight well, they
> will.

Later, in response to a query as to why the other side fights better than the Royal Lao forces, he said:

> Well, it is largely a question of explaining. The other side is very patient. They always explain to each soldier what he is doing, to encourage him. They send out many agents to talk to everyone, to keep talking and talking until they convince them. One man can spend all today and tomorrow and the next day, just talking to convince one other man. But our side [laughs]. All we do is talk on the radio, all the time, blah, blah, blah. But the radio is no good. It just goes in one ear and out the other. To convince people you have to talk with them personally.

American government sources, though naturally highly antagonistic, give a not dissimilar picture. From them one can also derive some idea of life in Pathet Lao areas, as interpreted by hostile observers. The Embassy in Vientiane supplied two documents by Edwin T. McKeithen, whom they described as one of their outstanding specialists on the Pathet Lao.[43] He writes:

> One of the most fundamental alterations [the Pathet Lao] seek in the Lao personality is the addition of persuasion and guilt to traditional authority as means of social control. P.L. cadres are urged to reason, to question and to discuss with villagers until the villagers agree with the P.L. viewpoint. Direct orders are not enough; people must be "taught" until they genuinely believe in what they are doing. At the same time, a villager who cheats or commits crimes against the state must be enlightened until he feels guilty for his actions. This guilt must arise from an internalized higher morality and not from a simple feeling of shame or loss of face among fellows.

These techniques he describes as the introduction of "the rather foreign concepts of persuasion and guilt ... as mechanisms of social control." McKeithen does not explain what he would regard as more humane or enlightened methods, nor does he explain wherein he objects to the goals of the Pathet Lao effort to transform Lao society:

> They have pressed for economic equality by introducing progressive taxation and discouraging the conspicuous consumption that establishes a wealthy villager's status. They have almost eliminated the "wasted resources" that are spent on bouns [Buddhist ceremonies],

marriages, funerals and traditional celebrations.[44] They have taken initial steps toward the communalization of property by establishing "public" padi [rice paddies], by closely controlling livestock sales and slaughter and by introducing public ownership of livestock in the school system…. The status of women has also been altered, as they have been given greater responsibility in administrative affairs and have assumed jobs traditionally restricted to men…. [They have set up] "youth organization[s]" devoted to lofty principles and dedicated to the advancement of long-range goals.

Being fair-minded, McKeithen does not limit himself to these comments, which he apparently regards as negative, judging by the paragraph that follows:

Finally, we should note the favorable aspects of P.L. rule as reported by the refugees. They favored the ideas of adult literacy and agricultural development but not the ways that the P.L. had been carrying them out. They also spoke favorably of the virtual elimination of official corruption.

Later on, he describes Pathet Lao measures to improve agriculture (use of fertilizers and irrigation, directed by North Vietnamese technicians); establishment of co-ops and local control of commerce, displacing the former Chinese and Vietnamese merchants[45]; progressive taxation to support teachers and medical personnel and a basic tax (15 percent after exemptions) "to help the state"; educational reforms, including primary schooling in virtually all villages and the introduction of textbooks which "emphasize hygiene and better agricultural practices, as well as self-denial, communal endeavor and solidarity against U.S. imperialism"; adult literacy programs; improved medical services; prohibition of polygamy and outlawing of the practice of bride abduction in Meo areas; and so on.

In his study of the role of North Vietnamese cadres, McKeithen also emphasizes their reliance on "patient counsel rather than direct command," their "softest of soft-sell approaches in dealing with their Lao counterparts," their "deep faith in the efficacy of endless persuasion" and in "the spirit of brotherhood that should bond their relationship." He claims that "virtually all important policy decisions are made by the NVN cadres, but in such a way that the decisions appear to be the work of Lao officials." However, he admits that he has very little evidence, since the refugees on whose testimony the report is based had little contact with Vietnamese advisers. The Vietnamese keep to themselves, even raising their own food. He reports that Vietnamese served as political advisers at higher levels, and that economic and other advisers work also at lower levels in giving technical assistance and as teachers. North Vietnamese products are also available at co-op stores, another way "in which their influence is felt." In listing government officials in Xieng Khouang Province he cites three North Vietnamese out of seventeen at the higher (Khoueng Group) level (one a "group representative," one an adviser, and one in charge of irrigation) and none out of fourteen at the lower (Muong) level.[46]

McKeithen claims that one of the goals of the North Vietnamese is "to annex Laos and to till its underpopulated land." Searching diligently through his material, I can find three bits of "confirmatory evidence" for this judgment. One is a "brief entry" in a diary of a North Vietnamese major found on the Plain of Jars, which states: "[We must] help Laos without restriction, but we have to keep Laos with us to realize permanent duty of [our] volunteer groups, [to] provide land, [to] marry natives, and to be settled in Laos." Second, "the North Vietnamese have requested permission from the NLHS to move in 20,000 families—dependents of the NVA troops in Laos." The request was turned down by the NLHS, and the plan apparently was not implemented. Finally, the North Vietnamese advisers were instrumental in instituting a second rice harvest and extensive irrigation projects, and McKeithen "cannot help but feel" that this is in anticipation of North Vietnamese migration, since there is so much unused land. Since McKeithen's papers are obviously propaganda documents of the American government, I assume that he made as strong a case as he could for his conclusion, which clearly must be regarded as without serious support.

The RAND Corporation has also published an extensive study attempting to demonstrate North Vietnamese domination of the Pathet Lao. Since it is accessible, I will not comment at length. The authors give a short summary of Pathet Lao social and economic changes, emphasizing the moderation of such efforts; "the ideal of an 'anti-imperialist, anti-feudalist, and progressive, democratic Laos'"; the "determined effort to raise the level of social consciousness and to instill ambition in the people"; educational programs; and, "the most drastic changes," the stress on "the need for equality of opportunity and close cooperation among all ethnic groups." They conclude that "Communist practice appears to live up to these principles." As to the Vietnamese advisers, they

> provide experienced, disciplined personnel who add competence to the operations of their Lao associates. We have found that these Vietnamese advisers are widely respected by the Lao for their dedication to duty. By their example, by on-the-job training, and by guidance, generally tactful, they goad the less vigorous Lao into better performance.[47]

They also provide medical and technical aid, and have trained native Lao, making "a beginning ... in developing indigenous technical skills." Their "doctrine places great emphasis on winning over the population ... one would expect considerable tension between the Lao and their Vietnamese mentors ... but we were struck by how successful the Vietnamese were in keeping such resentment at a minimum." A former Pathet Lao officer "spoke frankly about the respect that the Vietnamese advisers had gained among the Lao troops":

> The troops in Laos very much respected the Vietnamese advisers. They tried to give them good food, but the Vietnamese advisers wouldn't accept the food. They ate the same food as the soldiers, and stayed with them. The Lao officers, and some soldiers, seemed to be very grateful for their assistance.[48]

The information on North Vietnamese training is of some interest. Langer and Zasloff report an interview with a former second lieutenant who attended Thai Nguyen Technical School in North Vietnam for two years, 1961–1963, in "a class of 165 students, including Meo, Kha, and lowland Lao from fourteen Lao provinces ... [who] were taught auto mechanics, weapons repair, and electrical generator maintenance." Another informant had received five years of medical training (1959–1964) near Hanoi, along with 90 other Lao and 30 Vietnamese. The training, Langer and Zasloff claim, has a Maoist orientation: "It is unsophisticated and appeals primarily to the emotions of the Lao youth." As evidence, they quote this statement by a former Pathet Lao officer:

I was repeatedly told that I was the owner of Laos. Laos is a beautiful country, with an abundance of rivers and streams and natural resources. The Lao people could not do anything to use these resources because of the aggression and oppression of foreign countries. The French, for instance, had ruled Laos for more than sixty years. As the owner of the country and a member of the Issara, I should fight for freedom. Members of the Issara should never surrender.

They told us that now the principal enemy of the Lao people is the American imperialists. They said that the French had already withdrawn from Laos; and that the Americans seized the opportunity to dominate Laos by using Katay Sasorith as their tool. At that time there were no American troops in Laos—but later on the Lao troops would be commanded by Americans. From squad and platoon leader up to the commander in chief would be Americans. And so the country would be under the rule of the American imperialists.[49]

Langer and Zasloff do not explain wherein this approach is "Maoist," nor do they elaborate on their conception of a less emotional, more sophisticated approach.

They also note that in two decades there have been no defections of Lao Communist leaders.[50]

In discussing Pathet Lao social and economic programs with American Embassy officials, I had the impression that they were perhaps favorably impressed with what the Pathet Lao had done and might achieve, were it not for the "North Vietnamese aggression" which, they argue, is the cause of the problems of Laos. One agreed that the Pathet Lao educational reforms were particularly good, but said that the Royal Lao Government was now imitating these programs, specifically the adult literacy program. I tried to check this information with reporters and with Lao residents of Vientiane who were quite familiar with government activities. The responses ranged between skepticism and ridicule. I met no one outside the Embassy who believed that the RLG was capable of implementing such a program. Since I did not have the time to inquire further, I must leave it at that.

The American Embassy was also helpful in providing me with documentation to support their claim that North Vietnamese aggression is the fundamental problem of Laos. In addition to the documents cited above, they directed me to reports of the RAND Corporation and the International Control Commission. Particularly conclusive, they argued, was an ICC investigation of a complaint from the RLG on October 2, 1964, reporting the capture of three North Vietnamese prisoners.[51] The investigation confirmed the report. It concluded that these prisoners had entered Laos as members of complete North Vietnamese army units from February to September 1964, in groups ranging from 50 to 650 soldiers. The report also states:

> The Commission notes with interest that this was the first time, since the Commission's reconvening in 1961, that it had been brought to the attention of the Commission that prisoners, alleged to have been North Vietnamese, had been captured by the armed forces of the Royal Laotian Government and were available for interrogation.

The report opens by presenting the letter of October 2 from the RLG containing the complaints which it investigated, and also a letter of September 28 from Phoumi Vongvichit, Secretary of the Neo Lao Hak Sat at Vientiane, alleging that American aircraft based in South Vietnam had attacked Laotian territory and parachuted South Vietnamese military personnel into Laos, three of whom were captured (two identified by name). The latter charge is discussed in "a separate message," presumably *Message No. 36*. On returning to the United States I tried to obtain *Message No. 36*, but without success. I have been informed that it has not been declassified (by the British government). Though this fact naturally arouses suspicion, nevertheless it is likely that the message is perfunctory.

A second ICC document reports the investigation of a complaint that the Officers' School of the Royal Army at Dong Hene in southern Laos was attacked on March 8–9, 1965, by a combined Pathet Lao and North Vietnamese force. The investigation confirmed the allegation. Most of the captured prisoners testified that they were on their way to South Vietnam.[52]

The final supporting document is a report of interviews with a North Vietnamese adviser to a Pathet Lao battalion, Mai Dai Hap, who defected in December 1966.[53] The informant was a captain in the North Vietnamese army and a member of the Lao Dong (Workers) Party of

North Vietnam. He claims to have been one of thirty North Vietnamese assigned to Laos in February 1964 to serve as advisers. He trained the personnel of a Lao battalion and directed its operations. He served in the vicinity of Nam Tha near the Chinese and Burmese borders. In February 1966, his unit was sent to Muong Long in the area of the Co, a highland tribal minority, in northwest Laos, near Burma, to defend a Pathet Lao base that was under attack by RLG forces. This was a region in which "the Vietnamese and Pathet Lao had built resistance bases against the French, so that the Co people welcomed them heartily, especially after seeing the Vietnamese with the unit." Because of discouragement over the hardships of combat, a feeling that he had failed in his leadership, concern that the enemy—now supplied with artillery and bombers—was growing in strength and receiving support from the lowlanders, and a series of personal problems including a second marriage, he defected in December 1966.

Captain Hap reports that in addition to military tasks he had a political program with the following topics:

1. Objectives and tasks of the Laotian revolution
2. The land of Laos is beautiful and rich, the population of Laos is industrious; why are the Laotian people suffering?
3. Who is the enemy of the Laotian people?
4. The tasks and nature of the Laotian Liberation Army.

One comment of Hap's that is frequently quoted by American sources is this:

Generally speaking, everything is initiated by the North Vietnamese advisers, be it important or unimportant. If the North Vietnamese advisory machinery were to get stuck, the Pathet Lao machinery would be paralyzed.

This exhausts the documentary evidence that I was able to obtain. In reading these materials, one is struck by the low-keyed and generally constructive approach of the North Vietnamese, the limited evidence for actual North Vietnamese control over the Pathet Lao, and the gulf between the evidence and the claims it is used to support. It is, after all, hardly surprising that there were North Vietnamese troops in southern Laos a month after the regular bombing of North Vietnam was initiated (the Dong Hene incident). Nor is it surprising that North Vietnamese advisers should have arrived in northern Laos in early 1964 (note that the first complaint to the ICC was in October 1964), in view of the events outlined above. Recall that regular bombardment of northern Laos from Thai sanctuaries began in May 1964. Recall as well that the CIA established bases along the North Vietnamese frontier for sabotage and guerrilla action, as well as to guide the all-weather bombardment of North Vietnam.[54] It is interesting to compare the North Vietnamese involvement with the American program, aspects of which were discussed earlier. Also remarkable is the barely suppressed outrage over the North Vietnamese activities. How dare they assist friendly forces, on their border, that the United States is determined to destroy?

Suppose that the Pathet Lao were to take over Laos completely. What then would be the North Vietnamese role? Asked about this, the Lao defector quoted earlier (page 167) said that he expects them to leave when they finish their mission of helping the Pathet Lao: "It is just like when the Chinese went to help the Koreans. After they had won the war, they left." The urban intellectual whose remarks I reported earlier (pages 149–150) was less sure. He thought that Laotian independence would always be threatened by North Vietnam, Thailand, and China, though he felt there was a fair chance that all might agree that Laos should be left as a neutral buffer. Prince Souvanna Phouma, in an interview with us, had no doubts about the North Vietnamese intention to conquer Laos. He explains as follows:

> North Vietnam wants to colonize Laos with Vietnamese because their country is too overpopulated. It's obvious. Look at their flag with its five-pointed star. One is for Tonkin, one for Annam, one for Cochin China,[55] one for Laos, and one for Cambodia.[56]

He offered no other argument, apparently regarding this as conclusive. (Applying this reasoning to the American flag …)

A North Vietnamese spokesman described the interest of his country in Laos as purely strategic:

> It is on our western border. For our own security, we cannot allow Laos to turn into a base for the Americans to threaten us. You know that the Americans have been using Laos as a forward base both for

themselves and the Thais, and have guided their planes for bombing us from Laos.... Laos has been a historic invasion route into North Vietnam. The French took Laos first, originally, before setting out to colonize us. At the end of World War II they went back in and took Laos first, then used route 9 to transport men and materials to take Hue, and also route 7. Our only concern for Laos is that it remain strictly neutral. We cannot allow Laos to be a base for the Americans, with their planes, their soldiers, their special forces, their CIA, their Thais and other mercenaries.

Naturally, North Vietnam regards "the Lao territory bordering on North Vietnam, particularly in the provinces of Phong Saly, Luang Prabang, Sam Neua, and Xieng Khouang, as essential to its security and will strive to ensure that these areas are not controlled by hostile forces."[57] China also has an obvious security interest in these areas. As long as they are under attack by American forces or by forces which North Vietnam and China can regard, with justification, as American puppet forces, one can expect a continuing North Vietnamese involvement. It is difficult to see why North Vietnam should attempt to conquer Laos, thus being forced to control a hostile population and coming face to face with the Thai. Nor can I find any serious evidence for such an intent.

The aims of the Thai in Laos are also a subject of much speculation. The Pathet Lao view is expressed by Phoumi Vongvichit:

> Thai expansionism was conceived by the Thai bourgeoisie after it came to power in 1932. Its aim is to unify all countries inhabited by Thai people (South China, North Viet Nam, Laos and Northeastern Burma) into "Greater Thailand" around a core formed by present Thailand. The immediate target of this expansionism is Laos. The Thai feudalists had conquered almost half of Lao territory and five-sixths of its population had been assimilated. The Thai bourgeoisie, although none too powerful, has major trumpcards at its disposal for the carrying out of its designs on Laos: territorial bases, community of race, knowledge of the country, language, culture, etc.[58]

The Thai are also said to fear potential Lao expansionism, not through direct military aggression, but through guerrilla activity in northern and northeastern Thailand, which contain many more Lao than there are in Laos in addition to many dissident mountain tribesmen. The Meo, many of whom are organized by the CIA in Laos in the Clandestine Army,[59] are regarded in Thailand as "Communist sympathizers," and there is a concerted effort by the Thai military to remove them from their mountain homes by force. Reuters reports[60] that "Government authorities are uprooting thousands of Meo hill tribesmen from their homes in northern Thailand and moving them away from growing Communist influence there, official sources said today." According to reports in Vientiane, this is a bit of an understatement. It is reported that large-scale aerial attacks, with strafing, napalm, and explosives, have been used to drive Meo tribesmen into the valleys where, many observers believe, they cannot survive as an organized community. Some refer to this as a policy of virtual genocide. The future of the Meo in Laos is also grim.

Thailand is deeply involved in the Indochina war, with troops fighting for the United States in South Vietnam, Laos, and Cambodia. Its troops are—to an unknown extent—paid and "advised" by the United States.[61] Furthermore, Thailand has been a major American sanctuary for its war in Indochina since at least early 1964, when the bombing of Laos from Thai bases began. According to a map of military operations supplied by the Pathet Lao, the United States maintains B-52 bases at Utapao in the south and Khon Kaen in north central Thailand, while F-111 bombers are based in Taklee, north of Bangkok. These are used for strategic bombing in Laos and Vietnam. Bombing is also carried out with F-105s, F-4s, and other aircraft from Korat in central Thailand, and Ubon and Udorn near the border of Laos. Other smaller bases are also listed at Thoeng and Chieng Mai in the far north and elsewhere near the Laotian border. The Thai bases are also used for the bombardment of Cambodia, reported recently to be using 15,000-pound bombs for the first time. Thai jets are also reported on their way to Cambodian bases. Therefore naturally, the Thai are concerned about guerrilla activities in Thailand and neighboring countries, in part a response to their involvement in the American war in Indochina. According to recent, still unconfirmed reports from Vientiane, American "advisers" are leading Thai units in counterinsurgency operations now underway in northeast Thailand, about fifty miles from the Laotian border. It is a fair guess that information about these operations will be forthcoming in congressional investigations in five or ten years.

To return to Laos: according to American Embassy sources, over a million people in this nation of some three million remain in the areas controlled by the Pathet Lao. Harrison Salisbury, in his report from North Vietnam, quoted a foreign Communist visitor to these areas:

> You cannot imagine what it is like in the headquarters of these people. Never is there any halt in the bombing. Not at night. Not by day. One day we were in the cave. The bombing went on and on. The toilet was in another cave only 20 yards away. We could not leave. We could not even run the 20 yards. It was too dangerous.[62]

According to the same report, the Pathet Lao had set up a hospital, a printing press, a small textile mill, a bakery, and a shop for making arms and ammunition in the caves. The bombardment was said to include guided missiles that could dive into a cave, as well as high explosives and antipersonnel weapons. The people came out only at dusk and dawn to try to farm, but the planes attacked any visible target, even trails and cultivated fields. These reports attracted little attention, presumably because the source was not believed.

In June 1968, Jacques Decornoy of *Le Monde* traveled to Sam Neua Province and confirmed these reports.[63] For some excerpts, see Chapter 2.

Decornoy's harrowing account of life under perhaps the most intensive bombardment in history received little attention in the United States, but it did not go entirely unmentioned. Paul F. Langer, discussing Pathet Lao efforts at economic development for the RAND Corporation, observes that "The claims of substantial advances do not appear to be borne out by the testimony of refugees or sympathetic observers,"[64] referring to Decornoy's reports as his sole evidence. He did not go on to point out that "substantial advances" might be a bit difficult in an area where everything has been destroyed by aerial attack, where civilians can rarely emerge from caves without being torn to shreds by the constant bombardment.

Reports from eyewitness observers have also appeared in the Soviet press. Julian Semionov arrived in Sam Neua shortly before Decornoy. He reports that "everything is burned and ruined" and life is confined to caves. All targets having been destroyed, the bombing is simply "plowing up the ground" in selected sections. Even candlelight brings bombers, he reports.

He quotes a thirteen-year-old girl who tells how phosphorous bombs are used at cave entrances; "the smoke of the phosphorous bombs slowly crawls into a cave," blinding those inside and causing loss of consciousness and death. Those who escape the cave are attacked with high-explosive bombs.[65]

A Pathet Lao defector interviewed at Sam Thong reports that the town of Sam Neua was destroyed in 1965.

In Hanoi, I spoke to a member of a non-Communist embassy who had just returned from a trip to Sam Neua. He too reported that virtually nothing remains above ground, but that life continues in caves.

Probably the same is true of areas of southern Laos that are outside of government control. A Lao commander of a bomber squadron, interviewed in March 1970, designated large areas that are free-strike zones where all targets have been destroyed, though thousands of civilians remain in the area, living with the Pathet Lao in the forest. He assumes that anyone who stays with the Pathet Lao or the North Vietnamese is the enemy, civilian or not.

Some 700,000 refugees are said to have fled to government-controlled areas. The most recent arrivals are from the Plain of Jars. As noted earlier, this area was under Pathet Lao control from 1964 until 1969. In a fall offensive, the CIA Clandestine Army conquered the plain after an intensive bombardment, the first large shift in territorial boundaries since the outbreak of the civil war. When Communist forces were about to retake the Plain of Jars in February 1970, the population was evacuated and the area turned into a zone of devastation. It is estimated that about 15,000 refugees were taken, mostly by air, to Vientiane, where they are now scattered in refugee camps. Just prior to the Communist recapture of the Plain of Jars in February 1970, Henry Kamm reported:

> A flight low over the southern part of the plain—until now off limits to the press—confirmed the devastation. The only houses visible are those in refugee centers like Lat Sen and Khangsi, built after the Communists withdrew and the bombing stopped. Bomb craters pockmark the valleys, knolls and ridges of the plain as densely as the most embattled regions of South Vietnam.[66]

It is estimated that 150,000 people lived in this area prior to the bombardment.

I spent several days visiting a refugee camp near Vientiane. The camp consists of five long sheds, each with an aisle between two raised floors. Each family has about 15 square feet of space, without partitions, set off only by posts. There are perhaps 100 people housed in each shed. There are many children and old men and women, a few young mothers, some young men who were wounded in the fighting, and a few other young adults. Many observers believe, and have reported, that most of the young people joined the Pathet Lao before the evacuation. These refugees had been in the village for about two months.

The refugees give the impression of severe demoralization. Only rarely are any working. There has apparently been only a limited attempt to clear land for cultivation, though it is likely that they will stay in this area. Actually, they do not know what will happen to them. The government provides them with a rice ration, but little further care, and no information. Promises to reimburse them for lost property or to change their Pathet Lao money for government currency have not been fulfilled. The refugees asked—some begged—to have their money exchanged. Some said that they would starve otherwise, and this is possible, since apparently they have no food except for the rice ration and what they can find in the forest. But these people are not mendicants. They were, in fact, probably the most well-to-do of the Lao peasantry. Some had careful records of their possessions. One sixty-year-old man who had owned forty cows and nine buffalo estimated the total value of his belongings at about $3,600. Another, who showed us detailed records written up for the RLG but never honored, estimated his possessions at $5,000 before the bombing, Such reports were not unique, though some of the refugees had been very poor. Some had brought with them good clothes, occasionally a sewing machine or other possessions. All spoke with great longing of their wish to return to their homes in the Plain of Jars, with its fertile and abundant land, its cool climate, distant hills, rivers, and streams.

The refugees were acquainted with our translator from previous visits, and were superficially friendly, though wary. As I have already mentioned, they naturally assumed that we were connected with the American government, and they obviously were not going to tell us anything that might lead to some new catastrophe. One feels rather uncomfortable in taking extensive interviews. The refugees have good reason to dissimulate, and at the same time they are reluctant to be uncooperative. It is a simple matter, with repeated questioning, to discover inconsistencies and even absurdities in their answers, but it is not pleasant to take on the role of a police agent. Quite apart from this, it is heartrending to see their demoralization and despair, or to watch an old woman crouching down in unaccustomed supplication. Nor is it pleasant to see the children, many of them sitting quietly hour after hour in the oppressive heat and dust of the camp.

The first story told by virtually every refugee was simple and straightforward. They came to the government side because they hated the Pathet Lao, who were oppressive. Why did the Pathet Lao oppress the people? "I don't know; I guess they are just crazy," one man told us. Another man, who had been a rather poor farmer in their former village, spoke openly and in quite favorable terms about the Pathet Lao. As he went on, a small group collected and listened quietly. A very alert young man began to interrupt, correcting our informant and giving the negative, rather stereotyped answers to which we had already become accustomed. Within moments, our informant's answers also shifted. The same sequence was repeated in other interviews. We finally realized that as long as this man was present, there was no point in continuing the discussion. We were able to continue in a useful way only when he was occupied elsewhere. Who he was, of course, I have no idea—perhaps a Pathet Lao cadre. Certainly the reasonable approach, from their point of view, was to appear to be pro-government and antagonistic to the Pathet Lao.

We spoke to one young woman who had fled to the government side some years earlier, with several other young people. Asked why, she said it was because of the porterage that they were forced to do for the Pathet Lao. We asked whether she fled after her village was destroyed by bombing, "No, before," she answered. An older man interrupted: "No, after, you know, there were many people killed in the bombing." She then said, "Yes, we escaped after the bombing." "Were you afraid of the bombing or the porterage?" "Both," she answered.

Every refugee with whom I spoke said that everything he knew of—his own village, and all dwellings within several day's journey—had been destroyed by bombardment before they were evacuated. Prior to 1968 the bombing of the Plain of Jars was sporadic. In April 1968 it became more intensive, and the villagers soon had to leave their villages and dig trenches and tunnels in the surrounding forest. At first they were able to farm sometimes, mainly at night, but this became impossible as the bombing increased in intensity. One man told us that the people of his village had been forced to move eight or nine times, deeper and deeper into the forest into new systems of trenches, as the bombing extended in scope. He reported that by April 1969, his village had been destroyed by bombs and napalm. The Pathet Lao showed them how to dig trenches and tunnels, and identified the types of planes. Another reported that in February 1969 the bombing destroyed everything in the village. The first bombing of a nearby village was in June 1967. Later the bombing was constant, and the people lived in tunnels in the hills, coming out only on days when the bombing stopped. Our translator, who had taken about three hundred interviews with refugees, informed us that these stories were typical. Every refugee to whom he had spoken reported that everything he knew of personally or had heard about was destroyed by bombardment before the evacuation.

In September 1969, the Vang Pao army conquered the plain. The Meo soldiers were undisciplined and killed many of the cows and buffalo. Many of the young men joined the Pathet Lao; others were taken into the Vang Pao army. We asked why the Meo soldiers killed the cattle. One man said the soldiers told the villagers that they didn't want cattle left to nourish the Pathet Lao. The refugees were concentrated in new villages—strategic hamlets, apparently—when the Vang Pao army came. Then, when it was clear that the plain could not be held, they were evacuated,

The primary complaint against the Pathet Lao had to do with the compulsory porterage. Prior to the bombing, there was very little porterage, but when the bombing began, the Pathet Lao soldiers moved to remote areas and could no longer use trucks, as before. "The planes made the soldiers disperse, and they forced us to do porterage," one refugee said. One claimed that the porterage, had begun as early as 1964. Others gave later dates. All, when pressed, said that the porterage began when the soldiers were forced by the bombing to move to inaccessible places.

Few of the refugees had ever seen any Vietnamese, though one informant, when interrupted by the young man whom I mentioned earlier, agreed with this man that the Pathet Lao were really Vietnamese who spoke Lao. A moment before, in answer to the question, "What kind of people are they?" he had answered, "Oh, they are our own Lao people." He was unwilling to talk any longer at that point. The refugees did see some Pathet Lao soldiers, but for the most part they too stayed in the forests and hills.

There were other complaints about the Pathet Lao. One relatively rich farmer said he could not live comfortably with the Pathet Lao even if the bombing were to end, so that no more porterage would be necessary:

> They would take us to study all the time. There was no money, no commerce. They only respect you if you have torn clothing, so we have to wear torn clothing all the time.

The poor farmer I mentioned earlier gave a more sympathetic account. He described a mild land reform in 1965:

> They told the people who had a lot of land to give some to the people who had only a little. I didn't get any, and none was taken away. I had enough. They only took land to give to the really poor. The people from whom they took the land away sometimes were angry. In this case, the Pathet Lao would say, "Look, you have a lot of land and he doesn't have any. Do you want him to die?" They always explained. They rarely put anyone in jail. Only if they explained for a long time and they still didn't give any land. The people who were taken away were not put in prison. They were taken to Phonesavan to study and work. If a person caused trouble they also took him to study. Also lazy people. They would teach them not to steal or your friends will kill you. Being lazy or not giving up your land is stealing from your friends. The Pathet Lao never yelled. They really did well. They really acted nicely. They never stole. Never took anyone or beat anyone.

This informant had never been to school and was quite pleased with the Pathet Lao educational reforms. He said that the teachers were taken to Phonesavan to be taught and then returned to the village. Other boys joined the Pathet Lao to be soldiers, and some went to the towns for medical training or to join the civil administration. No Pathet Lao lived permanently in the village, he reported.

He was not sure what the Pathet Lao taught the teachers, but when they returned they taught only in Lao, no longer in French. Everyone was taught to read, the women in particular.

> The only people who didn't study were those who were blind. I knew how to read. I studied arithmetic. Before I didn't know anything. Before, the teacher didn't work as much. Now he worked much more. The teacher wasn't happy because he was working all the time. [General laughter]

We interviewed two of the village teachers. They said that when the Pathet Lao came in 1964, after driving the Kong Le forces off the plain, they took the teachers to the Phonesavan for ten days. They instructed them in teaching methods, and told them they must teach in Lao, not French. "They explained that Lao is our own language and Laos is our country and we don't need foreign languages." They also gave them political education.

> They taught us that under the French a French-style education was taught because they wanted people to love France. But now they taught us that our country was liberated and we have a liberated style of education and education would teach people to love their country. Education was now for everyone, not just for the rich. In the old days education was mainly in the towns and cities. Many villages had no schools. When the Pathet Lao came in they trained many teachers and many more people were educated, though schooling was still not universal.

Language teaching and mathematics were made more difficult than before, and four grades were to be instituted for everyone. The teacher was required to conduct an adult literacy program on Saturday and Sunday. Villagers who knew how to read also became literacy instructors. They described the literacy campaign as very good and virtually universal. The texts had political content, and dealt with agriculture and practical matters. Before, there had been just mechanical teaching of reading, with no content. Under the Pathet Lao, the texts dealt with agriculture and livestock and loving your country. The political content was something like this:

"Before, under the French, we had to pay taxes and money was sent to France. Now we're building our own country and are not working for foreign people."

The intention was to extend education to grades 5 to 7, but this program could not be carried out, because of the war.

An older man, formerly quite well off, added that the Pathet Lao made them study before work, and took some men from the village to study.

> They taught us mainly agriculture. One must produce more. Build the economy. One man should do the work of ten. If you produce more, you can exchange it for clothes and money. Then we can exchange the produce with other countries.

In theory, he said, it was a good idea, but he wasn't too happy about it, particularly because of the taxation. The Pathet Lao took 15 percent of everything above subsistence. This was for the soldiers, teachers, and medical personnel whom they trained and returned to the village. Others were taken to the town to study dancing and singing, the traditional folklore, and the national culture. This informant was rather skeptical about the medical training. He felt that it didn't do much good.

In Vientiane I was shown a collection of Pathet Lao texts. Parts were translated for me, and they did seem of remarkably high quality. Apparently, American officials are also impressed with the Pathet Lao educational program, and, as I noted earlier, they may be attempting to imitate it. A RAND study reports that "1967 constituted something of a landmark in Lao education: an American-financed secondary school got underway in Vientiane. Here, for the first time in the country's history, most of the instruction will be offered in the Lao language rather than in the traditional French."[67] The truth is that this new secondary school will be copying what the Pathet Lao has already accomplished in the villages of Laos—full teaching in the native language.

A refugee from the town of Phonesavan itself gave us a good deal more information on life under the Pathet Lao as it appeared to a participant who was willing to talk freely.[68] As he reports the recent history of the region, the Pathet Lao and the Kong Le neutralists worked together until after the Geneva agreements of 1962, when Kong Le's right-hand man, Ketsana, began to confiscate American arms and divert them to right-wing elements. This led to a split among the neutralists, and the Pathet Lao gave their support to the left-wing neutralists under Colonel Deuane, taking over the Plain of Jars in 1964. Prior to that, these groups cooperated in a land reform that eliminated absentee landownership and in setting up a legitimate local administration.

The activists, in this period, were intellectuals from Vientiane and Sam Neua who had studied in France. The Pathet Lao tended more to live among the people and recruited peasants from the area, while the intellectuals were, for the most part, with Kong Le. At first the Pathet Lao kept their identity secret. Later they began speaking more openly to people whom they felt they could trust, and built confidence through long, patient explanation. They always spoke nicely (this he reiterated over and over), and gave long explanations before suggesting any action. They lived like the poor peasants—for example, they refused to ride in trucks as the Kong Le soldiers did. They were very cautious and prudent.

The Pathet Lao cadres encouraged the people not to be afraid of important men or to use honorific forms of address:

> The Pathet Lao changed many things. They helped the villagers farm rice and build houses, and gave rice to people who didn't have enough. They changed the status of women. Women became equal to men. They became nurses and soldiers. Wives were not afraid of husbands any more.

At first some husbands got angry, but they were told that there was to be no more oppression: "Look, she's human, you don't have special rights."

Before, everything was for hire. After the Pathet Lao came, money wasn't necessary. They tried to induce cooperation among the villagers and to bring families to cooperate in agricultural work. They used no force, but tried to shame people into helping if they refused, to encourage them to see that all would benefit from cooperation.

They formed "awakening groups" of cadres from the village that were responsible for encouraging cooperation and collectivization. By 1967, virtually everyone was involved in collective farming, though they also kept private plots. The cadres never insulted anyone. They were very intelligent and spoke softly. They tried to make you like them. They would never take out guns and money to impress people. In 1967 they suddenly replaced all outsiders with local cadres drawn from the "awakening groups." Many of these had been taken away for training for a month or so.

Each village had a complicated system of organization: political, administrative, defense (police), young boys, young girls, women, cleanliness, education, cooperation. Everyone belonged. They elected their own leaders. There were also technical organizations concerned with irrigation, livestock, agriculture, adult literacy, forestry. Representatives of these groups would deal with experts from the outside in matters such as irrigation.

The first bombing began in May 1964. Phonesavan itself was bombed in 1965. In November 1968–January 1969 it was completely evacuated and destroyed. By September 1969, everything was destroyed. The Vang Pao army came through in September 1969.

In 1964–1965 there were some North Vietnamese soldiers in the vicinity, but very few. By 1969 there were many. The soldiers had a very strict discipline and kept away from the villagers. People felt sorry for them because of their enforced isolation. The Pathet Lao taught them that the North Vietnamese were their friends who had come to give them technical assistance and help them survive. They had enormous respect for the North Vietnamese. To illustrate, our informant told a story of a North Vietnamese irrigation adviser who was condemned to death by the Pathet Lao after he had killed a water buffalo. The people objected and protested to the general, who affirmed the sentence. The man then killed himself. In general, they regarded the North Vietnamese with awe.

The Pathet Lao also taught them not to hate the American pilots, some of whom were captured and led through the town, but only their leaders.[69]

I asked one man of about fifty, who looked strong and healthy, why neither he nor anyone else seemed to be working, why they were just sitting in the sheds when they surely should be preparing to farm. He said:

> Let the war end and we can return to our village. I don't know how to farm here, No one comes to explain or help or tell us how to do it. We don't have the strength to cut down the trees. The government says

nothing. They don't tell us whether we can ever go home. We don't know. All the land has trees or bushes. We are too tired to cut the bushes and the trees. There are no hills or mountains here. It is all flat. When we do *hai* [upland farming] where we come from, the trees all fall in one direction and it was easy to burn them. Here they just fall in all directions. We do not know how to farm here.

In fact, these people know well how to farm in this area, and the work would not be beyond their strength, at least if they had enough to eat. But the impression they give, as this answer indicates, is one of demoralization and hopelessness. The only work that I saw in the camp or the surrounding area was on one visit, when some men and women were constructing private huts with wood that they had cut in the forest. Some women were sewing, and others were cooking or collecting food. For the rest, they sat quietly, their interest aroused somewhat by our visit, but apparently with no plan, no hope for the future.

Other refugee interviews give a similar impression. One collection of interviews was taken with refugees from the southern village of Muong Phine, destroyed by bombing in 1964 with more than 100 killed, many by delayed-action bombs. A villager spoke of the antipersonnel bombs:

> The children used to play with them. The parents couldn't forbid them. They'd just go off into the forest and play. We were told not to go near the bombs by the village and hamlet chiefs. It was the rule, but the children did it anyway.

This village had been under Pathet Lao control since 1960. There was very little porterage until 1964, when the bombing began. Asked about Communist indoctrination, the informant said:

> They used to tell us that we should build ourselves up, work hard, and grow as much rice as possible. They also told us not to go over to the enemy side.

They tried to convince boys not to become monks, saying that people should work, but didn't bother those who went on to do so anyway. One monk said that many of the people who went with the Pathet Lao (about a third of the village) went willingly because they liked the Pathet Lao, but this was hotly denied by the village chief.

The villagers reported seeing no North Vietnamese until after 1964. When the bombing began in 1964, it was largely propeller-driven T-28s, but it shifted to jets and became far more intensive in 1966, and then again at the end of 1969. From 1965 the villagers lived in holes until they fled to a government-controlled city in late 1969.

North Vietnamese prisoners captured in that area report that the bombing did not bother them particularly. They kept far away from visible targets. Pathet Lao defectors also report that the bombing, though troublesome, was not a severe problem to them directly. The defector from the Plain of Jars, quoted earlier, said:

> I was not afraid of the planes. They killed many people, it is true. But for us soldiers it was not so dangerous. When it came low we could shoot it down. When it was up high it couldn't do us very much damage because it didn't know where we were. We had our own methods for hiding. So I wasn't afraid.

Asked whether he hated the pilots, he answered:

> Yes, I hated them. If they only came to shoot at me, I wouldn't care. I was a soldier. But they tried to kill all the villagers. And the villagers are just farmers, they just grow rice. They didn't do anything against the pilots. I am a Lao man. Those villagers are Lao. I must hate the men who try to kill them.

He estimates that for every soldier who was killed, fifty villagers were killed.

From other parts of the country, the same story is heard. Thus a report from Nam Tha in the northwest states that since 1966 villagers in that area have been living in trenches because everything they own has been destroyed and burned. The Pathet Lao representative in Vientiane, Colonel Soth Petrassi, says:

> From the province of Phong Saly at the extreme north to the province of Saravane in the south, everything has been razed. There no longer exist any villages, any peaceful agglomerations. The life in the liberated zones is so terribly difficult that the population must shelter themselves in natural caves or hide in the forests. Movement is restricted to nighttime, school is taught at night, work in the fields is done at night.

From the available information, one must accept this judgment as essentially accurate. A correspondent for the *Far Eastern Economic Review* summarizes as follows:

> For the past two years the US has carried out one of the most sustained bombing campaigns in history against essentially civilian targets in northeastern Laos. The area is a carpet of forest dotted by villages and a few towns. Refugees report that the bombing was primarily directed against their villages. Operating from Thai bases and from aircraft carriers, American jets have destroyed the great majority of villages and towns in the northeast. Severe casualties have been inflicted upon the inhabitants of the region, rice fields have been burned, and roads torn up. Refugees from the Plain of Jars report they were bombed almost daily by American jets last year. They say they spent most of the past two years living in caves or holes.[70]

It is doubtful that any military purpose, in the narrow sense, is served by the destructive bombing. The civilian economy may have been destroyed and thousands of refugees generated, but the Pathet Lao appear to be stronger than ever. If anything, the bombing appears to have improved Pathet Lao morale and increased support among the peasants, who no longer have to be encouraged to hate the Americans. It is exactly as in Vietnam, where, in the first year of the intensive American bombardment in the South (1965), local recruitment for the Viet Cong tripled to about 150,000, according to American sources. And as in Vietnam, the indigenous guerrilla forces are now more dependent on outside assistance as a result of the destruction of the civilian society in which they had their roots. The correspondent quoted above comments:

> By depriving communist forces of indigenous food stores, the bombing has caused them to rely on more dependable supplies from North Vietnam. For all that it has undoubtedly demoralized civilians, refugees report that the bombing has raised the morale of Pathet Lao fighting forces. Unlike most other soldiers in Laos, they finally have a clear idea of what they are fighting for. Refugees also say that volunteers for the Pathet Lao army have doubled … in the last few years. Before, many village youths were reluctant to leave their villages. Now the attitude has become, "better to die as a soldier than to die hiding from the bombing in holes in the ground."[71]

As in Vietnam, there is a military purpose to these tactics in a broader sense. Here again we see the tactic of "forced-draft urbanization" at work (see Chapter 1, section III, and Chapter 2). To fight against a people's war, it is necessary, here too, to eliminate the people, either by killing them, destroying their society, and forcing them into caves, or by "urbanizing" them—driving them into refugee camps or urban centers. Who can tell whether this tactic may not succeed?

We discussed the bombardment with Prince Souvanna Phouma. He simply denied that any destruction is taking place:

> There is no destruction. We only bomb the North Vietnamese. We have "teams" scattered throughout the country. When they see the North Vietnamese convoys they call for bombing. Laos is not like the United States. It is not densely populated, with many big cities. No cities or villages are destroyed. 700,000 refugees have come to our side. There are no people on the other side. Maybe a few huts destroyed, but no settled areas. People flee when they hear that the North Vietnamese are coming.[72]

We mentioned specifically that refugees have told us their villages were destroyed long before they left them. He replied:

> No, no. Sometimes North Vietnamese mix in with the population and we have to make a sacrifice of them and bomb the village, that's true. For example, recently in Paksane some North Vietnamese held a village and it took us three days to dislodge them. In that case unfortunately the villagers got bombed also.

He then showed us a large relief map of Indochina on the wall and repeated, "You see those mountainous areas controlled by the Pathet Lao and the North Vietnamese? Nobody lives there."

According to American figures, over a million people live there, well over a third of the population.

Part of the population of Laos lives in urban centers, Vientiane being the largest. Others live in the Pathet Lao-controlled areas under the conditions I have described. Still others remain in refugee camps. In addition, there are the Meo tribesmen who have been organized by the CIA, and that part of traditional Lao peasant society that is still untouched by the war.

Reports from the Vang Pao army of Meo indicate that they may be nearing the end of their ability to continue fighting. Several years ago, Robert Shaplen quoted Edgar "Pop" Buell, the American who is primarily responsible for the Meo operations:

> A few days ago I was with Vang Pao's officers when they rounded up 300 fresh Meo recruits. Thirty percent of the kids were 14 years old or less and about a dozen were only about 10 years old. Another 30 percent were 15 or 16. The rest were 35 or over. Where were the ones in between? I will tell you, they are all dead. Here were these little kids in their camouflage uniforms that were much too big for them, but they looked real neat, and when the King of Laos talked to them they were proud and cocky as could be. They were eager. Their fathers and brothers had played Indian before them, and now they want to play Indian themselves. But V.P. and I know better. They are too young and are not trained. In a few weeks 90 percent of them will be killed.[73]

Since then, the Vang Pao forces have suffered serious losses, and all credible reports indicate that their situation is far worse. In a recent congressional testimony, Ronald J. Rickenbach, who was AID refugee relief officer in northern Laos for three years, reported: "Now, they are all destitute, as a direct result of the attrition they have had to endure, from the battles we encouraged them to fight."[74] By inciting large numbers of Meo to fight against the Pathet Lao and North Vietnamese, the United States may have brought about their destruction as an organized group.

"Pop" Buell recently reported that "all his friends from his early days in Laos have died in combat."[75] He added: "The best are being killed off in this country and America will never be able to repay them for what they're doing." The American policy of sacrificing the Meo for America's anti-Communist crusade must be regarded, in my opinion, as one of the most profoundly cynical aspects of the American war in Indochina.

To try to get a sense of traditional Laos, we visited a village just a few miles from Vientiane which—incredibly—seems virtually untouched by the war, indeed by the modern age. We spent an evening at the home of an old peasant couple where our guide had lived for several years as an IVS volunteer. When we arrived, the old man was sitting on the large open porch outside the sleeping quarters, carving Buddhist verses on long strips of bamboo, deeply engrossed, unaware of our presence until, after a long conversation with his wife, our guide tapped him on the shoulder to greet him. The man and his wife seated themselves before us and wound knotted strings around our wrists while wishing us health and good fortune. The old woman explained that she had just received these particular strings from a Buddhist monk at a shrine where she had spent several days. Water buffalo, gentle beasts, trudged slowly along the dirt paths, past knots of people talking and laughing in the quiet of early evening. The villagers greeted our guide warmly, joking and chatting with him as we walked through the village. Several were at least half-stoned, contributing to the atmosphere of tranquility and abandon. We had brought some meat for dinner, which the peasant woman cooked. After a leisurely meal with the old couple, we returned, late that evening, to Vientiane.

Superficially, such a village seems a haven of peace in the turmoil and torture of Laos, but there is more to the story. Our guide, who had studied the village with great care, estimated that infant mortality may be as high as 50 percent. Dysentery is endemic, and much of the population is always ill. In fact, as we strolled through the village we saw ceremonies on several porches for those who were ill. There is no sanitary water supply, and very little medical care. The life of the village is less than delightful in many other ways. The old man we visited told us that he walks a long distance to fetch water. This seemed surprising, since there was a large pond nearby. When we walked to the pond, we discovered that it was fenced off, as was a large area surrounding it. Our guide explained that some years back a man had come to the village and simply taken the pond and the surrounding land for himself. When the villagers went to the village chief, they were told that was the way it was to be. The older inhabitants now speak sadly of the days when they could sit beneath the tall trees near the pond, and they complain of the difficulty and inconvenience and the loss of good land, but there is nothing they can do. When he arrived in the village and learned of the situation, the IVS worker tried to convince them to go to the city, barely five miles away, and undertake a lawsuit. It was quickly explained that this was impossible. The village chief had agreed, which means that higher officials were involved. Complaints would not be heeded and might even bring soldiers to the village. It is such abuses as these, typical of the traditional society and, if anything, given added harshness by colonialism, that the Pathet Lao seek to bring to an end.

Loring Waggoner, a community-development area adviser who has worked in Laos for a number of years in the USAID program, touched upon such matters in his testimony before the Symington subcommittee.[76] He described the peasants as "village oriented" and not concerned with Laos as a nation. With regard to the Royal Lao Government:

> The villager looks at the Government officials in Vientiane as people who have attained a position where they can ask and take things without consultation with the villagers, with the local population. They rarely make protests about this type of corruption or skimming off the top unless, of course, it begins to pinch them fairly badly.

He went on to describe the corruption of the elite in their dealings with the villagers, and observed that the villagers describe the Pathet Lao as "honest with them," though "much more authoritarian than the Lao Government seems to be." The villagers tend to view the Pathet Lao as traditionalists who emphasize "the old way of life, making it all Lao."

When I arrived in Laos and found young Americans living there out of free choice, I admit I was surprised. After only a week I began to have a sense of the appeal of the country and its people, along with a feeling of deep despair about its future.

Notes

1 For a good account of its operations, see Peter Dale Scott, "Air America: Flying the US into Laos," *Ramparts*, February 1970. See Chapter 1, Section II, for a brief discussion of the evolution of the Laotian crisis in the context of the Indochina war. I return to further details following.

2 Keith Buchanan, *The Southeast Asian World* (New York, Taplinger Publishing Company, 1967), pp. 140f. The present USAID administrator reports that as of today, "Laos has virtually no indigenous medical capability and there are only about a dozen foreign trained Lao doctors in-country." Hearings before the Subcommittee on United States Security Agreements and Commitments Abroad of the Committee on Foreign Relations (Symington subcommittee), United States 91st Congress, 1st session, Senate, October 20–28, 1969, p. 566, released with many deletions in April 1970.

3 *Ibid.*

4 Fred Branfman, "Education in Laos Today," a speech given at the IVS annual conference, February 10, 1968.

5 *Rapport sur la situation économique et financiére, 1968–9.* Other reports give ratios running as high as 60 to 1. The discrepancy may result from different methods of calculation. I have not had the opportunity to check details.

6 *Ibid.*

7 Branfman, *op. cit.* The reference is to the part of Laotian society administered by the Royal Lao Government. The figure of 6,669 students in secondary schools comes from the USAID report quoted before the Symington subcommittee (see Senate Hearings, p. 570).

8 Jacques Doyon and Guy Hannoteaux, "L'Ambiguité de l'engagement américain au Laos," *Figaro*, March 11, 1970.

9 "Laos: The Labyrinthine War," *Far Eastern Economic Review*, April 16, 1970, correspondent.

10 The CIA is also reported to be involved in the opium traffic. For background and discussion, see the articles by David Feingold and A. McCoy in N. Adams, A. McCoy, and F. Schurmann, *Laos Reader* (New York, Harper & Row, 1970). See also *Christian Science Monitor*, May 29, 1970, for a report of direct CIA involvement in opium shipment.

11 Embassy officials claim that this particular instance of corruption is exaggerated, and that USAID simply diverted other funds to the airport construction.

12 This was reported in the American press by Henry Kamm, *New York Times*, October 11, 1969, on the basis of interviews with refugees who had lived in caves and trenches for six months before they were airlifted from the area. Not a house remained standing when they left. My informants gave a slightly earlier date for the destruction.

13 After a long conversation with refugees in a camp, we asked what they thought we were doing there. They said that we were, of course, American soldiers in civilian dress.

14 A teacher whom we met in the refugee village confirmed this, saying that he was not permitted to teach because he was an opium addict.

15 Phoumi Vongvichit, *Laos and the Victorious Struggle of the Lao People Against U.S. Neo-colonialism* (Neo Lao Hak Sat Editions, 1969), pp. 139–40.

16 The Pathet Lao officially favor a return to the general lines of the agreements of 1962 that established a Government of National Union, and therefore has no embassy in Hanoi. There is a Royal Lao Government Embassy in Hanoi, staffed, I was informed, by Pathet Lao sympathizers. The Pathet Lao Information Office is the highest official Pathet Lao representation in Hanoi. There is also a Pathet Lao representative in Vientiane, accessible, though blockaded by RLG troops and, he asserts, harassed in many ways by the government. We were not able to penetrate the bureaucratic maze in the time available, but we did manage to speak to him

at the airport, on our way to Hanoi. The interview from which the observations in the text are taken appears in full in Adams, McCoy, and Schurmann, *op. cit.*

17   That USAID serves as a CIA cover, as has long been reported, has now been officially admitted by Foreign Aid Chief John A. Hannah, AP, *Boston Globe*, June 8, 1970.

18   See "Laos: The Labyrinthine War," *Far Eastern Economic Review*, April 16, 1970, for some comments on Allman's observations.

19   *New York Times*, May 25. AFP reports that Vang Pao "is trying to retake five small forward posts of his base at Sam Thong.... The base was captured by leftist forces in a surprise assault last week."

20   UPI, *International Herald Tribune*, April 4–5, 1970. There is some suspicion that the report that Communist troops had occupied Sam Thong was released in an effort to conceal the vandalism of the Clandestine Army.

21   In the words of the Department of State *Background Notes*, March 1969, "By the spring of 1961 the NLHS appeared to be in a position to take over the entire country." The strongly anti-Communist and very knowledgeable Australian reporter Denis Warner was more specific. Writing in July 1961, he observed that "the Neo Lao Hak Sat controls the countryside [and] the odds [in any election] are heavily in favor of that party, which has diligently built up an organization covering most of the country's ten thousand villages" (*Reporting Southeast Asia* [Sydney, Angus & Robertson, 1966], p. 171).

22   Paul F. Langer and Joseph J. Zasloff, *Revolution in Laos: The North Vietnamese and the Pathet Lao*, RM-5935, RAND Corporation, September 1969, p. 113.

23   Vongvichit, *op. cit.*, pp. 77–89. PEO is the Program Evaluation Office of the State Department, claimed by Vongvichit to be "a U.S. military command in Laos." MAAG is the Military Assistance Advisory Group; PAG, the Police Advisory Group; and USOM, the United States Operations Mission.

24   *op. cit.*, p. 171

25   See Jonathan Mirsky and Stephen E. Stonefield, "The United States in Laos, 1945–1962," in Edward Friedman and Mark Selden, eds., *America's Asia* (New York, Pantheon Books, 1971).

26   For background on events prior to the renewal of the civil war in 1963, see Arthur Dommen, *Conflict in Laos: The Politics of Neutralization* (New York, Frederick A. Praeger, 1964); Hugh Toye, *Laos: Buffer State or Battleground* (New York, Oxford University Press, 1968); Mirsky and Stonefield, *op. cit.*; Langer and Zasloff, *op. cit.*; Vongvichit, *op. cit.* See also Peter Dale Scott, "Laos, Nixon, and the CIA," *New York Review*, April 9, 1970. More recent events are more scantily covered in the available literature.

27   "From 1946 to 1963 Laos received more American aid per capita than any country in Southeast Asia. By 1958 the Royal Lao Army was the only foreign army in the world *wholly* supported by the taxpayers of the United States" (Mirsky and Stonefield, *op. cit.*).

28   This information comes from former IVS workers. I was not able to check other sources or the documents themselves, but I believe it to be fully accurate.

29   *Op. cit.*, p. 103.

30   Interrogation of William Sullivan, Deputy Assistant Secretary of State for East Asian and Pacific Affairs, and former Ambassador to Laos, by Mr. Paul of the Committee Staff, before the Symington subcommittee (Senate Hearings, pp. 532–33).

31   *Ibid.*, pp. 516–17.

32   *Ibid.*, p. 553.

33   *Ibid.*, pp. 585f. The subcommittee interrogator is more frank in his use of terminology. He asks what statutory authority USIA has for "involvement in propaganda of another country rather than the effort to portray the United States?" The answer is a bit obscure. Apparently

it lies in an interpretation of the USIA legislation given in a memorandum from President Kennedy which states: "The mission of the U.S. Information Agency is to help achieve U.S. foreign policy objectives by (a) influencing public attitudes in other nations...."

34 See Chapter 1, pp. 31–32. See also Peter Dale Scott, "Laos, Nixon, and the CIA," and Mirsky and Stonefield, *op. cit.*

35 Senate Hearings, p. 591.

36 The problems of initiating an insurrection are indicated by the American experience in North Vietnam. Since 1956, according to Bernard Fall, small saboteur groups have been parachuted or infiltrated into North Vietnam. The "infiltration of guerrilla teams" to the North, he wrote in 1964, "has been repeatedly attempted over the past years and has met with dismal failure." For several references, see my *American Power and the New Mandarins* (New York, Pantheon Books, 1969), pp. 242–43, 281–82.

37 Senate Hearings, p. 500. He continues with this pretense in the Kennedy subcommittee hearings on refugees, May 1970: "We established very clear rules putting all villages out of range of American air activity. Before I approved a strike, I insisted on photographic evidence to see the area and the target." He accepted the estimate of 700 sorties a day. See Murray Kempton, "From the City of Lies," *New York Review*, June 4, 1970.

38 For detailed documentation of other falsehoods in this speech, see Scott, "Laos, Nixon, and the CIA."

39 *Life*, April 3, 1970. Reprinted in an excellent selection of articles on the current situation in Laos inserted by Senator Kennedy in the *Congressional Record*, April 20, 1970, pp. S5988–92. See also Carl Strock, "Laotian Tragedy," *New Republic*, May 9, 1970.

40 *Washington Star*, April 19, 1970. Reprinted in the *Congressional Record* collection cited above.

41 See Symington subcommittee hearings (Senate Hearings, p. 380). The report adds that "of those killed in Laos up to October 22, 1969, something around one-quarter were killed with respect to operations in northern Laos." A UPI report from Geneva in the *International Herald Tribune*, April 4–5, 1970, gives the figure of 86 United States Air Force personnel held prisoner by the Pathet Lao in Laos. The figure, given by two clergymen, is claimed to be based on United States sources "confirmed by private sources in Geneva." The Pathet Lao claim to have shot down over 1,200 American planes in Laos.

42 A statement on this matter appears in the interview cited in note 16.

43 *Life under the P.L. in the Xieng Khouang Ville Area*, undated; *The Role of North Vietnamese Cadres in the Pathet Lao Administration of Xieng Khouang Province*, April 1970. McKeithen is not further identified in these documents. Presumably he is associated either with USAID, the CIA, or both. McKeithen's bias against the Pathet Lao is so extreme that he cannot even manage to maintain consistency. Thus he writes that Pathet Lao "minor officials are chosen on the basis of their contributions to the state and their reliability (strong back/weak mind)" (*Life under the P.L.*). A few pages earlier we read that "Government officials [under the Pathet Lao] are chosen almost entirely on the basis of merit, although there seems to be a general preference for the economically deprived villager as opposed to his wealthier counterpart." His prejudice also shows, for example, in his contemptuous description of the "principle of 'democratization'" : "i.e., everyone should rat on everyone else and punish former officials and reactionary merchants for exploiting the people, etc." How much more humane is the American approach, to support and enrich these officials and exploiters instead of getting people to rat on them.

44 Here McKeithen is a bit disingenuous. The virtual destruction of civil society by aerial bombardment is obviously a major reason why precious resources must be conserved. One refugee described his own marriage ceremony: few people could attend because of the bombardment and they had to dive into trenches during the ceremony because of a nearby raid.

Elsewhere McKeithen points out "There can be no doubt that the P.L. have reduced disguised unemployment in the areas they control to an all time low."

45 He notes that the market at Xieng Khouang city "frequently closes at dawn to avoid the possibility of air strikes." According to the *Washington Star*, August 20, 1969: "In May this year US jets blasted the Communist-held town of Xieng Khouangville off the map, killing some 200 civilians but very few communist troops, as they were in nearby caves." Cited in the Symington subcommittee hearings (Senate Hearings, p. 512). Colonel Robert Tyrell, USAF, United States Air Attaché in Vientiane, stated in sworn testimony that this report is "generally inaccurate," in his opinion. It is, however, borne out by refugee interviews. Recall Sullivan's testimony cited above, p. 161.

46 *Life under the P.L.* He also notes that "The Khoueng offices were located in a small cave" outside the city, but fails to mention the reason.

47 Langer and Zasloff, *op. cit.*, pp. 132–34, 146.

48 *Ibid.*, pp. 160–66.

49 *Ibid.*, pp. 156, 158.

50 *Ibid.*, p. 205.

51 *Message No. 35*, September 16, 1965, International Commission for Supervision and Control in Laos, to the Co-chairman of the Geneva Conference.

52 *Report of an Investigation by the International Commission for Supervision and Control in Laos of an attack on Dong Hene by North Vietnamese Troops.* This document, undated and unidentified, is a reproduction of parts of the original ICC document submitted on June 14, 1966.

53 Paul F. Langer and Joseph J. Zasloff, *The North Vietnamese Military Adviser in Laos*, RM-5688, RAND Corporation, July 1968.

54 The details are difficult to document, of course, since the RAND Corporation does not obligingly supply selected information to indicate the scope and timing of these activities. Some details appear in the Symington subcommittee hearings. See Chapter 3 for references. It is hardly necessary to emphasize that except for the ICC reports, documents of the sort reviewed here are of dubious value. The source material is not available, and there is no way of checking distortions, excisions, or omissions.

55 The three regions of Vietnam, in Western terminology. In Vietnamese: Bac-Bô, Trung-Bô, and Nam-Bô.

56 I did not take notes during the interview with Prince Souvanna Phouma. These remarks and those quoted below were reconstructed immediately after the interview and checked with other participants. The five points of the star do have a symbolic significance: they stand for intellectuals, workers, peasants, tradesmen, and soldiers, working together to defend and build the country.

57 Langer and Zasloff, *The Revolution in Laos.* p. 212.

58 *Op. cit.,* pp. 80–91.

59 There are also Meo fighting with the Pathet Lao, and Meo from North Vietnam are said to be working with these groups.

60 *New York Times*, March 19, 1970.

61 Some information is presented in the recently released Hearings of the Symington subcommittee of the Senate Foreign Relations Committee. See Chalmers Roberts, *Washington Post-Boston Globe*, June 8, 1970.

62 *Behind the Lines—Hanoi* (New York, Harper & Row, 1967), pp. 35–36. Salisbury assumed that he was referring to southern Laos, but the description is remarkably similar to what has since been reported from the north. Given what we now know, it is probable that the description is of Sam Neua Province.

63 Decornoy's reports are given in full, in translation, in Adams, McCoy, and Schurmann, *op. cit.*

64 *Laos: Preparing for a Settlement in Vietnam*, P-4024, RAND Corporation, February 1969.

65 *Pravda*, February 27, 1968. 1 do not have the original, and quote from a translation given to me in Vientiane.

66 *New York Times*, February 5, 1970. Kamm notes that the Lao peasants were not informed that they were to be evacuated, though those who wished to stay (in what would become a free-strike zone, in fact) would be permitted to do so. Reports in Vientiane indicate that a large part of the population (perhaps about half, including most young men and women) went over to the Pathet Lao, despite the abysmal conditions.

67 Paul F. Langer, *Laos: Search for Peace in the Midst of War*, P-3748, RAND Corporation, December 1967.

68 I quoted some of his observations, pages 150–51. Excerpts from the interview will appear in Adams, McCoy, and Schurmann, *op. cit.* The following is a fairly close, abbreviated paraphrase.

69 This is a constant refrain among the Communists of Indochina.

70 April 16, 1970. See note 9.

71 This paragraph is taken from the original text, parts of which appear in the *Far Eastern Economic Review*, April 16, 1970.

72 See note 56.

73 *New Yorker*, May, 1968, quoted in Symington subcommittee hearings (Senate Hearings, p. 552).

74 Kennedy subcommittee hearings on refugees, quoted by Kempton, *op. cit.*

75 Henry Kamm, *New York Times*, February 5, 1970.

76 Senate Hearings, pp. 574ff.

Chapter 5
North Vietnam

THE INTERNATIONAL Control Commission flight to Hanoi spirals upward around Vientiane until it reaches its assigned altitude, and then passes through a protected corridor over an area that has received some of the most intensive bombing in human history. A Phantom jet streaked close by us—much to the annoyance of the crew and regular passengers—but apart from that we saw nothing in the heavy clouds until the lights of Hanoi appeared below. The passengers on the flight were a curious mélange: Chinese diplomats, Russian journalists, an Italian novelist, several Poles, and three American visitors. We arrived on April 10, and departed on the same flight, a week later.

My visit to Vietnam was brief, and my impressions are necessarily superficial. Since I do not speak Vietnamese, an interpreter was generally necessary, and although the translators were highly skilled, the process is time-consuming and certainly retards communication. I will describe what I saw and what I was told. The reader should bear in mind the limitations of what I am able to report.

For a country at war, North Vietnam seems remarkably relaxed and serene. We took long walks, unaccompanied, in Hanoi and in the countryside. Occasionally, we were asked not to take pictures—for example, at the entrance to a cave in which a factory shop was hidden. Our Vietnamese hosts did not ask to develop or check any of the pictures that we took, including color photos. There was also very little security, so far as I could see. We visited Premier Pham Van Dong in a retreat outside the city, but noticed no guards or police anywhere near the residence. In the city there were many soldiers sitting by the lakes, walking through the streets, or in the dense waves of cyclists. Their appearance was that of soldiers on leave. There are also many young men in both city and country in civilian occupations. I noticed only a few police, mostly directing traffic and apparently unarmed.

In the countryside a crowd of children collected around us as we walked through a remote village, some distance from the administration buildings of Thanh Hoa Province, where we spent the night. They assumed we were Russians, as did the children who waved and shouted "Soviet Union" as we drove through towns and villages. We were invariably greeted with friendly smiles, and in the more remote areas, with some show of curiosity.

Everywhere we went, people seemed healthy, well-fed, and adequately clothed. There was no obvious difference between living standards in city and country. Consumer goods are scarce. Except for a bicycle, a thermos bottle, perhaps a radio, most people probably have very few consumer goods. I don't think I saw more than a few dozen cars in Hanoi. The center of the city looks not very different from the outskirts. The city is clean and quiet, except for the honking of truck horns, warning bicycles to clear the way. I had heard that there were loudspeakers everywhere blaring news and announcements, but I recall only one, playing music in a downtown park. The appearance of the city is drab. The scarce resources of the country are largely diverted to the countryside. Someday, if the war ends, Hanoi will be a beautiful city, with its wide tree-lined streets and many lakes and parks.

The most striking difference between Hanoi and the countryside is, of course, the devastation and ruin caused by the "air war of destruction." Hanoi itself, so far as I could see, was not badly hit, except near the Red River, where the bridge and surrounding areas must have been heavily bombed. But as soon as one leaves the city limits, the destruction is enormous. We traveled along the main highway to Thanh Hoa, about ninety miles to the south. The effects of the bombing are visible everywhere. From the road, one can see the entrances to caves where the population, particularly children, was dispersed during the bombing. Temporary wooden dwellings cluster at the base of the conical hills. The craters become more dense when a bridge lies ahead—sometimes, the "bridge" proves to be barely a few yards long. Where there was a bridge, there was often a village. The road and the nearby rail line were also heavily bombed, and the railroad stations remain a mass of debris. Of course, the stations are invariably situated in town or village centers.

Some of the names along the road were familiar to me from reading, for example Phu Ly, about ten miles south of Hanoi, which was visited by French and Japanese newsmen shortly after a particularly savage bombing raid. I asked my traveling companion—Professor Mai, formerly a professor of French, Vietnamese, and Chinese literature and now Chairman of the Association of Arts and Letters—to point out the town center when we reached it. The former market place is a flattened field of rubble in a bend of the river. A few of the buildings of brick and stone are still standing, but the rest of the town was wiped out. Much of the population has now returned and wooden dwellings are scattered among the ruins. The same is true of the village of Phu Xuyen, not far away.

Thanh Hoa itself is a rich agricultural province. Rice fields, a pattern of many shades of green, stretch far into the distance along the road, which also winds through foothills and the fringes of heavy jungle where tigers are said to roam. The vegetation, wild or cultivated, is lush and luxuriant. Watching the peasants working in the fields, the young boys leading their water buffalo, one almost forgets the war until a sharp reminder comes—a cratered field, the rubble of a village, the twisted wreck of a railroad car. We stopped to eat lunch on a wooded hillside where a few peasant women were collecting pine needles. Our hosts warned us to look carefully if we walked far away from the road, since there are still unexploded bombs.

The capital of Thanh Hoa Province—a city of 70,000, I was told—was heavily bombed. The details were related by Professor Mai, who was Province Chairman in 1947–1948, and had been a clandestine member of the Communist Party since its formation in 1930. We passed the wreckage of the provincial offices, now totally destroyed. One wall of a large hospital remains standing. A factory in Thanh Hoa city was also demolished; its separate shops are now dispersed in the surrounding countryside, hidden in caves. A nearby power station was severely damaged, but, I was told, never ceased to function. In the city itself there has been little reconstruction of the original buildings, but here too most of the population has apparently returned, and there are wooden structures everywhere alongside the ruins and buildings that remain.

Thanh Hoa is near the sea, and we drove to an attractive beach. Not far offshore, we were told, ships of the Seventh Fleet have been stationed, and there has been much naval shelling as well as aerial bombardment. Saboteurs and spies were landed in the area, but quickly caught, so we were informed. Wooden fishing boats line the beach. There used to be a resort area in the surrounding hills. It was demolished by the bombardment.

Near Thanh Hoa city, the Ham Rong bridge spans the Ma River. The largest of the bridges we crossed, it is now a rickety structure of twisted steel and shattered concrete. Traffic inches across in a single lane. We were told the story of the bridge one evening in the dim and flickering light of the provincial offices, now hidden near a village some distance from Thanh Hoa city, and indistinguishable from other clusters of dwellings. Later, we were shown a film recording the same events. The narrator was Miss Ham, twenty-five years old, the chief of the militia of Thanh Hoa township. Five years ago she was the militia chief of the village at the site of the Ham Rong bridge.

The bridge was attacked daily from early 1965 until the suspension of the bombing—in this region; in April 1968. The bridge and surrounding area were bombed with high explosives and aerial torpedoes, and shelled from ships offshore. Ninety-nine jet planes were downed in these attacks. A steep hill alongside the bridge was reduced to one-third its former size by the bombardment. The village nearby was destroyed, with many casualties.

We returned to the bridge the next day, this time accompanied by the head of the local branch of the Vietnam Fatherland Front, essentially the successor organization to the Viet Minh. To me he looked thirty at the most, but he obviously is considerably older, since his seventeen-year-old son is a university student in Hanoi. He related the outlines of the story again as we stood at the bridge in the chilling wind of the monsoon. The hill beside the bridge, a flag planted on its summit, was indeed far smaller than in the films we had been shown the evening before. Its rocky slope was torn and shredded. From where we stood to the hilly ridge in the distance, the fields were barren. There is no trace of the former village. The area has been bombed so heavily that even the craters are not delineated, as they generally are along the road. Only the shell of the building that houses the power station remains in the battered plain. Carved in the hills beyond, just visible from where we stood, are the words *Quyet Thang*—"determined to win."

The bridge still stands, severely damaged but proud and defiant, a symbol of deep significance to the people of Thanh Hoa. This scene summarizes, more than anything else, the mood of the people I met, from the Premier to students in the university, workers in the factory, and peasants in the villages. So far as I can tell, the country is unified, strong though poor, and determined to withstand the attack launched against Vietnam by the great superpower of the Western world.

The Vietnamese see their history as an unending series of struggles of resistance against aggression, by the Chinese, the Mongols, the Japanese, the French, and now the Americans. Over and over this history was recounted to us. A dozen times we were told how the Chinese had been beaten back, how the Mongols, who conquered most of Asia and Europe, were unable to cross the Annam Mountains into Vietnam because of the fierce resistance of the Vietnamese peasants, unified, even in feudal times, in opposition to the aggressor. As the director of the Historical Museum led us through exhibits, beginning with the Stone Age, the members of our entourage listened, with obvious fascination, to his account of the ancient culture and the details of each battle, each campaign. In the Military Museum, the same was true. Those who were with us had surely been through this innumerable times, but one could hardly guess it as they listened with rapt attention to each familiar detail. The Vietnamese see their history as a series of victories, each after a long struggle. A less optimistic view of the same events is that there have been periods of independence in a history of occupation by outside powers. It is striking that they do not interpret their past in this way. I am sure that had I suggested any such interpretation, it would have struck them as bizarre and perverse. There is also no mistaking the confidence with which they approach the future.

We spent an afternoon discussing the present situation with the head of the "Special Representation" of the Provisional Revolutionary Government of South Vietnam.[1] There we met several war victims from the South, hideously maimed, in Hanoi for extended medical treatment. The PRG representatives in Hanoi expect a long and bitter war in the South. They expect the United States to leave an army of 200,000 to 250,000 men, while providing direction and logistic support for a "puppet army" of about 800,000, and continuing or even extending the technological war. They calculate that under President Johnson, about 2 million tons of bombs were dropped in South Vietnam, while the Nixon administration has already reached the level of 1.2 million tons while intensifying the chemical war. The aim of "pacification" they see as concentration of the population in areas that can, it is hoped, be controlled by armed force, areas surrounded by a no man's land of devastation and destruction. They believe that this policy cannot succeed, that there will be internal decay within the region administered by the increasingly authoritarian and repressive Saigon authorities. They look forward to a coalition government that will organize free general elections and elect a national assembly, and specifically mentioned such people as Duong Van Minh and Tran Van Don as representatives of a possible "third force" with which, if I understood correctly, they feel they could cooperate. But they see no present sign that the United States would be willing to permit a representative coalition government in South Vietnam.

I believe that the leadership of the Democratic Republic of Vietnam also expect a long, continuing war and see no indication that the United States intends to abandon its efforts to subjugate South Vietnam and to dominate the Indochinese peninsula. They do not see any sign of American seriousness in Paris, and interpret each American proposal—quite correctly, I believe—as one or another scheme to maintain the American puppet regime in power in South Vietnam. They expect that the bombing of the North may be resumed as the American position erodes elsewhere in Indochina. They anticipate, with confidence, that the American position will deteriorate. Because of the likelihood of resumption of the air war, cities are not being reconstructed and factories remain dispersed. Although North Vietnam has considerable potential for development of hydro-electric power, no dams are being built. Quite apart from the toll taken by the war itself, the threat of further war is a great barrier to development and industrialization.

We spoke one evening to Hoang Tung, the director of *Nhan Dan*, the major newspaper of North Vietnam, and a member of the Central Committee of the Lao Dong (Workers) Party since 1950. In the 1930s he took part in the youth movement and was jailed from 1940 until 1945, when the Japanese overthrew the French colonial government. He was in charge of the Hanoi section of the victorious insurrection in August 1945, and then took part in the First Indochina War against the French, fighting in the Red River Delta region. He too outlined to us the course of Vietnamese history, and described the present political and social organization and the plans for development. He spoke softly, with great feeling, about these long struggles, about the suffering of the people, and about the problems that still face them in the future.

> The aggressors [he said] have forced the whole of the population to fight or accept death. Our country and other Indochinese countries have experienced all kinds of policies and war methods. Our countries have been a testing ground for the French, the Japanese, and now the Americans. We think that in the whole of history there has not been a people that has had to undergo so many kinds of war. Take only the United States. They have tried strategic hamlets, the special war of Kennedy, the local war of Johnson, the special-local war of Nixon. We have had to deal with all kinds of theories and doctrines. Our people have not been destroyed. In fact, the United States imperialists have put into use all the forces they can gather. Take the strategic hamlets. This was a great effort. They destroyed tens of thousands of villages and carried away millions of people. Then, they brought in half a million troops. They undertook the air war against the North. We cannot find in history such a concentration of bombardment. In South Vietnam alone, 3 million tons of bombs, and in addition other kinds of ordnance. It far exceeds World War II. The Vietnamese are a small people. Only 37 million. Now we have reached this stage. We can go to the end.

In 1954, he added, "we were not vigilant enough; we did not expect another war." But now, he said, it is understood that the United States ruling forces do not wish to leave Asia to its own people. Nixon may succeed in gathering the reactionary forces of Asia, but the forces opposing imperialism will also gather together. There will be a long struggle: the reactionary forces against the popular forces in Asia. But the feeling of nationalism runs very high, and the reactionary forces cannot win.

Premier Pham Van Dong spoke in a similar vein. President Nixon, he said, seems to want to expand the war. Cambodia is an example.[2] But "the

sorcerer is not always in a position to control what he has created." Prince
Sihanouk has called for armed struggle, and the three peoples of Indochina
will now combine their patriotic struggles. "In the end, justice is the deci-
sive factor, and justice will prevail."

We asked whether he conceived of some kind of federation of the peoples of Indochina in the long run, and mentioned Senator Fulbright's
recent statement that North Vietnam, as the strongest and most dynamic
society, would be likely to dominate the region. The Premier agreed that
North Vietnam is stronger than its neighbors in Indochina, but forcefully
dismissed any possibility of its dominating the region and rejected any
thought of federation in the foreseeable future. Even for the reunification
of Vietnam, he said, it is impossible now to provide a specific plan, "a blue-
print."

> The Indochinese peninsula must be free and independent. South
> Vietnam, Cambodia, and Laos will be neutral. Given the present sit-
> uation, this is a likely prospect. Only Nixon is opposed to this.

It is interesting that Pham Van Dong reiterated the formula proposed
by the National Liberation Front in 1962 and ignored, in fact suppressed,
in the United States: namely, that South Vietnam, Laos, and Cambodia be
neutral. Then as now, this was a very reasonable proposal, and a likely outcome if the United States were to withdraw from the region. Then as now,
there are no prospects for achieving the neutralization of South Vietnam,
Laos, and Cambodia, because of the American insistence on retaining
these countries within the American orbit, along with the periphery of the
Asian land mass.

The Premier also expressed confidence in the future. "B-52s and computers can't compete with a just cause and human intelligence," he said.
The Vietnamese people and the other people of Indochina must still
undergo great suffering, but ultimately they will win.

It is, of course, not surprising that the leaders of the country should
wish to appear confident before foreign visitors. However, I sensed no
deviation from this mood in discussions with others. The people I met
exhibited no bravado, only quiet confidence in the justice of their cause and
the eventual achievement of independence and the defeat of foreign
aggression.

The personal stories they tell are sometimes painful beyond words. We had a few hours to spare on our last afternoon in Hanoi, and were taken on a tour of the city. In Reunification Park, near a lake surrounded by newly planted trees that are characteristic of the southern part of Vietnam, my translator told me something of the story of his life. He is a native of the South, from Quang Ngai Province. He had joined the Viet Minh as a young man, and then came north with his father in 1954, leaving his mother and sisters behind and expecting to return in 1956 after the promised elections that were to reunify the country. Since that time, he has heard not a word from any member of his family in the South. The United States not only prevented the elections but moved at once to block all communication, even mail, between North and South Vietnam. He can guess what his family and friends have suffered since. With some reluctance, I told him what I knew of the recent history of Quang Ngai Province, more savagely attacked than any other part of Vietnam. Now that I have returned home, shall I send him Jonathan Schell's book on the American destruction of Quang Ngai Province? Or the reports by Dr. Alje Vennema, director of a Canadian tuberculosis hospital in Quang Ngai Province until August 1968, when he left because he felt he could do nothing useful there any more, because, he said, "My service was futile?" Dr. Vennema reports that he did nothing about the My Lai slayings, which he knew of at once, "because it was nothing new":

> They were being talked about among the Vietnamese people, but no more than other incidents [for example, a massacre at Son Tra in February 1969 and another similar incident during the summer in the Mo Duc district].... I had heard this type of story many times before, however, and had spoken to U.S. and Canadian officials about the senseless killings of civilians that were going on ... [the] senseless bombings.

The province, he reports,

> had become "a no man's land" with half the population in refugee camps, children starving and much land and foliage destroyed. His patients were constantly telling him of the shootings of their family and friends, and every time he treated a child for war wounds, "five more were brought in." ... Claire Culhane, who worked in 1968 as an administrator in the Canadian TB hospital in Quang Ngai, said a

report filed from the hospital in April '68 mentioned the difficulties of working in an area with Americans "who boasted about the brutalities and massacres they were engaged in."[3]

Shall I send him the books now appearing about the My Lai massacre, or about the incomparably greater atrocity of the war itself in Quang Ngai, or any other part of the country that resists American rule?

Mr. Tri, my translator, knew about most of this and spoke of it with an uncanny calm. It is remarkable that one senses no hatred, no hostility toward Americans, but rather a great curiosity about American life, sympathy for the "difficult situation" of those in the peace movement who are forced to "struggle against their government," even sympathy for the soldiers and pilots who are misled into participating in the "*sale guerre*" of the Americans in Vietnam.

In Thanh Hoa Province, near the province capital, we visited a factory buried inside a mountain. Some 30 to 35 men and women work there with machine tools, making parts for buses and trucks. Generally there are two people at a machine, one a skilled worker, one an apprentice. Over tea and beer, in one corner of the dank and dimly lit cave, the manager told us how the entire factory had been dispersed during the "air war of destruction" to such sites as this one. The mountain itself had been heavily bombed, but no damage had been caused to the facilities inside the cave that was hewed out by hand while the bombing proceeded. Afterward, the workers in the cave grouped themselves at the end of the table where we were sitting and, as a gesture of welcome, sang songs, patriotic and sentimental, and declaimed poems. The whole experience was intensely moving. As I left, I swore to myself not to speak or write about it, knowing how a sophisticated Westerner might react. Let the reader think what he may. The fact is that it was intensely moving to see the spirit of the people in this miserable place, working in the face of all the obstacles that American power can erect, to defend their country and to find their way into the modern age.

We left the factory on an unpaved road through the heavily cratered fields, and went on to a remote agricultural cooperative quite far from the main highway. Over more tea and beer, the mayor, a young woman who looked in her mid-twenties, provided us with details about production and village organization, and answered some questions about their plans and hopes. Two-thirds of the workers are involved in handicrafts, mostly weaving. They hope to receive machinery from the state for this industry, now partially collectivized. The fields are intensively cultivated, as we could see driving past, and like most villages they have now achieved two harvests a year in their rice fields, more than doubling former production levels while at the same time diversifying their crops considerably. The road to the village and the fields within sight are lined with young pine trees, planted during a recent reforestation campaign, the signs of which are visible everywhere.

We spent several hours in the cooperative, visiting a small dispensary and two schools. The dispensary, clean and moderately well equipped, had separate sections for Western and Oriental medicine. Outside the Oriental pharmacy were baskets of many different types of herbs, most of them from the garden of the dispensary. All children are now born in the maternity section of the dispensary. The wards were empty when we were there. A few patients were in the clinic, and in the maternity section several women were chatting with a young mother whose newborn baby was in a crib in the next room. We were told that the traditional diseases (malaria, trachoma) are virtually nonexistent. They intend to maintain traditional and Western medicine side by side, but I noticed that in the Oriental section the practitioners and the pharmacist were considerably older. There is a larger district hospital for more serious cases. I did not ask whether the large province hospital, destroyed during the air war, had been rebuilt somewhere else.

We sat in a mathematics class (seventh grade, children of twelve to fourteen) for some time. There were 45 children, studying geometry. I looked through some of the children's notebooks, which contained neatly done, quite advanced algebra problems. The lesson was lively. Children tried to work out proofs of theorems as the teacher sketched their proposals on the blackboard. The level was remarkable, easily as advanced as anything I know of in the United States. It was particularly striking to find such work in a remote village, barely a generation removed from illiteracy. We were told that literacy among adults has been nearly universal for some years, and that in this agricultural province of 2 million everyone receives ten grades of schooling[4] and about 800 students go to the university each year, about 200 of them abroad, most (perhaps all—I am not sure) to Eastern Europe. In principle, most are expected to return to the village. The war, however, has disrupted the intended normal pattern.

Later, we were told that this village was of a medium level from an economic point of view, not among the poorest or the richest in the area, and I gather that our visit was intended as something of a gesture of encouragement for the villagers. The peasants have private gardens, and there is a free market alongside the state market—literally alongside, as we saw later in Hanoi while walking through the market area, where both are housed under one roof. On street corners in Hanoi one still sees peasant women selling their produce. However, there seems to be little incentive for the peasants to use the free market, since agricultural prices set by the state are, I understand, made artificially high in accordance with the policy of equalizing standards in country and city. There are still some peasants who have not joined the cooperatives, but apparently not many, the advantages of joining being obvious, not only because of the state assistance but also because of the benefits achieved through mutual aid. Along the road to the village we saw groups working on irrigation projects, constructing large earthen dikes and channels, and the completed irrigation works from earlier projects can be seen everywhere. The larger irrigation projects are constructed by the state; local projects are developed under regional organization and by the villages themselves.

In principle, the cooperative is expected to put aside from 1 to 5 percent of its income from agricultural production and a varying percentage of its income from other production for development, presumably under independent village-based initiative. A general meeting of the cooperative makes decisions about such matters and sets the rate of accumulation and the program for development, deciding, for example, whether to build a school, to work for extra profits, and so on. An annual meeting of all adult members selects an administrative committee for the cooperative.

We were also told that in traditional Vietnamese peasant society, there was a certain degree of mutual aid and some communal land, and also considerable village and regional independence. Landholdings were limited in size by the "law of the king." Under the French, this was changed.

Free ownership of land was permitted, and large plantations were developed as well, particularly in the South. Catholics were particularly privileged, and many priests and archbishops became great landowners. Large feudal holdings grew "where the stork can fly and never get tired." There was very little development, either industrial or agricultural. Now great efforts are being made, apparently with success, to expand agricultural production and to develop regional industry that is related to local needs.

The New Zealand geographer Keith Buchanan has discussed the early achievements of the Vietnamese revolution in the context of a general review of problems of development in Asian peasant society. He concludes:

> The achievements of the North Vietnamese in the economic field have been considerable and they demonstrate to the rest of Southeast Asia the conditions under which real economic progress is possible. The achievements in the socio-cultural field, more specifically in the field of minority policy, have been equally striking and these, in the long run, may prove of even greater relevance to the neighbouring countries of Southeast Asia.[5]

Of course, he was writing before the bombing destroyed most of the early achievements of industrialization.[6]

The process of regional diversification was spurred by the air war, and is now apparently to be maintained and extended. It is surely a very healthy development. "The price may be higher and quality not always good, but goods are produced for local needs and self-supply in each province," we were told by Hoang Tung, in a discussion of these questions back in Hanoi. Special attention is given to training of skilled workers. Heavy industry will have to wait, as present plans are to develop agriculture and small industry related to agriculture and local needs. The country has rich supplies of metals, coal, and other material requirements for industrialization, and can develop ample hydroelectric power when the threat of bombing is removed. With remarkably high standards of education and health extending to the remote areas as well as the urban centers, there seems every possibility that these goals can be realized, and that North Vietnam can be spared a Manila, a Bangkok, or a Saigon—an artificial consumer culture for a minority of the privileged in the midst of urban slums and rural stagnation.

Although there appears to be a high level of democratic participation at the village and regional levels, and some degree of leeway—limited, to be sure, by the exigencies of war—for independent planning at these levels, still major planning is highly centralized in the hands of the state authorities. As Hoang Tung explained, the Central Committee of the Lao Dong Party sets the general lines of policy. These plans are implemented by governmental bodies selected by the National Assembly, which also drafts specific plans. The ministries are responsible to the Assembly, which is chosen by direct election from local districts that extend over the entire country, including the mountain tribesmen, who are well represented. The managers of local enterprises are selected by the government ministries in charge of various branches of the economy. Each factory has a congress once a year of all workers, to which the manager reports. A party cell in the factory, containing 10 to 20 percent of the work force, gives advice to the manager. There is also a trade-union organization, which seems to concern itself largely with education and welfare programs. There are also, in each workshop, production teams of skilled and unskilled workers, and apparently there are plans, the details of which I had no time to investigate, to rearrange the internal organization of enterprises.

This account is based on information provided in conversations with officials at various levels of administration and other knowledgeable people whom I met. Evidently, I am in no position to flesh out the account with detailed impressions or the results of personal investigation.

The central planning role of the Lao Dong Party is stressed in the major government documents. Le Duan, in his recent "analysis of the great problems, essential tasks, and principles and methods of action of the Vietnamese revolution,"[7] lays great stress on this governing role:

> An important task of economic organization is to determine correctly the *relationships between the Party, the State, and the popular masses* in the matter of economic management. As director and general staff of the army of builders of the economy, the Party has the mission of defining the line and fundamental measures, fixing the leading principles, the programs and methods, mobilizing the masses for a power-

ful offensive on the economic front, supervising the activity of the governmental services. Party direction is a historical necessity which guarantees for our economy a development conforming to a fixed orientation, safeguards the rights and interests of various strata of the population, and reinforces incessantly the governing role of the people. In the revolution in general and economic development in particular, our Party has no interest particular to itself. The totality of the national economy, just like each factory and each rice field, is the property of the people, under different forms and in various economic and technical conditions. This objective reality requires the Party to arrange for different modes of direction that fit each case (industry, agriculture, factories, cooperatives) and that permit the Party to maintain its directing role, making sure that the managerial prerogatives of administration are respected and at the same time assuring to the popular masses the direct exercise of their right to rule.

Le Duan's policy statement reveals clearly the extent to which the Vietnamese revolution, in its current state at least, is a revolution of modernization and development:

"To tighten the belt," to reduce all nonessential expenditures, and to resolutely commit capital for accumulation, is a dominant necessity, and testifies to a high level of political understanding with respect to the construction of socialism.

This revolution of development, Le Duan stresses, must be the work of the masses of the population and must involve direct participation and self-education. In the present state of Vietnamese society, management of the economy

must be very flexible, in conformity with the economic laws of socialism and of the process of development proceeding from small-scale to heavy production; it must combine unified central direction with the right of governance of the various branches, regions, and units of the base; it must extend the system of planning while making use of market relations where appropriate [for regulating economic indices and economic activities of secondary importance not provided for by the general plan] and extending the domain of general accounting; it must promote both the material interest and the political and ideological education, the socialist education, of the great masses of the population.

That all these tasks are compatible is not obvious, and it remains to be seen how they can be realized. The present plans appear to be a composite of Communist Party ideology, traditional Vietnamese sociocultural patterns, the necessity of running a wartime economy, and the general problems of modernization and development. My personal guess is that, unhindered by imperialist intervention, the Vietnamese would develop a modern industrial society with much popular participation in implementation and direct democracy at the lower levels of organization, a highly egalitarian society with excellent conditions of welfare and technical education, but with a degree of centralization of control which, in the long run, will pose serious problems that can be overcome only by eliminating party direction in favor of direct popular control at all levels. At the moment, the leadership appears to be approaching these problems in a flexible and intelligent fashion. But the problems of creating a modern, egalitarian, democratic industrial society are not slight. They have not been solved successfully anywhere in the world as yet, and it will be extremely interesting to see how they are faced in the future, if the Vietnamese are given the opportunity to deal with their internal problems under the conditions of independence and peace that they are presently struggling to achieve.

Richard Gott, a journalist with much experience in underdeveloped countries, summed up his impressions after his recent trip as follows:[8]

> To anyone familiar with the underdeveloped rural areas of the world, especially in Latin America, North Vietnam is by no means an abjectly poor country. The population is poor, of course, but there is no "misery"—that appalling hopeless poverty one encounters too often in the Third World.
>
> Of course there are inequalities. Hanoi is better off than the countryside. The delta areas are richer than the "panhandle." The mountainous regions have less pressure of population and more access to wood. But by getting rid of the rich, and avoiding extremes of poverty, Vietnam gives the impression of a prospering, cohesive society, unique in the underdeveloped world.

He quotes an old man in a southern province:

> When a landlord passed in the road, the peasants used to fold their arms and bow. Not until we had the land reform could we get rid of the influence of the landlords. This was our greatest difficulty.

Vietnamese peasants lived under feudal lords for thousands of years. They were psychologically subservient to landlords. Whenever they wanted to do anything, they felt they ought to ask the landlord first. Basically, peasants have a very conservative attitude and are very mean. They have to be educated. This was the biggest problem.

As Gott notes, the land reform of 1954 took a fearful toll; it was "a chaotic affair, with thousands of people using the opportunity to pay off old scores," and thousands were killed in an eruption of violence and terror.[9] It also laid the basis for a new society which has overcome starvation and rural misery and offers the peasant hope for the future:

The most important change of all is in the peasants themselves. It would be hard to find now a more purposeful or determined people. There is none of that awful cringing deference that you encounter among Latin-American peasants—who remain beaten into apathy by centuries of landlord oppression. The departure of the landlords has lifted a yoke from the peasantry and liberated an almost unprecedentedly powerful force.

The British China scholar Jack Gray recently summarized Mao's socioeconomic theory of development as stressing the need for "inducing the villagers gradually, through their own efforts toward an intermediate technology, to mechanize out of their own resources and to operate the machines with their own hands, in a milieu in which local industry, agricultural mechanization, agricultural diversification, and the education (both formal and informal) growing out of these activities mutually enrich each other."[10] Similarly, "the collectives will be run by peasant cadres for the peasants." My impressions, from what I have seen and read, are that North Vietnam is successfully applying these concepts of development.

To understand just how remarkable is the achievement of development in North Vietnam, it is useful to return to some of the forecasts made by the most knowledgeable experts at the end of the First Indochina War. Bernard Fall, writing in 1954, regarded the situation in the North as almost hopeless:

The southern part of the country is its "iron lung," with its huge rice surplus and dollar-earning exports of rubber, pepper, coffee, and precious woods. It is obvious that, deprived of the south, the Ho Chi Minh regime would face either starvation—as in 1946 when it was deprived of southern imports—or a type of integration into the Red Chinese economy that would be the equivalent of annexation.[11]

The Democratic Republic of Vietnam was cut off from the South by American duplicity and force. It has been severely bombed and drawn into a ruinous war. But there is no starvation—far from it. And it has not been integrated into the Chinese economy. Its achievements are, indeed, quite remarkable.

One purpose of the American bombing of the North, in Gérard Chaliand's characterization, was "to demoralize ordinary citizens until, directly or indirectly, they pressurized the Hanoi government into sueing for peace." Thus the bombing aimed at

> undoing the hard, patient work of many years. In a world whose basic problem is surely the backwardness and penury of two thirds of the planet, the United States government—whatever excuses it may invoke—has systematically destroyed the economic infrastructure of one of the three or four "underdeveloped" countries which have seriously laid the foundations for their own industrialization…. In the view of most countries—especially the newer ones—the American intervention in Vietnam is an attempt to stifle national independence and dignity.[12]

This assessment is, I believe, entirely correct. The attempt has failed, dismally. There is no doubt that the spirit of national independence and dignity is high, and that the Vietnamese are proceeding to lay the basis for a modern society.

I have some sense of their achievement in this regard from discussions with Vietnamese scientists and intellectuals. After a long and very productive meeting, I was asked to lecture about current work in linguistics at the Polytechnic University, and was able to do so for about seven hours, to a group of 70 to 80 linguists and mathematicians. Their work, in this rather remote area of science and scholarship, was at an international level. I lectured approximately as I would at Tokyo, Oxford, or the Sorbonne. They are not familiar with the most recent work, because of the unavailability of recent materials, but they are, I believe, in a position to close the gap quickly if this problem is overcome—and to help them overcome it, in all fields, is one tiny effort that Americans might make in the hopeless task of compensating for the destruction of much of what the Vietnamese have created with remarkable enterprise, diligence, and courage. One of the members of the group had studied in East Berlin in one of the outstanding world centers of linguistics. Beyond what he could supply, they made good use of the meager resources available. Other scientists and intellectuals too were extremely eager to discuss current work and educational curricula, and to hear about colleagues whom they knew by reputation or had occasionally met at international conferences. So far as I could judge, the work in some branches of mathematics was also excellent, though here as well there was a general problem of access to recent work. The problem is not limited to technical and scientific areas. Thus a professor of American literature approached me to speak about current writing—he had not seen an American novel for fifteen years and wanted to know, in particular, what Norman Mailer had been doing lately.

The students generally read English, but having little familiarity with the spoken language, were not able to follow a technical lecture. The translators, though excellent in general discussion, had considerable difficulty as the material became more technical and complex. One tried for about an hour, and then, apologetically, asked to be relieved. A second translator also made a noble effort, but the problems were severe. When they floundered, an older man in the audience intervened, and corrected mistakes or explained obscure points. It was obvious that he had followed everything very well and understood the material I was trying to present. Finally he took over completely, and translated for several hours without a break. I was introduced to him later. He was the Minister of Higher Education of North Vietnam, Ta Quang Buu, a mathematician of note who had, in fact, sent me a reprint on mathematical linguistics several years ago that I could not read, since it was in Vietnamese, but that astonished me by its familiarity—in the midst of the air war—with current technical material. I did not think to ask, but I assume that this is the same Ta Quang Buu who was a general during the First Indochina War. We only had a brief chance to talk afterward, to my great disappointment. I think there are few countries where the Minister of Higher Education could have taken over the task of translating an advanced technical lecture of this sort, or would have been willing to do so; and I was also impressed by the easy familiarity of relations within the group, the quality of the debate and discussion, as we proceeded.

After my last lecture I was presented with several gifts, one a Vietnamese dictionary that the linguists had compiled and printed while they were dispersed in the forests and mountains during the air war. With justifiable pride, they observed that this work had been done while the American government was attempting to "drive them back to the Stone Age." In fact, at the Polytechnic University the Vietnamese are training scientists of whom any society could be proud.

I was quite surprised to find myself lecturing on technical material in Hanoi and spending hours with colleagues in discussion of work in progress in the United States. This surprise is a result of my own failure to overcome regrettable stereotypes. The Vietnamese are devoting themselves not only to securing their independence in a bitter war but also to creating a modern society with a high level of general culture. Given half a chance, they will succeed in this, I am sure. It was a great personal pleasure for me to have the opportunity to meet with Vietnamese colleagues, to explore our common interests, and to learn of their work and plans.

In his Will, President Ho Chi Minh wrote that though the war may last long and though new sacrifices will be necessary, still "our rivers, our mountains, our men will always remain." With nuclear weapons, the United States could destroy these hopes, but short of that, I doubt that it can overcome the resistance of the Vietnamese or impose client governments on the people of Indochina.

I left Southeast Asia, after this brief stay, with two overriding general impressions. The first was of the resilience and strength of Vietnamese society. It is conceivable that the United States may be able to break the will of the popular movements in the surrounding countries, perhaps even destroy the National Liberation Front of South Vietnam, by employing the vast resources of violence and terror at its command. If so, it will create a situation in which, indeed, North Vietnam will necessarily dominate Indochina, for no other viable society will remain.

The American intervention, like imperialist wars in general, has stirred up ethnic and class hatreds, set groups in conflict, and raised every conceivable antagonism to the level of a bloody conflict. The Vietnamese and the Thai, the two strongest and most dynamic societies in the region, are virtually at war. The Cambodian army has massacred Vietnamese. The Meo have been set against the Lao and other hill tribesmen. The Thai are driving the mountain tribesmen from their homes, and fear the native Lao population. The Thai and Saigon elites are now laying plans to devour Cambodia. Chinese Nationalist troops remain active in border areas. Khmer mercenaries fight the Viet Cong, alongside Thai and South Koreans brought by the Americans. Native elites, dependent on the flow of American goods and war expenditures, have been drawn into a brutal war against the peasantry. Not all of this is a direct consequence of the American war in Indochina, but there is no doubt that every potential conflict, every form of latent hostility, has been exacerbated as a result of the American intervention, often by design and direct manipulation. Even if the United States were to leave Indochina to its own people—and there is, for the moment, not a sign of any such intention—this legacy of hatred will remain, embittering the lives of the people of Indochina and denying them the hope of creating a decent future.

Notes

1 The PRG does not have an embassy, I presume because they hope to join in a larger coalition government for South Vietnam.

2 The reference is to the March 18 coup and the subsequent attacks in Cambodia by the Saigon Army. The date of this interview was April 16, two weeks before the American invasion of Cambodia. Some form of direct American intervention in Cambodia was clearly anticipated, though it may be that the scale of the American invasion came as something of a surprise.

3 *Ottawa Citizen*, January 12, 1970.

4 I did not think to ask whether this is also true of the many mountain tribesmen in the province, who are said to retain much of their original culture. Our guide for part of the trip was the assistant province chairman, a member of the Muong minority of hill tribesmen, the minority that is said to be closest in language and cultural pattern to the Viet lowlanders.

5 Keith Buchanan, *The Southeast Asian World* (New York, Taplinger Publishing Company, 1967), p. 153.

6 For a detailed investigation of rural Vietnam, see Gérard Chaliand, *The Peasants of North Vietnam* (Harmondsworth, Eng. Penguin Books, 1969). See also the report by Richard Gott of a seven-week trip, *Guardian* (London), February 24–27, 1970.

7 *La révolution Vietnamienne: problémes fondamentaux, tâches essentielles* (Hanoi, 1970), introduction.

8 *Guardian* (London), February 24–27, 1970.

9 According to the very well-informed French journalist Georges Chaffard, the land reform "was carried out in an excessively brutal manner by inexperienced cadres mostly originating from the armed forces, who had only received a few weeks' training [in land reform problems] prior to being sent into the villages, their heads full of badly assimilated theories." Quoted by Bernard Fall, *Viet-Nam Witness* (New York, Frederick A. Praeger, 1966), p. 97, from *Le Monde Weekly Selection*, December 5, 1956. Much American discussion of the land reform is based on Hoang Van Chi, *From Colonialism to Communism* (New York, Frederick A. Praeger, 1964). This book, subsidized (without acknowledgment) by USIA, is an extremely dubious source. For a careful analysis of errors and hopeless bias, see Steven Seltzer, "The Land Reform in North Vietnam," *Viet Report*, June–July, 1967. In the introduction, P. J. Honey writes that the author, in his various writings, "has explained the reasons for the failure of communist agriculture, not only in Vietnam, but in China and North Korea too." In fact, North Vietnam has succeeded, contrary to general expectation, in resolving successfully an extremely difficult problem of agricultural production. For some discussion by a serious observer, see Keith Buchanan, *The Southeast Asian World* (New York, Taplinger Publishing Company, 1967). On the "failure" in China, see John Gurley, *Bulletin of Concerned Asian Scholars*, April–July, 1970. For some recent comment on the North Korean "failure," as seen by a hostile though knowledgeable observer, see Joungwon Kim, *Foreign Affairs*, October 1969. It is remarkable that Honey is taken seriously as a commentator on North Vietnam. Where his statements can be checked, they often prove merely ludicrous. For a few examples, see my *American Power and the New Mandarins*, p. 290.

10 "Economics of Maoism," in Dick Wilson, ed., *China After the Cultural Revolution* (New York, Random House, 1969), selections from the *Bulletin of the Atomic Scientists*. Gray also notes that Western theorists of development are belatedly coming to some of the same conclusions.

11 *The Nation*, March 6, 1954. Reprinted in *Viet-Nam Witness*, pp. 15–21.

12 Chaliand, pp. 68–69.

Chapter 6
On War Crimes*

> We are not judges. We are witnesses. Our task is to make mankind
> bear witness to these terrible crimes and to unite humanity on the side
> of justice in Vietnam.

WITH THESE WORDS, Bertrand Russell opened the second session of
the International War Crimes Tribunal, in November 1967. The American
people were given no opportunity, at that time, to bear witness to the terrible crimes recorded in the Proceedings of the Tribunal. As Russell writes
in his introduction to the first edition, "it is in the nature of imperialism
that citizens of the imperial power are always among the last to know—or
care—about circumstances in the colonies." The evidence brought before
the Tribunal was suppressed by the self-censorship of the mass media, and
its Proceedings, when they appeared in print, were barely reviewed.

Russell wrote "that it is in the United States that this book can have its
most profound effect." He expressed his faith in the essential decency of the
American people, his faith that the ordinary man will react in a civilized
way when he is given the facts. We have yet to show that this faith is justified. Russell hoped to "arouse consciousness in order to create mass resistance … in the smug streets of Europe and the complacent cities of North
America." By now, there are few who can honestly claim to be unaware of
the character of the American war in Vietnam. There are few, for example,
who can now claim ignorance of the "new Oradours and Lidices"
described, in testimony to the Tribunal, by a West German physician who
spent six years in Vietnam. But consciousness has yet to create mass resistance. The streets of Europe and the cities of North America remain smug
and complacent—with the significant and honorable exception of the student youth.

The record of the Tribunal stands as an eloquent and dramatic appeal
to renounce the crime of silence. The crime was compounded by the

silence that greeted its detailed documentation and careful studies. However, although no honest effort was made to deal with the factual record made public in the proceedings of the Tribunal, its work did receive some oblique response. The Pentagon was forced to admit that it was, indeed, using antipersonnel weapons in its attacks against North Vietnam (though it could not resist the final lie that the targets were radar stations and anti-aircraft batteries). The hypocritical claim that the American bombing policy was one of magnificent restraint, that its targets were "steel and concrete," was finally exploded beyond repair. A State Department functionary who had become an object of general contempt for his unending deceit regarding Vietnam demeaned himself still further by informing journalists that he had no intention of "playing games with a ninety-four-year-old Briton," referring to one of the truly great men of the twentieth century. Those who were prepared to go beyond the mass media for information could learn something about the work of the Tribunal from such journals as *Liberation*, as could readers of the foreign press, in particular *Le Monde*. The Tribunal Proceedings, along with the documentary study *In the Name of America*[1] which appeared in the same year and the honest and courageous work of many fine war correspondents, helped to crumble the defenses erected by the government, with the partial collusion of the media, to keep the reality of the war from popular consciousness.

Though not reported honestly, the Tribunal was sharply criticized. Many of the criticisms are answered, effectively I believe, in Part I of the Proceedings. There are two criticisms that retain a certain validity, however. The participants, the "jurors" and the witnesses, were undoubtedly biased. They made no attempt, in fact, to conceal this bias, this profound hatred of murder and wanton destruction carried out by a foreign invader with unmatched technological resources.

A second and less frivolous criticism that might be raised is that the indictment is, in a sense, superfluous and redundant. This is a matter that deserves more serious attention.

The Pentagon will gladly supply, on request, such information as the quantity of ordnance expended in Indochina. From 1965 through 1969 this amounts to about 4.5 million tons by aerial bombardment. This is nine times the tonnage of bombing in the entire Pacific theater in World War II, including Hiroshima and Nagasaki—"over 70 tons of bombs for every square mile of Vietnam, North and South ... about 500 pounds of bombs for every man, woman and child in Vietnam."[2] The total of "ordnance expended" is more than doubled when ground and naval attacks are taken into account. With no further information than this, a person who has not lost his senses must realize that the war is an overwhelming atrocity.

A few weeks before the Tribunal began its second session, forty-nine volunteers of the International Voluntary Services wrote a letter to President Johnson describing the war as "an overwhelming atrocity." Four of the staff leaders resigned. These volunteers, who had worked for many years in Vietnam, were among the few Americans who had some human contact with the Vietnamese people. Their activities, and even the letter of protest, indicate their belief—surprisingly uncritical—in the legitimacy of the American effort in Vietnam.[3] In this letter they refer to "the free strike zones, the refugees, the spraying of herbicide on crops, the napalm ... the deserted villages, the sterile valleys, the forests with the huge swaths cut out, and the long-abandoned rice checks." They speak of the refugees "forcibly resettled, landless, in isolated desolate places which are turned into colonies of mendicants"; of "the Saigon slums, secure but ridden with disease and the compulsion towards crime"; of "refugees generated not by Viet Cong terrorism, but by a policy of the war, an American policy"—a process described by cynical American scholars as "urbanization" or "modernization."

Experts in pacification ("peace researchers," to use the preferred term) assure us that "the only sense in which [we have demolished the society of Vietnam] is the sense in which every modernizing country abandons reactionary traditionalism."[4] The methods of "urbanization" by which we have so advanced the modernization of Vietnam are described, for example, by Orville and Jonathan Schell:

> We both spent several weeks in Quangngai some six months before the [Song My] incident. We flew daily with the F.A.C.'s (Forward Air Control). What we saw was a province utterly destroyed, In August 1967, during Operation Benton, the "pacification" camps became so

full that Army units were ordered not to "generate" any more refugees. The Army complied. But search-and-destroy operations continued.

Only now peasants were not warned before an air-strike was called in on their village. They were killed in their villages because there was no room for them in the swamped pacification camps. The usual warning by helicopter loudspeaker or air dropped leaflets were stopped. Every civilian on the ground was assumed to be enemy by the pilots by nature of living in Quangngai, which was largely a free-fire-zone.

Pilots, servicemen not unlike Calley and Mitchell, continued to carry out their orders. Village after village was destroyed from the air as a matter of *de facto* policy. Air-strikes on civilians became a matter of routine. It was under these circumstances of official acquiescence to the destruction of the countryside and its people that the massacre of Song My occurred.

Such atrocities were and are the logical consequences of a war directed against an enemy indistinguishable from the people.[5]

Elsewhere, Orville Schell quotes a *Newsweek* correspondent returning from Quang Ngai Province: "Having had experience in Europe during World War II, he said what he had seen was 'much worse than what the Nazis had done to Europe.'" Schell adds, "Had he written about it in these terms? No."[6]

Vietnamese-speaking field workers of the American Friends Service Committee describe more recent stages of modernization, as seen from the ground:

In one such removal, during Operation Bold Mariner in January 1969, 12,000 peasants from the Batangan Peninsula were taken to a waterless camp near Quang Ngai over whose guarded gate floated a banner saying, "We thank you for liberating us from communist terror." These people had been given an hour to get out before the USS New Jersey began to shell their homes. After 8 weeks of imprisonment they were ferried back to what was left of their villages, given a few sheets of corrugated metal and told to fend for themselves. When asked what they would live on until new crops could be raised, the Vietnamese camp commander said, "Maybe they can fish."[7]

Reports by Western observers are limited to areas more or less under American control. The most intensive attacks are therefore unreported in the West. We do, however, have Vietnamese reports, which will perhaps be given somewhat greater credence than heretofore now that the incident at Song My, which they described with accuracy at the time, has finally been made public. To select one such report virtually at random:

> In Trang Bang on the evening of October 24 [1969], three flights of B-52's made three sorties, killing 47 people, wounding many others (mostly children and old folks), completely levelling 450 houses and devastating 650 hectares of fields. On the night of October 25, B-52's flew 9 attacks in Quang Tri and Quang Nam provinces, dumping more than 1,000 tons of bombs, killing 300 people, wounding 236 others, setting afire 564 houses and damaging hundreds of hectares of fields and orchards. In Pleiku, a fertile region, many flights of B-52's came in on the morning of October 17 and released 700 tons of bombs which wrought havoc in hundreds of hectares of fields and orchards....
>
> In the area of Nui Ba and the villages of Ninh Thanh, Hiep Ninh Thanh, Hiep Ninh of the Tay Ninh Cao Dai persuasion, the US-puppets resorted to toxic chemicals to destroy the crops and kill civilians. American hovercraft dumped tens of thousands of CS cans while helicopters dropped hundreds of thousands of toxic bombs on the villages. Moreover, enemy guns and mortars fired more than 5,000 gas shells over 1,000 people affecting 13 children under 13 killed (Ninh Thanh and Hiep Ninh villages) and more than 100 hectares of crops completely destroyed.[8]

And on and on, without end.

The facts are, of course, familiar in a general way to the highest authorities in the United States. The Under-Secretary of the Air Force, Townsend Hoopes, wrote a memorandum in March 1968, in which he pointed out that:

> ARVN [Army of the Republic of Vietnam] and US forces in the towns and cities are now responding to mortar fire from nearby villages by the liberal use of artillery and air strikes. This response is causing widespread destruction and heavy civilian casualties—among people who were considered only a few weeks ago to be secure elements of the GVN [South Vietnamese government] constituency....

The present mode and tempo of operations in SVN is already destroying cities, villages and crops, and is creating civilian casualties at an increasing rate.[9]

Hoopes describes the savage American reaction to the conquest of many cities by the National Liberation Front in the Tet offensive in January 1968—for example, in Saigon, where in an effort to dislodge the 1,000 soldiers who had taken the city, "artillery and air strikes were repeatedly used against densely populated areas of the city, causing heavy civilian casualties"; or in Hue, where the American reoccupation left "a devastated and prostrate city." "Eighty percent of the buildings had been reduced to rubble, and in the smashed ruins lay 2,000 dead civilians.[10] ... Three-quarters of the city's people were rendered homeless and looting was widespread, members of the ARVN being the worst offenders." Elsewhere, the story was much the same:

> Everywhere, the U.S.-ARVN forces mounted counterattacks of great severity. In the delta region below Saigon, half of the city of Mytho, with a population of 70,000, was destroyed by artillery and air strikes in an effort to eject a strong VC force. In Ben Tre on February 7, at least 1,000 civilians were killed and 1,500 wounded in an effort to dislodge 2,500 VC.[11]

According to Hoopes, the combat photographer David Douglas Duncan, whose war experience covers World War II, Korea, Algeria, and the French war in Vietnam, "was appalled by the U.S.-ARVN method of freeing Hue." He quotes him as saying:

> The Americans pounded the Citadel and surrounding city almost to dust with air strikes, napalm runs, artillery and naval gunfire, and the direct cannon fire from tanks and recoilless rifles—a total effort to root out and kill every enemy soldier. The mind reels at the carnage, cost, and ruthlessness of it all.[12]

Hoopes also reports that of the North Vietnamese force of 1,000 that had taken Hue in a day, a "sizable part" escaped. Compare the figures on casualties, cited above.

These events occurred too late to be considered by the Tribunal. I need not elaborate on what has been revealed since. Some indications are given in earlier chapters. For far more, see the study by Edward Herman, cited in footnote 2.

I have mentioned all of this in connection with the question raised earlier, whether it is necessary, today, to publicize the detailed reports of the Tribunal. Is it not true that by now the monstrous character of the war has penetrated the American consciousness so fully that further documentation is superfluous? Unfortunately, the answer must be negative. To see why, consider again the case of Townsend Hoopes, who is now a leading "dove." A reviewer of his book in *The New York Times* describes it as the most persuasive presentation of the case for American withdrawal from Vietnam. It is instructive to compare his position with that of the "hawks" on the one hand and that of the Tribunal on the other. Such a comparison shows how narrow is the gap between the hawks and the doves, and how far removed the dove-hawk position still remains from the consciousness that Russell hoped would be aroused by the factual record and historical and legal argument of the Tribunal. I want to stress that Hoopes's is one of the most humane and enlightened voices to be heard within the mainstream of American opinion today, surely among those who have had any significant role in the formation and implementation of policy. For this reason, his views are important and deserve careful consideration.

Our early strategy, as Hoopes describes it, was to kill as many Viet Cong as possible with artillery and air strikes:

> As late as the fall of 1966 … a certain aura of optimism surrounded this strategy. Some were ready to believe that, in its unprecedented mobility and massive firepower, American forces had discovered the military answer to endless Asian manpower and Oriental indifference to death. For a few weeks there hung in the expectant Washington air the exhilarating possibility that the most modern, mobile, professional American field force in the nation's history was going to lay to rest the time-honored superstition, the gnawing unease of military planners, that a major land war against Asian hordes is by definition a disastrous plunge into quicksand for any Western army.[13]

But this glorious hope was dashed. The endless manpower of Vietnam, the Asian hordes with their Oriental indifference to death, confounded our strategy. And our bombing of North Vietnam also availed us little, given the nature of the enemy. As Hoopes explains, quoting a senior United States Army officer, "Caucasians cannot really imagine what ant labor can do." In short, our strategy was rational, but it presupposed civilized Western values:

> We believe the enemy can be forced to be "reasonable," i.e., to compromise or even capitulate, because we assume he wants to avoid pain, death, and material destruction. We assume that if these are inflicted on him with increasing severity, then at some point in the process he will want to stop the suffering. Ours is a plausible strategy—for those who are rich, who love life and fear pain. But happiness, wealth, and power are expectations that constitute a dimension far beyond the experience, and probably beyond the emotional comprehension, of the Asian poor.[14]

Hoopes does not tell us how he knows that the Asian poor do not love life or fear pain, or that happiness is probably beyond their emotional comprehension.[15] But he does go on to explain how "ideologues in Asia" make use of these characteristics of the Asian hordes. Their strategy is to convert "Asia's capacity for endurance in suffering into an instrument for exploiting a basic vulnerability of the Christian West." They do this by inviting the West "to carry its strategic logic to the final conclusion, which is genocide." The Asians thus "defy us by a readiness to struggle, suffer, and die on a scale that seems to us beyond the bounds of humanity…. At that point we hesitate, for, remembering Hitler and Hiroshima and Nagasaki, we realize anew that genocide is a terrible burden to bear."

Thus by their willingness to die, the Asian hordes, who do not love life, who fear no pain and cannot conceive of happiness, exploit our basic weakness—our Christian values which make us reluctant to bear the burden of genocide, the final conclusion of our strategic logic. Is it really possible to read these passages without being stunned by their crudity and callousness?

James Thomson, East Asian specialist at the Department of State and the White House between 1961 and 1966, has written of

> an unprovable factor that relates to bureaucratic detachment: the ingredient of *cryptoracism*. I do not mean to imply any conscious contempt for Asian loss of life on the part of Washington officials. But I do mean to imply that bureaucratic detachment may well be com-

pounded by a traditional Western sense that there are so many Asians, after all; that Asians have a fatalism about life and a disregard for its loss; that they are cruel and barbaric to their own people; and that they are very different from us (and all look alike?). And I *do* mean to imply that the upshot of such subliminal views is a subliminal question whether Asians, and particularly Asian peasants, and most particularly Asian Communists, are really people—like you and me. To put the matter another way: would we have pursued quite such policies—and quite such military tactics—if the Vietnamese were white?[16]

Let us continue. Seeing that our strategy, though plausible, has failed, the Air Force Staff worked out several alternative strategies, which they presented to the new Secretary of Defense, Clark Clifford, in March 1968. The Air Staff preferred the following:

> an intensified bombing campaign in the North, including attacks on the dock area of Haiphong, on railroad equipment within the Chinese Buffer Zone, and on the dike system that controlled irrigation for NVN agriculture.[17]

But Hoopes and Air Force Secretary Harold Brown demurred. Why? They felt "there was little assurance such a campaign could either force NVN to the conference table, or even significantly reduce its war effort"; furthermore, "it was a course embodying excessive risks of confrontation with Russia." If they had any other objections to intensified bombing of the dike system of North Vietnam, Hoopes does not inform us of them.[18] Hoopes himself preferred, rather, the following tactics:

> a campaign designed to substitute tactical airpower for a large portion of the search-and-destroy operations currently conducted by ground forces, thus permitting the ground troops to concentrate on a perimeter defense of the heavily populated areas … the analysis seemed to show that tactical air-power could provide a potent "left jab" to keep the enemy in the South off balance while the U.S.-ARVN ground forces adopted a modified enclaves strategy, featuring enough aggressive reconnaissance to identify and break up developing attacks, but designed primarily to protect the people of Vietnam and, by population control measures, to force exposure of the VC political cadres.[19]

As we know from other sources, the VC political cadres thus "exposed" were to be eliminated by "Operation Phoenix," which, in the year 1968, is claimed to have killed 18,393 persons.[20]

D. Gareth Porter, a graduate student in Southeast Asian studies at Cornell, states that the Phoenix program is responsible for the death or capture of 35,000 people: "the majority of those arrested are merely low-level propagandists, supply agents and others who are part-time helpers in the NLF ranks."[21] He concludes his article with the following paragraphs:

> What is most significant about the program is that provincial police officials are expected to meet specific quotas for eliminating enemy "cadres" each month, although the official term for these quotas is "goals." As in the "anti-Communist denunciation campaign" and the Strategic Hamlet program, those officials who fail to meet the goals lose favor with the government; those who produce results are promoted. Thus quotas are likely to be met by applying practices which are already routine for the police. The victims are the people of South Vietnam, who must suffer yet another intensification of the terror which they have come to associate with the police.
>
> This totalitarian-oriented machinery of arbitrary arrest and political surveillance, which the United States helped shape with money and advice, will not be dismantled if the Nixon Administration manages to keep the present military regime in power. The men who have been put in office through American intervention have been frank enough to say that the façade of liberal institutions is only for American consumption. Perhaps this police state will be one of America's legacies to the Vietnamese people.

Len Ackland, a former IVS worker in South Vietnam and then a team leader and analyst in Vietnam for the RAND Corporation, comments on the Phoenix program:

> What this all means is that civilians are being murdered—people who serve the political party, the National Liberation Front, as tax collectors, clerks, postmen, etc. This policy would be analogous to the Administration murdering dissidents in the Internal Revenue Service, the "juvenile delinquents" of the Moratorium Committee, or the Democratic National Committee.[22]

Those who would counter by pointing out that there is (more precisely, was) a civil war in South Vietnam might remember that the Viet Minh did (naively) accept the terms of political struggle after Geneva until forced by the South Vietnamese government and the United States "to use counter-force to survive," as the American government specialist Douglas Pike puts it.[23]

Returning to Hoopes, in a letter of February 13, 1968, to Clark Clifford he explains his preferences in terms similar to those quoted above (page 231). We should, he urges, stop the militarily insignificant bombing of North Vietnam and undertake a less ambitious ground strategy in the South, trying merely to control (the technical term is "protect") the popu-lated areas. This policy

> would give us a better chance to develop a definable geographical area of South Vietnamese political and economic stability; and by reduc-ing the intensity of the war tempo, *it could materially improve the prospect of our staying the course for an added number of grinding years without rending our own society....*[24]

Compare these recommendations with the tactics now being followed by the Nixon administration. Secretary of the Army Stanley Resor, testify-ing before the House Appropriations Committee,[25] refused to predict how long the war would last, but he sees time as "running on our side":

> Therefore if we can just buy some time in the U.S. by these periodic progressive withdrawals and the American people can just shore up their patience and determination, I think we can bring this to a suc-cessful conclusion.

To this remark General Westmoreland added, "I have never made the pre-diction that this would be other than a long war."

Thus the present Secretary of the Army agrees with the Hoopes letter of February 1968 that we may be able to stay the course for "an added number of grinding years" if the American people will consent, if this pol-icy will not rend our own society. And with this judgment, finally, Mr. Hoopes disagrees:

> Vietnam is not of course the only source of division in America today, but it is the most pervasive issue of our discord, the catalytic agent that stimulates and magnifies all other divisive issues. In particular, there can be no real truce between the generations—no end to the bit-terness and alienation of even the large majority of our youth that is

neither revolutionary nor irresponsible—until Vietnam is termi-
nated.[26]

This is the primary reason why, he urges, we must withdraw from
Vietnam.

I do not want to suggest that the spectrum from Hoopes to Resor
exhausts the contemporary debate over Vietnam, but there is little doubt
that it represents the range of views and assumptions expressed within the
mainstream of "responsible" American opinion. With this observation, we
can return to the Tribunal. Its assumptions, of course, fall entirely outside
this spectrum. It is unfortunate but undeniable that the central issue in the
American debate over Vietnam, in respectable circles, has been the question, Can we win at an acceptable cost? The doves and the hawks disagree.
Hawks become doves as their assessment of the probabilities and costs
shifts, and if the American conquest were to prove successful, they would
no doubt resume their former militancy. The Tribunal is concerned with
very different questions. It does not ask whether the United States *can* win
at an acceptable cost, but rather whether it *should* win, whether it should
be involved at all in the internal affairs of the Vietnamese, whether it has
any right to try to settle or even influence these internal matters by force.

Inevitably, despite disclaimers, the Russell Tribunal will evoke memo-
ries of Nuremberg and Tokyo. With the revelation of the Song My atrocities, the issues raised in the War Crimes trials have become, at last, a matter of public concern. We can hardly suppress the memory of our initiative
at Nuremberg and Tokyo, or the explicit insistence of the United States
prosecutor, Robert Jackson, that the principles of Nuremberg are to be
regarded as universal in their applicability. After the trials, he wrote:

> If certain acts and violations of treaties are crimes, they are crimes
> whether the United States does them or whether Germany does them.
> We are not prepared to lay down a rule of criminal conduct against
> others which we would not be willing to have invoked against us.[27]

It might be argued that the verdicts of Nuremberg and Tokyo were merely
the judgment of victors, who sought vengeance and retribution rather
than justice. I think there is some merit in this accusation, but right or
wrong, it does not affect the broader question of the legitimacy of the principles that were recognized in the Charter of the War Crimes Tribunals.

Legal niceties aside, the citizen is justified in taking these principles as his guide.

A classic liberal doctrine holds that "Generally speaking, it is the drawn sword of the nation which checks the physical power of its rulers."[28] It is the fundamental duty of the citizen to resist and to restrain the violence of the state. Those who choose to disregard this responsibility can justly be accused of complicity in war crimes, which is itself designated as "a crime under international law" in the Principles of the Charter of Nuremberg. This is, in essence, the challenge posed to us by the Russell Tribunal.

Richard A. Falk has written about this matter in an important recent article.[29] He points out that "Song My stands out as a landmark atrocity in the history of warfare, and its occurrence is a moral challenge to the entire American society." Nevertheless, it would "be misleading to isolate the awful happenings at Song My from the overall conduct of the war." Among the war policies that might, he argues, be found illegal are these: "(1) the Phoenix Program; (2) aerial and naval bombardment of undefended villages; (3) destruction of crops and forests; (4) 'search-and-destroy' missions; (5) 'harassment and interdiction' fire; (6) forcible removal of civilian population; (7) reliance on a variety of weapons prohibited by treaty." That these policies have been followed on a massive scale is not in question. Falk argues that "if found to be 'illegal,' such policies should be discontinued forthwith and those responsible for the policy and its execution should be prosecuted as war criminals by appropriate tribunals." He also notes how broad was the conception of criminal responsibility developed, under American initiative, in the War Crimes trials. In Falk's paraphrase, the majority judgment of the Tokyo Tribunal held as follows:

> A leader must take affirmative acts to prevent war crimes or dissociate
> himself from the government. If he fails to do one or the other, then
> by the very act of remaining in a government of a state guilty of war
> crimes, he becomes a war criminal.

And Falk emphasizes the obligation of resistance for the citizen, if the evidence is strong that the state is engaged in criminal acts.

It is correct, but irrelevant, to stress the vast differences in the political processes of America and the fascist states. It is correct, but hardly relevant, to point out that the United States has stopped short of carrying "its strategic logic to the final conclusion, which is genocide" (Hoopes). Thus one cannot compare American policy to that of Nazi Germany, as of 1942. It would be more difficult to argue that American policy is not comparable to that of fascist Japan, or of Germany prior to the "final solution." There may be those who are prepared to tolerate any policy less ghastly than crematoria and death camps and to reserve their horror for the particular forms of criminal insanity perfected by the Nazi technicians. Others will not lightly disregard comparisons which, though harsh, may well be accurate.

Nazi Germany was *sui generis*, of that there is no doubt. But we should have the courage and honesty to face the question whether the principles applied to Nazi Germany and fascist Japan do not, as well, apply to the American war in Vietnam. Recall the objectives of "denazification," as formulated by those who were responsible for this policy. General Lucius D. Clay, in 1950, described the primary objective as follows: "to safeguard the new German democracy from Nazi influence and to make it possible for anti-Nazi, non-Nazi and outspoken democratic individuals to enter public life and replace the Nazi elements which had dominated all life in Germany from 1933 to 1945." He reports:

> This was, perhaps, the most extensive legal procedure the world had ever witnessed. In the U.S. Zone alone more than 13 million persons had been involved, of whom over three and two-thirds million were found chargeable, and of these some 800,000 persons were made subject to penalty for their party affiliations or actions. All this was, of course, apart from the punishment of war criminals many of whom were high-ranking Nazis.[30]

Field Marshall Sir Bernard Montgomery saw one of the most important objects of the Allied forces in Germany as "to change the heart, and the way of life, of the German people." Denazification involved a cultural and ideological change, to proceed side by side with economic reconstruction.[31] We can certainly ask whether three and two-thirds million Germans in the United States Zone were more guilty of complicity in war crimes than any Americans. And we can ask whether a cultural and ideological change in the United States, at the very least, is not imperative if many others, who fear neither pain nor death, are to be spared the fate of Vietnam.

Some of these questions arise in a revealing exchange between Townsend Hoopes and two journalists who published an interview with him in the *Village Voice* (see footnote 27). Hoopes insisted that:

> War crimes tribunals would be the worst thing that could happen to this country. That would amount to McCarthyism. You're proposing a system of legal guilt for top elected officials. The traditional way to deal with these top officials is to throw the rascals out.

In an article in which he comments on "the curious piece of reporting" of Judith Coburn and Geoffrey Cowan, Hoopes explains further that "a democratic and an entirely elective form of retribution" has already been visited upon Lyndon Johnson, and that his "closest collaborators" may also be excluded from high office.[32] Hoopes does not say whether this form of "retribution" would also have been more appropriate in the case of the Japanese and German war criminals—should the West, then, merely have guaranteed a democratic election in which they might have been deprived of office? He does, however, reject the suggestion that civilian officials be held accountable for such incidents as the Song My massacre, or for the bombing of North Vietnam, or for such policies as those enumerated by Falk, cited above. In fact, Coburn and Cowan report that "in the friendliest possible terms, he accused our 'generation' of wanting to impose a totalitarian system of morality" which would lead to "universal anarchy." Coburn and Cowan, in turn, ask:

> If Tojo can be sentenced to be executed by an American war crime tribunal for leading Japan into a "war of aggression," should the only punishment for an American President be that he is voted out of office while his Secretary of Defense serves a secure term as President of the World Bank?

This seems a not unreasonable question, certainly not unreasonable for those who take seriously the statement of Justice Jackson, quoted earlier. Nor do Coburn and Cowan appear unreasonable when they add: "The 'anarchists' who frighten us most are those who wield the big bombs, control the courts, and assume for themselves the power to declare all their enemies outlaws."

Hoopes strongly disagrees. It is these strange conclusions that make the Coburn-Cowan article such a "curious piece of reporting." To him it is "crystal clear … that such views could not conceivably be held or expressed by anyone who was a young man during the Second World War or who was engaged in the mortal struggles of its aftermath—in Greece, in Germany, in Berlin, in Korea." Only "sensitive, clever children" could be moved to such harsh judgments, "unshaped by historical perspective and untempered by any first-hand experience with the unruly forces at work in this near-cyclonic century." Those who designed our Vietnam policy were "struggling in good conscience to uphold the Constitution and to serve the broad national interest according to their lights"; they were, "almost uniformly, those considered when they took office to be among the ablest, the best, the most humane and liberal men that could be found for public trust," and "no one doubted their honest, high-minded pursuit of the best interests of their country, and indeed of the whole noncommunist world, as they perceived these interests." To be sure, they were deluded by the "tensions of the Cold War years." The tragedy of Vietnam, as he sees it, is that these good men were unable to perceive that the triumph of the national revolution in Vietnam would be "neither a triumph for Moscow and Peking nor a disaster for the United States." Furthermore, their policies received wide public support. "Set against these facts, the easy designation of individuals as deliberate or imputed 'war criminals' is shockingly glib, even if one allows for the inexperience of the young." Similarly, it would be "absurd" even to ask whether a war crimes tribunal, even in principle, should try Nixon and Kissinger as "war criminals" (even though they continue to "buy some time in the U.S." so that the war can be brought "to a successful conclusion," in the words of the present Secretary of the Army).

One should, I believe, agree with Townsend Hoopes that "what the country needs is not retribution, but therapy in the form of deeper understanding of our problems and of each other." No one, to my knowledge, has urged that those responsible for the massacre of the people of Vietnam, their forced evacuation from their homes,[33] and the destruction of their country be jailed or executed, or even that "denazification" procedures of the sort instituted against 13 million Germans in the United States Zone be applied to the American population. Let us, by all means, try rather to achieve a deeper understanding of our problems. Among these problems is the fact that one of the most liberal and enlightened commentators on contemporary affairs can assure us that Asian hordes care nothing for death, fear no pain, and cannot conceive of happiness, while as for us—it is our Christian values that impel us to stop short of a final solution. Among our problems is the fact that the same spokesman can summon up the kind of historical perspective that sees our intervention in Greece in the 1940s as a "mortal struggle" (against whom?); or the fact that those who were, quite possibly, the most humane and liberal men that could be found for public trust could set out to annihilate the Vietnamese in the belief (whether honest or feigned—it hardly matters) that they were combating a Communist monolith that included Moscow and Peking (in 1965!). One of our problems is the doctrine developed by Mr. Hoopes, in accordance with which—to take his words literally—no policy carried out by the best American leaders with wide public support could be criminal, could in principle demand any response other than "to throw the rascals out."

In fact, is it not a trifle naive (or even "glib") of Mr. Hoopes to suggest that we throw the rascals out? Did we vote the rascals in?

No one who considers carefully the role of the executive in civil-military decisions in the postwar world, or the role of the private economic empires in determining national policy (either in their own protected domain or within the parliamentary system itself), or the kinds of choices presented by the two competing candidate-producing organizations can so easily speak of throwing the rascals out. It would require social revolution, leading to a redistribution of power throughout the industrial as well as the political system, for a significant change to take place in the top decision-making positions in American society. For this reason alone, one must fully accept the judgment that "what the country needs is not retribution, but therapy in the form of deeper understanding of our problems"—and appropriate action to remedy these problems, which, given our enormous power, are problems of life and death for a good part of the world.

These problems should be on the agenda for any thinking person. More immediate, however, is the problem of bringing about a withdrawal of American forces from Vietnam. There is no indication that any such policy is envisioned at present. Rather, it is clear that the United States government is hoping to stay the course until victory is achieved, adjusting tactics where necessary to buy some time at home. For this reason, the Proceedings of the Tribunal are a document of first importance; the spirit and convictions that underlie it must, as Russell hoped, become a part of the consciousness of all Americans.

Richard Falk concludes the article I quoted earlier:

> Given the perils and horrors of the contemporary world, it is time that individuals everywhere called their government to account for indulging or ignoring the daily evidences of barbarism … the obsolete pretensions of sovereign prerogative and military necessity had better be challenged soon if life on earth is to survive.

The Tribunal takes one step—small, perhaps, but significant. The Tribunal, or another like it, should turn to Czechoslovakia, to Greece, to a dozen other countries that are suffering in the grip of the imperialist powers or the local forces that they support and maintain. Still more important, the work initiated by the Tribunal should be carried further by groups of citizens who take upon themselves the duty of discovering and making public the daily evidences of barbarism, and the still more severe duty of challenging the powers—state or private—that are responsible for violence and oppression, looking forward to the day when an international movement for freedom and social justice will end their rule.

Notes

* This is an edited and extended version of the introduction to *Against the Crime of Silence: Proceedings of the Russell International War Crimes Tribunal*, 2nd ed. (New York, Simon & Schuster, 1970).

1 Published by Clergy and Laymen Concerned About Vietnam (Annandale, Va., Turnpike Press, 1968).

2 Edward S. Herman, *"Atrocities" in Vietnam: Myths and Realities* (Boston, Pilgrim Press, 1970). In a careful analysis, Herman estimates South Vietnamese civilian casualties at over 1 million dead and over 2 million wounded, and he notes that two years ago the total number of refugees, "generated" mainly by the American scorched-earth policy, was estimated at almost 4 million by the Kennedy Committee of the 90th Congress.

3 The letter appears as an appendix in Don Luce and John Sommer, *Vietnam: The Unheard Voices* (Ithaca, N.Y., Cornell University Press, 1969), pp. 315–21.

4 Ithiel Pool, *New York Review*, letter, February 13, 1969.

5 *New York Times*, letter, November 26, 1969. The war in Quang Ngai and Quang Tin provinces is described in unforgettable detail by Jonathan Schell, *The Military Half* (New York, Vintage Books, 1968).

6 "Pop Me Some Dinks," *New Republic*, January 3, 1970.

7 *Vietnam: 1969*, AFSC White Paper, May 5, 1969, 160 North 15th Street, Philadelphia, Pa. 19102.

8 *South Viet Nam: The Struggle*, publication of the NLF Information Commission, No. 48, November 15, 1969.

9 *The Limits of Intervention* (New York, David McKay Co.), p. 199.

10 The NLF claims that 2,000 victims of the American bombardment were buried in mass graves (see Wilfred Burchett, *Guardian* (New York), December 6, 1969). This is consistent with Hoopes's account. Hoopes states that after ten days of fighting, 300 local officials and prominent citizens were found in a mass grave. This corresponds roughly with the estimate of Police Chief Doan Cong Lap, who estimated the total number executed as 200; he also gives the figure of 3,776 civilian casualties in the battle of Hue (Stewart Harris, *The Times* [London], March 27, 1969). Apart from Harris, I know of only one journalist who has given a detailed eyewitness report from Hue at the time, namely Marc Riboud. United States authorities were unable to show him the mass graves reported by the United States Mission. Riboud reports 4,000 civilians killed during the reconquest of the "assassinated city" of Hue (*Le Monde*, April 13, 1968). American Friends Service Committee staff people in Hue were unable to confirm the reports of mass graves, though they reported many civilians shot and killed during the reconquest of the city (see the report by John Sullivan of the AFSC, May 9, 1968). For attempts to evaluate government propaganda on mass killings in Hue, see D. Gareth Porter and Len E. Ackland, "Vietnam: The Bloodbath Argument," *Christian Century*, November 5, 1969; *Vietnam International*, December 1969, 6 Endsleigh Street, London WC1; Tran Van Dinh, "Fear of a Bloodbath," *New Republic*, December 6, 1969. The only other accounts I have seen merely convey information given out by American government sources.

11 Hoopes, *op. cit.*, p. 141.

12 *Ibid.*, p. 142.

13 *Ibid.*, p. 64.

14 *Ibid.*, pp. 79, 128–29.

15 This is not quite accurate. He does provide a brief philosophical discussion of Buddhist beliefs, which tend "to create a positive impetus toward honorable death."

16 James C. Thomson, Jr., "How Could Vietnam Happen?" in Robert Manning and Michael Janeway, eds., *Who We Are: An Atlantic Chronicle of the United States and Vietnam 1966–1969* (Boston, Little, Brown and Co., 1969), p. 206; reprinted from the *Atlantic Monthly*, April 1968.

17 Hoopes, *op. cit.*, p, 176.

18 As Gabriel Kolko notes, in testimony to the Russell Tribunal, the barbarism of Seyss-Inquart in opening the dikes in Holland was considered one of the most monstrous crimes of World War II, and was prominent among the charges that led to his death sentence at Nuremberg. Note also Kolko's discussion of the bombing of dikes in the Korean War, and the testimony given regarding American bombing of dikes in North Vietnam. Eyewitness reports of the bombing of dikes in the Red River Delta have appeared in the American press. See *Christian Science Monitor*, September 8, 1967, quoted in my *American Power and the New Mandarins* (New York, Pantheon Books, 1969), p. 15.

19 Hoopes, *op. cit.*, pp. 176–77.

20 See Senator Charles E. Goodell, *New Republic*, November 22, 1969, cited in Herman, *op. cit.*; also Judith Coburn and Geoffrey Cowan, "Training for Terror: A Deliberate Policy?" *Village Voice*, December 11, 1969. On "population control measures," see William Nighswonger, *Rural Pacification in Vietnam* (Praeger Special Studies; New York, Frederick A. Praeger, 1967). For some discussion, see my *American Power and the New Mandarins*, pp. 37ff., and for earlier precedents during the Japanese occupation of Manchuria, *ibid.*, pp. 195–203. The exact figures of those "neutralized" by Operation Phoenix vary in the several available accounts. William Colby, principal official in charge of pacification programs in Saigon, claims that in 1969, 6,187 Viet Cong were killed, 8,515 captured (their fate is unrecorded), and 4,832 rallied to the government. The Senate Foreign Relations Committee, February 2, 1970, states that 15,000 Viet Cong infrastructure (i.e., civilians) were neutralized in 1968, and a somewhat larger number in the first ten months of 1969 (see Herman, *op. cit.*).

21 "Saigon's Secret Police," *The Nation*, April 27, 1970.

22 *The Peace Times*, publication of the Vietnam Moratorium Committee, March 7, 1970.

23 See my *American Power and the New Mandarins*, pp. 46ff., 365–66, for relevant quotes from Pike.

24 Hoopes, *op. cit.*, pp. 154–55. My italics.

25 October 8, 1969, released December 2. Quoted in *I. F. Stone's Weekly*, December 15, 1969.

26 *Op. cit.*, p. 236.

27 Quoted in an article by Judith Coburn and Geoffrey Cowan, "The War Criminals Hedge Their Bets," *Village Voice*, December 4, 1969.

28 Wilhelm von Humboldt, *The Limits of State Action* (1792) ed. J. W. Burrow (Cambridge, Cambridge University Press, 1969).

29 "The Circle of Responsibility," *The Nation*, January 26, 1970. Falk is Milbank Professor of International Law and Practice at Princeton University.

30 *The Present State of Denazification*, reprinted in Constantine Fitzgibbon, *Denazification* (New York, W. W. Norton & Co., 1969), pp. 130, 133.

31 Fitzgibbon, *ibid.*, p. 120.

32 "The Nuremberg Suggestion," *Washington Monthly*, January 1970.

33 Coburn and Cowan report the views of Ambassador Ellsworth Bunker, who says in a statement to Congress on the refugee situation that the figures may be misleading, since the war-torn Vietnamese are used to disruption and "have been moving around for centuries." Since this is true, to a far greater extent, of the American population, there would presumably be even less reason to protest if they were driven from their homes by a foreign invader.

Ordering Information

AK Press
674-A 23rd Street,
Oakland, CA 94612-1163,
USA

Phone: (510) 208-1700
E-mail: akpress@akpress.org
URL: www.akpress.org
Please send all payments (checks, money orders, or cash at your own risk) in U.S. dollars. Alternatively, we take VISA and MC.

AK Press
PO Box 12766,
Edinburgh, EH8 9YE,
Scotland

Phone: (0131) 555-5165
E-mail: ak@akedin.demon.co.uk
URL: www.akuk.com
Please send all payments (cheques, money orders, or cash at your own risk) in U.K. pounds. Alternatively, we take credit cards.

For a dollar, a pound or a few IRC's, the same addresses would be delighted to provide you with the latest complete AK catalog, featuring several thousand books, pamphlets, zines, audio products and stylish apparel published & distributed by AK Press. Alternatively, check out our websites for the complete catalog, latest news and updates, events, and secure ordering.

AK Press Books, CDs, & DVDs by Noam Chomsky

Radical Priorities by Noam Chomsky edited by C.P. Otero
$18.95. ISBN 1 902593 69 3
In *Radical Priorities*, C.P. Otero sets out to "provide relatively easy access to Chomsky's libertarian philosophy and political analysis". Taken from a wide variety of sources, many never widely published—some never in a book at all and spanning four decades, the reader is furnished with a truly comprehensive window into Chomsky's anarchist convictions. Convictions which, while ever-present in his analysis are left largely misunderstood or worse-ignored. In seeking to combat the great challenges facing humanity, Chomsky's analysis and the traditions that bore it must not be left in obscurity.

Distorted Morality DVD by Noam Chomsky
$25.00 ISBN 1 905293 76 6
Here Chomsky offers a devastating critique of America's current War on Terror—arguing that it is a logical impossibility for such a war to be taking place. Chomsky presents his reasoning with refreshing clarity, drawing from a wealth of historic knowledge and analysis. The DVD includes a shorter; more recent talk on the danger, cruelty, and stupidity of the U.S. and Israel's policy of Pre-emptive War and a lively Q&A session all in an easily searchable user friendly format.

The Emerging Framework of World Power CD by Noam Chomsky
$14.98. ISBN 1 902593 75 8
Chomsky's state-of-the-world address. America's leading foreign policy critic surveys the role of the U.S. in a post-911 world—and finds nothing has changed.

The New War on Terrorism: Fact and Fiction CD by Noam Chomsky
$14.98. ISBN 1 902593 62 6
"We certainly want to reduce the level of terror... There is one easy way to do that... stop participating in it."—Noam Chomsky, from the CD
What is terrorism? And how can we reduce the likelihood of such crimes, whether they are against us, or against someone else? With his vintage flair, penetrating analysis, and ironic wit, Chomsky, in perhaps his most anticipated lecture ever—delivered a month after 9/11, and his first public statement—makes sense of a world apparently gone mad.

An American Addiction: Drugs, Guerillas, Counterinsurgency—U.S. Intervention in Colombia CD by Noam Chomsky
$13.98. ISBN 1 902593 44 8
"Colombia has been the leading recipient of US arms and training in the Western Hemisphere through the 1990s. It has also had the worst human rights record by far in the Western Hemisphere during these years. That correlation is one of the best correlations in contemporary history....It's a very important correlation that should be known and understood by the people who are paying for it. That's us. And it will get worse." (From the CD)

Propaganda and Control of the Public Mind 2×CD by Noam Chomsky
$20.00. ISBN 1 873176 68 6
"The war against working people should be understood to be a real war. It's not a new war. It's an old war. Furthermore it's a perfectly conscious war everywhere, but specifically in the U.S... which happens to have a highly class-conscious business class... And they have long seen themselves as fighting a bitter class war, except they don't want anybody else to know about it." [Noam Chomsky, from the CD]

Case Studies In Hypocrisy: U.S. Human Rights Policy 2×CD by Noam Chomsky
$20.00. ISBN 1 902593 27 8
With the recent celebration of the fiftieth anniversary of the Universal Declaration Of Human Rights, and America's undisputed position as the world's only superpower, the contrast between the rhetoric and the reality of U.S. foreign policy has never been more stark. With his inimitable penetrating analysis and dry wit, Chomsky leads us through the murky blood-soaked reality of America's New World Order.

For A Free Humanity: For Anarchy 2×CD by Noam Chomsky/Chumbawamba
$18.00 ISBN 1 873176 74 0
A Double CD with Noam Chomsky and Chumbawamba. Disc One comprises the Noam Chomsky lecture 'Capital Rules'—another articulate, and immediately accessible description of Corporate America's unrelenting attack on poor and working class people. Disc Two is Chumbawamba's best collection of live sounds—Showbusiness!, previously only available as an expensive import. Recorded live in '94. The double CD is accompanied by a 24 page booklet, with extensive interviews with both Noam Chomsky - discussing corporate structure as private tyranny, domestic surveillance of activists, and visions for a new society - and Chumbawamba discussing their past, politics, and anarchism.

Prospects For Democracy CD by Noam Chomsky
$14.98 ISBN 1 873176 38 4
Beginning with a broad review of democratic theory and political history, he argues that classical democrats such as Thomas Jefferson would be shocked at the current disrepair of American democracy. The enormous growth of corporate capitalism has already devastated democratic culture and government by concentrating power in the hands of the wealthy. And the future looks no brighter. In spite of this dark assessment, Chomsky maintains that any hope for democracy rests ultimately with you and me—on whether we can shake off our political malaise and build a democratic future.

Free Market Fantasies: Capitalism in the Real World CD by Noam Chomsky
$13.98. ISBN 1 873176 79 1
There is endless talk about the free market and its virtues. Entrepreneurs compete on level playing fields and the public benefits. The chasm between such fantasies and reality is acute and growing wider. Megamergers and monopolies are limiting competition. Fewer than 10 corporations control most of the global media. The existing free market depends heavily on taxpayer subsidies and bailouts. Corporate welfare far exceeds that which goes to the poor. Economic policy is based on the dictum: take from the needy, and give to the greedy. The captains of industry of today make the robber barons of the 19th century look like underachievers. The gap between CEO and worker salaries has never been sharper. One union leader put it this way, "Workers are getting the absolute crap kicked out of them."

Other Books Available from AK Press

What is Anarchism? book by Alexander Berkman
$13.95. ISBN 1 902593 70 7
A reprint of perhaps the first and best exposition of Anarchism by one of its greatest propagandists (by both word and deed) and thinkers. In a clear conversation with the reader Berkman discusses society as it now exists, the need for Anarchism and the methods for bringing it about. Combines the oft-reprinted texts of *What is Communist Anarchism?* and the *ABC of Anarchism* back into its original format. Forewords by his comrade and lover Emma Goldman and Barry Pateman.

Addicted to War: Why the U.S. Can't Stop Militarism book by Joel Andreas
$10.00. ISBN 1 904859 01 1
Addicted to War takes on the most active, powerful and destructive military in the world. Hard-hitting, carefully documented, and heavily illustrated, it reveals why the United States has been involved in more wars in recent years than any other country. Read *Addicted to War* to find out who benefits from these military adventures, who pays—and who dies.

"A witty and devastating portrait of U.S. military policy."—Howard Zinn

Other Titles from AK Press

Books

MARTHA **ACKELSBERG**—*Free Women of Spain*

KATHY **ACKER**—*Pussycat Fever*

MICHAEL **ALBERT**—*Moving Forward: Program for a Participatory Economy*

JOEL **ANDREAS**—*Addicted to War: Why the U.S. Can't Kick Militarism*

ALEXANDER **BERKMAN**—*What is Anarchism?*

HAKIM **BEY**—*Immediatism*

JANET **BIEHL** & PETER **STAUDENMAIER**—*Ecofascism: Lessons From The German Experience*

BIOTIC BAKING BRIGADE—*Pie Any Means Necessary: The Biotic Baking Brigade Cookbook*

JACK **BLACK**—*You Can't Win*

MURRAY **BOOKCHIN**—*Anarchism, Marxism, and the Future of the Left*

MURRAY **BOOKCHIN**—*Social Anarchism or Lifestyle Anarchism: An Unbridgeable Chasm*

MURRAY **BOOKCHIN**—*Spanish Anarchists: The Heroic Years 1868–1936, The*

MURRAY **BOOKCHIN**—*To Remember Spain: The Anarchist and Syndicalist Revolution of 1936*

MURRAY **BOOKCHIN**—*Which Way for the Ecology Movement?*

DANNY **BURNS**—*Poll Tax Rebellion*

CHRIS **CARLSSON**—*Critical Mass: Bicycling's Defiant Celebration*

JAMES **CARR**—*Bad*

NOAM **CHOMSKY**—*At War With Asia*

NOAM **CHOMSKY**—*Language and Politics*

NOAM **CHOMSKY**—*Radical Priorities*

WARD **CHURCHILL**—*On the Justice of Roosting Chickens: Reflections on the Consequences of U.S. Imperial Arrogance and Criminality*

HARRY **CLEAVER**—*Reading Capital Politically*

ALEXANDER **COCKBURN** & JEFFREY **ST. CLAIR** (ed.)—*Dime's Worth of Difference*

ALEXANDER **COCKBURN** & JEFFREY **ST. CLAIR** (ed.)—*Politics of Anti-Semitism, The*

ALEXANDER **COCKBURN** & JEFFREY **ST. CLAIR** (ed.)—*Serpents in the Garden*

DANIEL & GABRIEL **COHN-BENDIT**—*Obsolete Communism: The Left-Wing Alternative*

EG SMITH COLLECTIVE—*Animal Ingredients A–Z (3rd edition)*

VOLTAIRINE de **CLEYRE**—*Voltarine de Cleyre Reader*

HOWARD **EHRLICH**—*Reinventing Anarchy, Again*

SIMON **FORD**—*Realization and Suppression of the Situationist International: An Annotated Bibliography 1972–1992, The*

YVES **FREMION** & **VOLNY**—*Orgasms of History: 3000 Years of Spontaneous Revolt*

DANIEL **GUERIN**—*No Gods No Masters*

AGUSTIN **GUILLAMON**—*Friends Of Durruti Group, 1937–1939, The*

ANN **HANSEN**—*Direct Action: Memoirs Of An Urban Guerilla*

WILLIAM **HERRICK**—*Jumping the Line: The Adventures and Misadventures of an American Radical*

FRED **HO**—*Legacy to Liberation: Politics & Culture of Revolutionary Asian/Pacific America*

STEWART **HOME**—*Assault on Culture*

STEWART **HOME**—*Neoism, Plagiarism & Praxis*

STEWART **HOME**—*Neoist Manifestos / The Art Strike Papers*

STEWART **HOME**—*No Pity*

STEWART **HOME**—*Red London*

STEWART **HOME**—*What Is Situationism? A Reader*

JAMES **KELMAN**—*Some Recent Attacks: Essays Cultural And Political*

KEN **KNABB**—*Complete Cinematic Works of Guy Debord*

KATYA **KOMISARUK**—*Beat the Heat: How to Handle Encounters With Law Enforcement*

NESTOR **MAKHNO**—*Struggle Against The State & Other Essays, The*

G.A. **MATIASZ**—*End Time*

CHERIE **MATRIX**—*Tales From the Clit*

ALBERT **MELTZER**—*Anarchism: Arguments For & Against*

ALBERT **MELTZER**—*I Couldn't Paint Golden Angels*

RAY **MURPHY**—*Siege Of Gresham*

NORMAN **NAWROCKI**—*Rebel Moon*

HENRY **NORMAL**—*Map of Heaven, A*

HENRY **NORMAL**—*Dream Ticket*

HENRY **NORMAL**—*Fifteenth of February*

HENRY **NORMAL**—*Third Person*

FIONBARRA **O'DOCHARTAIGH**—*Ulster's White Negroes: From Civil Rights To Insurrection*

DAN **O'MAHONY**—*Four Letter World*

CRAIG **O'HARA**—*Philosophy Of Punk, The*

ANTON **PANNEKOEK**—*Workers' Councils*

BEN **REITMAN**—*Sister of the Road: the Autobiography of Boxcar Bertha*

PENNY **RIMBAUD**—*Diamond Signature, The*

PENNY **RIMBAUD**—*Shibboleth: My Revolting Life*

RUDOLF **ROCKER**—*Anarcho-Syndicalism*

RON **SAKOLSKY** & STEPHEN **DUNIFER**—*Seizing the Airwaves: A Free Radio Handbook*

ROY **SAN FILIPPO**—*New World In Our Hearts: 8 Years of Writings from the Love and Rage Revolutionary Anarchist Federation, A*

ALEXANDRE **SKIRDA**—*Facing the Enemy: A History Of Anarchist Organisation From Proudhon To May 1968*

ALEXANDRE **SKIRDA**—*Nestor Mahkno—Anarchy's Cossack*

VALERIE **SOLANAS**—*Scum Manifesto*

CJ **STONE**—*Housing Benefit Hill & Other Places*

ANTONIO **TELLEZ**—*Sabate: Guerilla Extraordinary*

MICHAEL **TOBIAS**—*Rage and Reason*

JIM **TULLY**—*Beggars of Life: A Hobo Autobiography*

TOM **VAGUE**—*Anarchy in the UK: The Angry Brigade*

TOM **VAGUE**—*Great British Mistake, The*

TOM **VAGUE**—*Televisionaries*

JAN **VALTIN**—*Out of the Night*

RAOUL **VANEIGEM**—*Cavalier History Of Surrealism, A*

FRANCOIS EUGENE **VIDOCQ**—*Memoirs of Vidocq: Master of Crime*

GEE **VOUCHER**—*Crass Art And Other Pre-Postmodern Monsters*

MARK J **WHITE**—*Idol Killing, An*

JOHN **YATES**—*Controlled Flight Into Terrain*

JOHN **YATES**—*September Commando*

BENJAMIN **ZEPHANIAH**—*Little Book of Vegan Poems*

BENJAMIN **ZEPHANIAH**—*School's Out*

HELLO—*2/15: The Day The World Said NO To War*

DARK STAR COLLECTIVE —*Beneath the Paving Stones: Situationists and the Beach, May 68*

DARK STAR COLLECTIVE —*Quiet Rumours: An Anarcha-Feminist Reader*

ANONYMOUS —*Test Card F*

CLASS WAR FEDERATION —*Unfinished Business: The Politics of Class War*

CDs

THE **EX**—*1936: The Spanish Revolution*

MUMIA **ABU JAMAL**—*175 Progress Drive*

MUMIA **ABU JAMAL**—*All Things Censored Vol.1*

MUMIA **ABU JAMAL**—*Spoken Word*

FREEDOM **ARCHIVES**—*Chile: Promise of Freedom*

FREEDOM **ARCHIVES**—*Prisons on Fire: George Jackson, Attica & Black Liberation*

JUDI **BARI**—*Who Bombed Judi Bari?*

JELLO **BIAFRA**—*Become the Media*

JELLO **BIAFRA**—*Beyond The Valley of the Gift Police*

JELLO **BIAFRA**—*High Priest of Harmful*

JELLO **BIAFRA**—*I Blow Minds For A Living*

JELLO **BIAFRA**—*If Evolution Is Outlawed*

JELLO **BIAFRA**—*Machine Gun In The Clown's Hand*

JELLO **BIAFRA**—*No More Cocoons*

NOAM **CHOMSKY**—*American Addiction, An*

NOAM **CHOMSKY**—*Case Studies in Hypocrisy*

NOAM **CHOMSKY**—*Emerging Framework of World Power*

NOAM **CHOMSKY**—*Free Market Fantasies*

NOAM **CHOMSKY**—*New War On Terrorism: Fact And Fiction*

NOAM **CHOMSKY**—*Propaganda and Control of the Public Mind*

NOAM **CHOMSKY**—*Prospects for Democracy*

NOAM **CHOMSKY/CHUMBAWAMBA**—*For A Free Humanity: For Anarchy*

WARD **CHURCHILL**—*Doing Time: The Politics of Imprisonment*

WARD **CHURCHILL**—*In A Pig's Eye: Reflections on the Police State, Repression, and Native America*

WARD **CHURCHILL**—*Life in Occupied America*

WARD **CHURCHILL**—*Pacifism and Pathology in the American Left*

ALEXANDER **COCKBURN**—*Beating the Devil: The Incendiary Rants of Alexander Cockburn*

ANGELA **DAVIS**—*Prison Industrial Complex, The*

JAMES **KELMAN**—*Seven Stories*

TOM **LEONARD**—*Nora's Place and Other Poems 1965–99*

CHRISTIAN **PARENTI**—*Taking Liberties: Policing, Prisons and Surveillance in an Age of Crisis*

UTAH **PHILLIPS**—*I've Got To know*

DAVID **ROVICS**—*Behind the Barricades: Best of David Rovics*

ARUNDHATI **ROY**—*Come September*

VARIOUS—*Better Read Than Dead*

VARIOUS—*Less Rock, More Talk*

VARIOUS—*Mob Action Against the State: Collected Speeches from the Bay Area Anarchist Bookfair*

VARIOUS—*Monkeywrenching the New World Order*

VARIOUS—*Return of the Read Menace*

HOWARD **ZINN**—*Artists In A Time of War*

HOWARD **ZINN**—*Heroes and Martyrs: Emma Goldman, Sacco & Vanzetti, and the Revolutionary Struggle*

HOWARD **ZINN**—*People's History of the United States: A Lecture at Reed College, A*

HOWARD **ZINN**—*People's History Project*

HOWARD **ZINN**–*Stories Hollywood Never Tells*

DVDs

NOAM **CHOMSKY**—*Distorted Morality*

ARUNDHATI **ROY**—*Instant Mix Imperial Democracy*